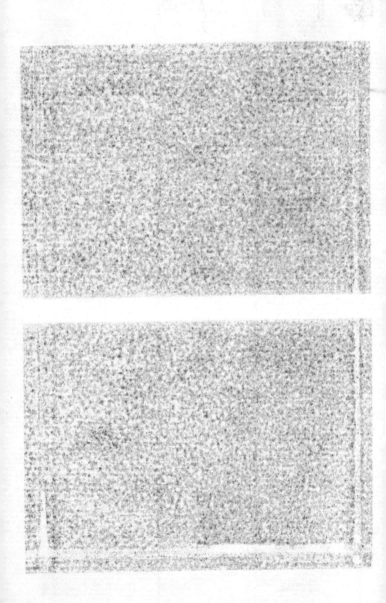

ENGLISH RECUSANT LITERATURE
1558–1640

Selected and Edited by
D. M. ROGERS

Volume 372

A Manual of Prayers
1583

A Manual of Prayers
1583

The Scolar Press
1978

ISBN o 85967 443 6

Published and printed in Great Britain by
The Scolar Press Limited, 59-61 East Parade,
Ilkley, Yorkshire and
39 Great Russell Street,
London WC1

A MANVAL OF PRAYERS

NEVVLY GATHERED OVT OF MANY
and diuers famous authours afwell
auncient as of the tyme prefent.

*Reduced into. 13.chap. very commodious
and profitable for a deuout Chriſtian.*

PRAYER,
IS GOOD,
WITH FAS
TYNG AND
ALMES.

TOB · 12.

1.*Pet.cap.*4. Be wiſe therfore & watch in
prayers. But before all things, hauing mu-
tual charitie cõtinual among your ſelues.

CVM PRIVILEGIO. 1583.

This is the Iuſtice of man in this
life, Faſting, Almeſ-deedes, Prayer.

Ibidem in ſerm. 59.

He that wyll haue his prayer to
flye to heauen, muſte make it two
wynges, Almeſ-deedes, & Faſting,
and it ſhall ſpedelye aſcende and
bee harde.

THE COLLECTOVR AND

traunslatour of this presente Manual, to the Catholicke aud Christian Reader.

Ost deare Countrymē vvhose desires are to serue God in holines of life, crauing aide for the acccomplishment of your religiouse intentes at the handes of his Maiestye, by the merites of Christe, and intercession of the blessed virgin Mary, and all Angels and saynts : to the intente that you may proceede dayly from one vertue to another, and to be helped by the labours of God his seruauntes and sayntes, (vvhoe from time to time to increase the deuotions of the people, haue lefte manye holye prayers and exercyses, as a treasure for to comforte and strengthen the dull soule of man) I haue thought good to collect and translate certayne deuoute prayers verye fitte and conueniente for this time,
vvhi[ch]

vvhich is done the more vvillingly in respecte of the greate and zelouse desire that many of our poore countrye hath, rather to occupye them selues deuoutly by begging pardone for their sinnes, thē curiously by searching the secrete misteries of God, to spende their time in vnprofitable and insolente contradictions, tendinge to no other ende, but onely to roote out of the mindes of christian catholickes all true fayth, firme hope, and perfecte charitie, vvhich dayly by deuotion and other spirituall exercyses is vvonderfully increased, to the greate admiration, euen of the very aduersaries of all pietie and catholicke religion, as doth vvell appeare to the vvhole vvorld sece the time that some vertuous, holy & learned men haue applyèd some parte of their time in compyling, translating and collecting particular vvorks of deuotion, vvhich in the iudgement of many are presently more necessary, than

farther

farther to treate of any controuersie, seeinge that heresie is growen to suche rypenes, that the simplest man of all, can novv discypher the poyson hid vnder her: but deuotion is so decayed that the learned themselues haue neede of helpes for to attayne thereunto: yet is it not my mynde that any man shoulde so tye himselfe to any deuoute prayer, or to anye number of prayers here colected, that thereby he shoulde omit the accustomable publique prayers of our holy mother the Catholicke Churche, as hereafter more at large I haue noted. Farther good Christian Reader I am to let thee vnderstand, that this litle Manual hath bene collected and transated in greate haste, and vpon earnest requeste of dyuers godlye and vertuouse catholickes: yet not vvithout the iudgemente and opinion of some number of the learned forte in this studye, vvhoe finde it very conuenient and necessary for this time, specially

specially for that they are collected and translated out of dyuers famous and holy Authors, as vvell auncient as of the time preſ̃et, and are to the great increaſe of deuotion publiſhed in many countries and in dyuers tongues, before this my collection & tranſlatiõ: vvhich if I may requeſt to be gratefully accepted of thee good catholicke and chriſtian Reader, it ſhall gyue me the radiar occaſion, to take the lyke paynes in any ſuch profitable action, vvhich hereafter maye be offred: and thus vviſhing, that increaſe of grace to the reader, vvhich I deſire to my ſelfe, and deſiring hartye repentaunce to be vvrought in the hartes of all my deare country-men, I bid thee gentle reader hartely fare-vvell.

Thy harty welwiller
to commaunde in
Chriſte Ieſus.
G. F.

THE ARGVMENTE OF THE
Chapters.

Auinge expreſſed the
cauſes that moued me
to the collection and
tranſlation of this ma-
nuall, I am now to lay
downe a direction
whereby thou mayeſt with more facili-
tye finde out ſuch particular prayers as
ſeemeth beſte to thy diſcrete deuotion:
that ſeeing the particular praiers of this
booke deuided into certayne chapters,
thou mayeſt as tyme, place and neceſſitye requireth, vſe theſe kynde of prayers . whiche ſhall bee moſte to Gods
glory, thy owne ſoules health, and the
profit of thy euen-chriſtian.

The firſte and ſecond chapters are
ſuch, as whereby the Chriſtian Catholicke may learne and knowe howe to
craue the ayde and ſuccour of God in
all his endeuours, enterpryſes and actions , which that daye he purpoſeth and
meaneth to take in hand : and before he
goe to bed, to thanke God for his benifites receyued that day : and to knowe

a   h w

how to examine his confcience, callirg to minde his finnes committed the day paft : but fpecially in the feconde chapter, the catholicke man may learne howe to behaue him felfe at the tyme of the dreadful mifteries, which chriftian people commonly call the Maffe. Further he may there learne what to craue of God, and what kinde of meditations to vfe in the Church, and withall howe to moue him felfe to fpirituall deuotion.

The reft which are ten chapters, are put in a feuerall Index, whereby the catholicke fhall eafely finde what prayers are thought mofte conuenient for euerye day in the weeke : that fo he may as leafure and deuotion ferueth him, reade either the whole, or parte, as they are fet downe in this Index following.

Read vpon. Soundaye thefe chap.	{ 10. *Prayers to the holy Trinitie.* 8. *Of thankefgyuing to God for his benefites.*
Vpon. Moundaye thefe chap.	{ 11. *To the B. Virgin Marie and to the holy Saintes.* 3. *For obteyning remißion of finnes.*
Vpon. Tewefdaye thefe chap.	{ 4. *For ayde and comfort in tribulations and afflictions.* 5. *For obteyning of God neceffaries for body and foule.*
Vpon. VVednefday thefe chap.	{ 9. *For the Churche, our friendes, and others.* 13. *For the departed foules.*
Vpon. Thurfdaye thefe chap.	{ 5. *For obteyninge of God, neceffaries for body & foule.* 8. *Of thankef-gyuinge to God for his benefites.*
Vpon. Fydaye thefe chap.	{ 3. *For obteyninge remißion of fynnes.* 6. *Prayers of the lyfe and Paßion of our Sauiour Iefus Chrift.*
Vpon. Saturdaye thefe chap.	{ 13. *For the departed foules.* 9. *To the B. Virgin and to the holy Saintes.*

THe firste weeke shall be read the chapters which are put in the firste rankes for euery daye: and the nexte weeke after, the chapters put in the second ranckes: So shalt thou reade ouer all the within named ten chapters in the Index twyse euery moneth, and some of the sayed chapters foure tymes: As for the other three chapters they are conuenient at certayne times, and for certayne persones, for which cause they are not meete to be put in order with the other as aboue named.

But those that haue neither time nor leasure to read euery day a whole chapter, may yet reade of the same chapter some of the sayde prayers, and suche as they thincke conueniente for the aduancement of God his glory, their profit and for the profit of others: notwithstading, in no wise may they omit their dayly prayers, or those prayers which they ought to say in Masse time.

Also when any holy day falleth, that you haue no saynte by name in your chapter of Saintes, then must you take one of the prayers which be common to any Apostle, Martyr, Confessor or Virgin.

Fur-

Further it is neceſſary for all devout Catholickes to knowe, that the accuſtomed prayers vſed in the Church according to the auncient and laudable maner of our forefathers, and obſerued by continuall practiſe of both the learned and vnlearned, (to the greate glorye of God, and increaſe of deuotion, religion and pietie of lyfe) are not to be omitted for the deſire that any may haue to any ſpeciall prayers either in this or anye other pamphlet, tranſlated or collected by any priuate perſons, which is done to moue men to deuotion, but not to withdrawe men from obedience or any receyued Catholicke cuſtome or tradition.

And therefore I counſayle the Catholicke Reader that of deuotion hath accuſtomed him ſelfe to theſe prayers folowing, not to omit thē in any caſe (for they are not deuiſed by the wit and priuate deuotiō of mā, but by the holy ſpirit of God, the Author and delyuerer of all trueth) which are the ſeuen canonicall houres in the Breuiarye or in the Primer, commonly called our Ladyes mattins: the ſeuen penitentiall pſalmes, with
the

the lytanies: the dyrige for the foules departed: the houres of the holy Ghost: the houres of the Crosse: prayers of the passion: the fiftiene graduall psalmes: the beades which consisteth in a certayne number of pater nosters, angelicall salutations, with the Creede of the Apostles: commonly is called the Rosarye of our Lady.

Thus hauinge gyuen thee an order (gentle Reader) to vnderstand this litle Manuall of prayers, with my opinion touching the vse of the same: I will conclude with earnest request and humble supplication vnto thee, desiring thee to remember me in thy vndistracted deuotions, saynge this prayer folowinge for me and others, whose helpes I vsed in collecting this sayed worke out of many authors, and translating many prayers out of latin and french into this our vulgar tonge.

O Omnipotent almightie and euerliuinge God, haue mercye vpon thy seruaunt N. for the loue of thy sweete soane our sauiour Iesu Christ, the true lighte and lyfe of all that shall be saued:

O

O Iesu the seconde person in Trinitie,
equall God with the Father and the holy
Ghoste, conserue and keepe him in thy
grace, fauour and loue, and suffer him
not to be drawen from thee through a-
ny suttle perswasions of the enemy : O
holy Ghost proceedinge from the father
and the sonne, the comforter of the e-
lect: the inspirer of all good giftes: the
onely schole-maister and teacher of all
truth : graunte that through thy giftes
he maye euermore dwell in thy trueth:
replenishe his harte with all charitable
desires and heauenlye inspirations ne-
cessarye to his saluation : graunt this O
holye Trinitie for the bitter passion of
our Sauiour : by the merites and
intercession of the glorioufe
Virgin Marye and all
Angels and faintes.
Amen.

S.Peter. 1. *cap.* 4.

Be wyse therefore:and watche in
prayers. But before all thinges hauing mutual charytie continual a-
monge your selues,&c.

Aug. in Psal. 42.

This is the Iustice of man in this
life, Fasting, Almes-deedes, Prayer

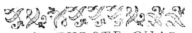

THE FYRSTE CHAP-
TER CONTEYNINGE QVO-
tidiane or dayly prayers, accom-
modated & prescribed to certayne houres or times bothe
for the day and night.

*A briefe exhortation to praye conti-
nually, extracted and taken out of Saint
Chrisostome.*

In lib. De orando Deum.

'T is very meete and
profitable, that we
occupy all the course
of our life in prayer,
that thereby our harts
may receaue cōtinually the sweete
dewe of gods grace: of the which
all persons haue no lesse neede,
than trees and herbs haue of the
moysture of waters. For as trees

A   can

can not bringe furth fruite except
the rootes be cõforted with moy-
fture:in like maner,it is impoffible
for vs to be replenifhed with beautifull fruites of pietie,if our hartes
be not refrefhed by prayer: for
which caufe we ought to forfake
our bedds,and preuent the fonne-
rifing,in gods feruice.

The like we ought to do when
we goe to meate, & at night when
we mufte of neceffitye take our
reft : yca it behoueth at all houres,
to offer fome one prayer to God,
to the ende both daye and nighte
together,might be fpent in prayer: efpecially in time of winter,it
is conuenient to imploye the moft
parte of the night in prayer, and
fo to fpende the time vppon our
knees in diuine feruice.

Tell me I praye thee, how canft
thou beholde the fonne, if thou
doeft

doeſt not honour him firſte, that
made thine eyes to ſee that moſte
beautifull light? How can ye goe
to the table to eate,if you do not
firſt honour him who geueth and
furniſheth vs daily with ſuch great
beniſites ? How canſt thou truſte
to paſſe the darcke night, and to
auoyde ſuch dreames & thoughts
as may come to thee, if thou defend not thy ſelfe by prayer. If
thou be not countergarded by
prayer , thou ſhalt eaſely yelde
thy ſelfe to wicked ſpirites, which
goeth cõtinually about vs,eſpying
if they can perceaue any one vnar-
med,that ſoudainly they may deuoure him.

But if they ſee him furniſhed
with prayer, they retyre preſent-
lye, euen as wicked theeues when
they ſee the ſworde towardes
them.

Hoolſome

A MANVAL

Hoolſome meditations and exerſice for the morninge.

1 Fyrſt preſently in the morninge when thou art awake, thou ſhalt pray to God, that he woulde ſo lighten the eyes of thine hart, with the holy lighte of his holy ſpirite, that thou be not allured or entyced to conſente to ſinne, & ſo conſequently ſeduced to death.

2 Secondly after thou art riſen, bleſſe thee with the ſigne of the croſſe, ſaying the prayer that foloweth.

3 Thirdly when thou art appareled, geue not thy ſelfe preſently to babling or ianglinge, or to vaine thoughtes or fanſies: but lift vp thy harte vnto God in ſilence, and prepare thy ſelfe to ſaye theſe prayers folowing.

4 Fourthly after prayer, thou ſhalt purpoſe firmelye and conſtantly

ſtantly in thy ſelfe, not to committ willingly that day any thinge,
whereby God or thy neighbour
might be offended.

5 Fyſtly it ſhall be very neceſſary beſides theſe afore-ſayed, to
call to minde thine affayres, and
with quicknes of ſpirit ſett downe
with thy ſelfe howe thou wilt ſpēd
the day to come.

*A prayer in the mornyng vvhen
ye avvake.*
Dauid in Pſal

Lighten myne eyes O Lorde,
leſte at any tyme I ouerſleepe
in ſinne, & leſte myne enemy doe
ſaye, I haue preuailed againſt him.

VVhen ye doo aryſe.
F. Sonn. 3. tract. 11. Chriſt. Inſt. for.

IN the name of oure Lorde Ieſus
Chriſte crucified, I doo ryſe : he
bleſſe me, ✠, gouuerne me, keepe
me

me, faue me, and bringe me vnto
euerlaſting lyfe. Amen.
Pater noſter. Aue. Credo. & Confiteor.

A morning prayer vvhen
ye are ryſen.
Ex Viridario ſpirit.

O Heauenly Father, omnipotente and euerlaſtinge God,
vnto thee I yealde innumerable
thankes, whiche haſte vouchſafed
to keepe me this nighte through
thy great mercy, and I beſeech thy
aboundaunt clemencye, that thou
graunt me ſo to ſpende the day to
come, in fayth, hope, charity, pa-
tiēce, feare & careſulnes of minde,
that my ſeruice maye pleaſe thy
heauenly Maieſtie.

A morninge prayer vvhereby to com-
mende thy ſelfe to God.
B. Aug. cap. 40. Medit.

O Holy Trinitie heare me moſt
miſerable ſinner, and keepe
me

me from all euill, from all occasion of euill, from all mortall sinne,
from all the deceptes and wilynes
of the deuill, and of mine enemies
visible and inuisible, by the prayers of the Patriarkes, by the merits of the Prophets, by the suffrages of the Apostles, by the constancie of Martyrs, by the faith of
the Confessours, by the chastitie
of Virgins, and by the intercession of al Sainctes, which haue pleased thee from the beginninge of
the worlde. Amen.

*A prayer to be sayed goinge out
of the house.*
Ioan Fab. in prec. Christ.

O All ye holy Angels and saints
of God, I beseech you, that
your intercession may geue me
ayde and power, that no enemie
may hurt me in the way that I shal
walke, neither sleepinge nor wa-
kinge,

king, and that neither fier, nor water, nor any other noyſome thing,
doe oppreſſe or harme me. Amen.

A prayer deſiring God to order
and directe vs.

De imit Chriſt.li.3 cap. 16.

Ord God thou knoweſt what
thing is to me moſt profitable
to doe, this or that, after thy will.
Geue me what thou wilt, as much
as thou wilt, and when thou wilt.
Doe with me as thou knoweſt beſt
to be donne, and as it ſhall pleaſe
thee, and as ſhal be moſt to thy honour: put me where thou wilt, and
freely doe with me in all thinges
after thy will. Thy creature I am,
and in thy handes, leade me, and
turne me where thou wilt. Loe I
am thy ſeruaunt redie to all things
that thou commaūdeſt: for I deſire
not to lyue to my ſelfe but to thee,
would to God it might be worthely

ly & profitably to thy honor. Amē.

A prayer to perseuere in goodnes.

Imitatio Christ.l.r.cap 19.

Elpe me my Lord Iesu Christ, that I may perseuere in good purpose, and in thy holy seruice vnto my death, and that I may now this present day perfectly beginne, for it is nothinge that I haue done in time paste.

An exercise to be dayly vsed in meditating the passion of our Lord & Sauiour.

An Exhortation.

If thou wilt profit and growe in the loue of God, thou must haue an often and frequent memorie, & as it were an Image before thine eyes, of thy Lord and Sauiour crucyfied for thee : and it shall be verye profitable for thy dayly exercyse, to call to thy mind (with a deuoute. and diligente attention and consideration) one or moe of these fiftiene litle meditations, and in the ende of the same meditation, say the prayer folowing for the same purpose

O mylde and innocēt Lambe. &c.

O Good & gracious IESV, thou beinge highest and almightie God, of the infinite charitie wherwith thou louedst me, wouldest be made man, thou didest vouchsafe, to be borne in a stable, to be laide downe in an oxe stall, and after that to be circumcised, and to flee into Egipte. Thou didest vouchsafe to be baptized, to fast, to be tempted, to watch, to teach to preach, and to heale the dyseased. Thou diddest vouchsafe to suffer manifolde labours, painfull cares and persecutions three and thirtie yeres, and at the length to come to Hierusalem and to suffer death for me.

This prayer folovving is to be sayed after one or moe of these meditations, as the leasure of the deuoute person shall serue, according to the tyme and deuoction

tion that the partye shall haue.

O Myld and innocent Lambe of God, thus hartely thou didest loue me, thefe thinges thou didest for me, thefe paines moft meekely, moft patiently and louingly thou fufferedft for me. VVhat fhail I render againe vnto thee? I adore, laud, and glorifie thee. I praife thee, and geue vnto thee thankes as hartely and as well as I can. All haile fweete I E S V, the fonne of the liuing God king of all kinges, the very king of glorie. All haile the precious ftone of the diuine nobilitie, that quickneth and geueth lyfe, the flower that neuer fadeth of mankinds high dignitie. O mercifull and kinde redeemer, haue mercy vpon me for thy goodneffe fake. Put awaye all my finnes. Deftroye and mortifie in me what focuer difpleafeth thee. Make me one according vnto thy blefled

blessed harte, making me like vnto
thy holy humanitye, Graunte, my
Lord, that I may to my litle power,
most diligently folowe thy blessed
lyfe and vertues. O blessed father
celestial, I offer vnto thee, the most
holy incarnation, conuersacion, &
passion of thy most deere beloued
sonne Iesu, for my saluation, and for
the saluation of all men, as for full
amendmente and purgation of all
our sinnes and offences. Graunte
most mercifull father by the same
onelye begotten sonne of thyne,
vnto them that are alyue, mercy &
grace, and vnto the soules departed, rest and lyfe euerlasting. Amen.

Medita. 2.

O Good and gracious IESV,
thou didest eate the pascall
lambe in Hierusalé with thy derebeloued disciples: and arising from
supper, thou diddest girdde thy
selfe

selfe about with a Towel, and pow-
redst water into a bason, and knee-
ling vpon thy knees, thou meekely
didest washe the feete of thy disciples, and wypedst them with a To-
well.

Medita. 3.

O Good and gracious IESV, thou,
before thou shouldest suffer,
did bequeth a most excellēt good
thinge vnto thy children, leauinge
for vs thy most sacred body to be
our meate, and thy most precious
bloude to be our drincke. There
can no witt nor vnderstanding pe-
netrate and throughly see the bottomles deapth of this thy charytie.

Medit. 4.

O Good and gracious IESV, thou
cominge vnto the garden of
Oliuet, begannest to feare and to
be heauy: whereupon thou saidest
vnto thy disciples.

My

My soule is soro vfull vntill death.
And then diuided & sondred from
them, thou settest thy selfe vpon
thy knees: and fallinge vpon the
earth flatte on thy face, thou pray-
edst vnto thy father, and fully and
wholly thou resignest and yeldest
thy selfe vnto him sayinge: Father
thy will be done.

And at length through most payn-
full agonye (where-with thou was
greuouselye opprest and afflicted)
thou swettest throughout all thy
body a bloodye sweate.

Medita. 5.

O Good and gracious IESV, thou
kindled and burning, with the
ineffable desire to redeeme me,
thou wentest to meete thyne enemies, and suffered Iudas the traitor
to kisse thee: and suffered thy selfe
to be taken, and to be bound with
all confusion and shame: and most
in-

indignely to be ledd with bondes
from thence, and that of moſt vile
and wicked perſons, vnto Annas:
where thou ſuffered moſt mekely,
a verye ſore ſtroke on thy face,
moſt iniuſtly geuen thee of a moſt
vyle manciple and ſlaue.

Medita. 6.

O Good and gracious IESV, thou
being faſt bound like a notori-
ous malefactour, waſt led vnto the
houſe of Cayphas the high Prieſt:
where the Iewes moſte vniuſtely
condemned thee, and moſt filthi-
ly and vily all beſpetted and ſpaw-
led thy royall and moſte amiable
face, and moſt ſpitefully they laied
on thee manye a ſore buffette and
blowe, and ſkornefully in mockage they did blindfolde and couer
thy face, and ſtrykinge thee, they
with mocke & ſcorne ſayed: Pro-
phecy Chriſt, who is he that ſtroke
thee

thee? doinge vnto thee innumerable iniuries all that nighte.

Medita. 7.

O Good and gracious IESV, thou
in the morninge was brought
before Pilate: and with most sweet
and pleasaunt countinaunce, cast-
ing thine eyes downe, stoodest before him in the iudgemente hall.
And when thou wast moste falsely
accused of the Iewes, and many a
rebuke and reproche was geuen
thee: thou most meekely heldest
thy peace and madest no answere.

Medita. 8.

O Good and gracious IESV, thou
was sente from Pylate vnto
Herode: This Herode of a vayne
and curious minde, couetinge to
see some miracle at thy hande, as-
ked and demaunded many things
of thee. And the Iewes sturdi-
lye accused thee still. But thow
amonge

amonge all thefe, moofte wifely heldeft thy peace. For this caufe Herode and all his, defpyfed and contemmed thee, put vpon thee a white garment, a dezerds cote : & lyke a fot he fent thee thus againe vnto Pylate, O howe vnmeafurable is this humilitie and obediéce? At the will and pleafure of thine ennemyes thou wenteft foorthe, & thou returnedft againe without gaine faying, fuffering thé to dooe to thee what foeuer they would.

Medita. 9.

O Good and gracious IESV, thou in the iudgement hall ftripped naked, and without all côpaffion being bounde faft to a pillar, was moofte cruelly fcourged. There was thy virginall & tender fleshe, cutte with whippes & torne with ftripes, all together mangled and deformed, with blacke and blewe

B   and

and many a wounde, so that the
streames of thy moste precious
bloude, ranne downe on euery
syde vpon the earthe.

Medita. 10.

O Good and gracious IESV, after
that sore and sharpe scour
gyng of thine, to put thee to more
shame and vilanye, thou was clothed of Sathanas souldiours with
a purple reade garment vyle and
torne. They also makyng a crowne
of thorne, painefully pressed the
same vpon thy moste holy heade:
And while the sharpe thorns pric-
ked greuously, and wounded sore
thy head, thy moost pure bloude
ranne downe aboundantly ouer all
thy louely face and necke. Then
they puttynge a reede into thy
ryght hande, and kneelyng downe
before thee in scorne, saluted thee
saying: All hayle Kynge of Iewes.
And

And then tooke they the reede,&
with many a fore ftroke they fmit-
te thy venerable heade. They alfo
fpette in thy mellifluous vifage &
ftroke thee on the bleffed face.

Medita. 11.

O Good and gracious IESV, thou
was brought foorthe by Pylate vnto the furious Iewes, to bee
gafed and looked vpon, wearinge
thy crowne of thorne and purple
garment: but they cried out with
more cruelneffe to haue thee crucified.

Medita. 12.

O Good and gracious IESV, thou
was delyuered vpp vnto the
will & pleafure of the Iewes, which
by & by led thee to bee crucifyed,
layinge the heauy croffe vppon
thy fore and bloudie fhoulders.
Thus didft thou beare mofte mekely

kely thyne owne crosse, whose
greate weyghte payned thee full
sore:and comyng vnto the place,
all werie & breathlesse with paine,
for my sake thou dydst not refuse,
to taste wyne mingled with gall &
myrre,which was there geuen vnto thee.

Medita. 13.

O Good and gracious IESV,
when thou was stripped naked,then were thy sore woundes
by the violent pullynge of thy
clothes, renewed.

Oh what a bytter and cruell
payne dyddest thou suffre, whan
thy tender handes and vndefyled
feete were with blounte & rough
nayles,faste nailed vnto the crosse,
and when the ioinctes of thy lim-
mes were loosed. Oh with what
loue and swetenesse of charitye,
didst thou offre thy handes and
feete

feete to be bored through. Then
out of the woundes of thy handes
and feete, as it had been out of wel-
les, thy precious bloude plentifully gufhed out.

Medita. 14.

O Good and gracious IESV, thou
hangynge vpon the croffe in
the middes betwene two theues,
was affayled with blafphemyes:
but thou praydft vnto thy father
the while, faying: Father forgeue
it them, they wote not what they
do. Then diddeft thou promife paradife vnto the theefe. Then ga-
ueft thou thy deere-beloued mother (who perfed with the fworde
of forowe, ftoode by the croffe)
vnto thy difciple Iohn , and vnto
vs all to be our mother. And after
that thou hadeft fuffred three long
houres intollerable paynes, and
thirfted verye vehemently, they
gaue

gaue thee eyſell to drinke, which
when thou hadeſt taſted, bowing
downe thy venerable head, thou
yeldeſt vp thy ſpirite.

Medita. 15.

O Good and gracious I E S V, O
good ſhepherde, thus thou
beſtowedſt thy lyfe for thy ſhepe,
and the right ſide of thy dead body was opened with a ſpeare, out
of the which flowed both water
and bloud for vs. Thou wouldeſt
that thy tender and louinge harte
ſhould be wounded for my ſake.
Afterwarde thy immaculate body
taken downe from the croſſe, thy
moſte bleſſed mother tooke it in
her lappe, ſhe kiſſed it, and wett it
with teares: At the length Ioſeph
and Nicodeme wounde it vpp in
Sindon, and layed it in the ſepul-
cher. My dere beloued, yea the
deare beloued of all my deſires,
thou

thou diddeft vouchfafe thus to die,
& to be buried for my fake, which
lyueft and reygnefte bleffed and
glorious for euer, and euer world
without ende. Amen.

*Thefe afperations and ghoftlye figh-
inges and prayers are needefull for
deuoute Chriftians to haue by harte:
(and often times to reuollue in minde
fome of them at the leafte) for attayning
to a ghoftly and perfecte lyfe.*

O Good Iefu, o gracious Iefu, o
fweete Iefu, o my hope, my
refuge, and my helth, haue mercy,
haue mercy, haue mercy vpō me,
I am poore, nedy, and weake, I am
naught, I haue naught, I know nothinge, I can dooe nothing of my
felfe but finne, helpe me therfore
fwete Iefu.

O Lorde bee mercyfull vnto
me mofte vile, mofte abominable
fynner, vnworthie to lyue on the

ca th

earth, verily it is but ryghte, that
euery man fhould defpife me, per-
fecute me,afflicte me,& ouertreade
me with their feete. I refigne and
furrendre me, yelding me wholy
vnto thee.Thy mofte bleffed and
thankeful will, bee euer done vpō
me and in me.

Graunt me(O good Lord)full
remiffion of all my finnes,wafhing
me in thy precious bloude.

Graunt me perfecte mortifi-
cation and denyinge of my felfe.
Deftroye in me myne owne will
and the fekyng of my felfe.

Graunt me true humilitye, perfecte patience &charitie, & of my
tounge & of all my fenfes perfecte
temperaunce.

Graunt vnto me, the puritie,
fimplicitie, nuditie, and libertie
of mynde, and alfo an exacte and
effenciall In-turnyng,that I maye
bee

bee one accordynge to thy hartes desire.

Lo, my singular beloued Lord, lo, I salute and honour thy rose-ruddy and swete woundes.

All hayle all haile moste plea-saunte and healthsome woundes of my Lorde.

All hayle moste bountifull harte of my deare louer, wounded for my sake: of all goodnesse, of all blisse the moste pleasaunt treasure house.

O My Lord Iesu Christ, I moste humblye thanke the for thy venerable woundes.

Oh Lord drowne me in them, hyde me in them: write and prynte them deepely in my harte, that I may burne al together in thy loue, and that I maye take compassion vpon thee from the harte.

Graunt that all fraile creatures

may

may bee vyle and of ſmall eſtima-
cion with me:and that thou onely
mayeſt pleaſe and bee ſwete and
delectable vnto me:Make me lyke
vnto thy holy humanitie.

O derely-beloued,derely-be·
loued,derely-beloued:O the moſt
derely-beloued of all derely-be-
loued:O my onely beloued.O my
freſhe and flouriſhinge ſpouſe : O
my melliſluous and hony-ſweete
ſpouſe : O the ſweteneſſe of my
harte,& the lyfe of my ſoule:ſette
me on fier,burne me,make me a
newe,and tranſforme me,that nothinge beſide thee,liue in me.

Oh, wounde very depely my
harte,with the darte of thy loue.
Then turne thy mynde to the godhead
of Chriſt , and quyetly thincke or ſaye
thus.

O My Lord God,o my delectable principle and beginnynge,
O

O amiable depth bottomleſſe, O
the clere lighte of my intrailes, and
bottome of my verye herte : O
moſte ſincere & delectable goodneſſe, my very and incomparable
goodneſſe: O my God & all thing:
what deſire I beſides thee? Thou
arte my highe & full contentacion,
and only ynough for me. Oh when
ſhall I luckely fynde thee? when
ſhall I ardently and mooſte feruently loue thee? when wilt thou
rauiſhe me all together into thee?
when wilt thou conſume me all
wholy into thee? when wilt thou
moſte faſt and ſure knytte me vnto
thee.

Oh remoue awaye mercifully
all impedimétes, and make me one
ſpirite with thee, to the laude and
prayſe of thy name.

All hayle glorious, ſhyninge
and euerlaſtinge quiet Trinitye,
fathe,

father, ſonne, and holy ghoſte, one
God. Oh voucheſafe to feede my
ſoule with thy goſtly influence.

*In lyke maner to the bleſſed mother of
God ſaye thus.*

HAyle MARIE full of grace,
oure Lorde is with the : hayle
ſweete Virgin, the bleſſed mother
of God: The very excellēt Quene
of heauen : Hayle bright ſhinynge
ſtarre : Roſe verye delectable and
pleaſaunt: The Orient white lyllie
of the Trinitye : O bleſſed ladye,
take pitye vpon me moſte poore
baniſhed man.

*In lyke maner to ſuch a Sainte of God
as thou haſt ſpeciall deuotion vnto, and
to thy holy Angell.*

ALhayle derebeloued of God,
bleſſed and holy ſaincte. N. or
all haile noble ſpouſe of Chriſte,
holy and bleſſed ſaincte. N.

Hayle holy Angell of God, my
faith-

faithfull keper. All hayle all ye
blessed sainctes of God, and all ye
blessed spirits Angelical, which are
fulfylled perpetually with the ve-
hemente streame of all diuine vo-
luptuousnesse & heauely pleasure:
pray for me now, and at the houre
of my death.

O mercifull IESV, I beseche
the, for thy moste venerable Passiõ
and death, graunt vnto the quicke,
mercy & grace, and vnto the deade
reste and euerlasting light.

An other briefe exercise to be vsed
dayly accordinge to the choyse of the
deuoute christian, as his opportunitie
shall serue.

O Good IESV, be mercyfull
vnto me abhominable sinner,
I haue sinned, I haue offended, I
haue done amisse before the Lord
perdon me. All my iniquitye, my
negligences, and all my immortifi-
cations

cations, I put thē all into thy moste derebeloued woundes, and I caste them into the bottomlesse depthe of thy mercy & merites. O would to God I had neuer offended thee: would to God I had neuer letted thy grace in me: I purpose now (by thy helpe) to correcte and amende my selfe. Oh Lorde, put awaye all my sinnes, washe me cleane with thy precious bloude : Make me whole with thy precious woundes Sanctifie me with thy bitter Passiō and deathe: Clense me perfectlye: Restore againe vnto me the inno-cencye, whiche thou gaueſt me in baptisme, that I maye trulye pleaſe thee: I worſhyp, I laude & glorifie thee, I prayſe & geue thankes vnto thee my Lorde IᴇSV CHRISTᴇ for all thy mercies and benefites. I thanke thee (O ſonne of the lyuing God) moſte higheſt GOD: whiche
for

for thy excedinge greate charitye,
that thou didſte beare towarde me,
haſt vouchefaſſed to bée made mã:
Thou wouldeſte for my ſake be
borne in a ſtable,and an infant be-
wrapt in clothes,to be layd downe
in a manger,to be fed with the litle
milke of the mayden thy mother,
to ſuffre nedineſſe and pouertye,
to be fore troubled thyrtie three
yeres with manifolde labours and
carefull paines.Thou wouldeſt for
very inwarde paine and agonie,be
all in a bloudy ſweate,to be appre-
hended and taken ſhamefully, to
bee bound vnworthily,to bee cõ-
demned vniuſtly, to bee defyled
with ſpettle, to be ſtricken vvith
buffettes & blowes,to bee clothed
& ſcorned as it were a madde man,
in a white garment in mockage:
Thou wouldeſt bee beatẽ & torne
moſte cruellye with ſtripes,moſte
cruelly

cruellye crowned with thornes,
ouerlodē with a painfull & heauye
croſſe, furiouſly and boyſteouſly
nailed vnto the croſſe with ſturdie
nailes,vnkyndely to haue offred to
thee in thy thyrſte,eyſell and gall.

Thou, the noble clother and
garniſher of the ſtarres, hangeſt all
naked,deſpiſed,wounded,and with
innumerable ſorowes afflicted vpō
the croſſe for my ſake.

Thou ſhedſt for me thy moſte
pure and precious bloude, thou
dyedſt for me. I embrace in the
armes of my ſoule thy venerable
croſſe:and for the loue & honourē
of thee I kyſſe the ſame. Graunte
that I may with whole & full deſire
attayne vnto thee,and that I maye
pauſe & reſte in thee,moſt ſweeteſt
of all.Lo my Lord lo,I repute and
ſet my ſelfe in the loweſt place vnder all creatures. For I am vnwor-

thy

thie, that the earth fhoulde beare
me.I caſte my felfe downe,& putt
my felfe vnder the ſtate of all men:
I ſincerely loue all men as well as
I can:I forfake and leaue all corruptible thinges for thy fake,I refuſe
what foeuer thou arte not: I forfake & renounce all fenſuall pleafure and delite:I renounce all vanitie and impuritie:I forfake al the
fekyng of my felfe and all immor-
tifications:I refygne and put me
wholy into thy hande & pleafure:
All my whole will I chaunge into
thyne:Thy onely will(Lorde)thy
onely will be done in me,and on
me:thy bleffed will be doone in all
times and euerlaſtyngly.I offre me
redie to fuffre,(with the helpe of
thy grace,)whatfoeuer it ſhal pleafe thee.

Oh moſte fweete and mercifull IESV,mortifie whatfoeuer lyueth

ueth naughtillie and senfuallye in me, and what foeuer is vicious and inordinate in me, what foeuer difpleafeth thee in me: mortifye in me all propertye: Garnyfhe and adourne me with thy merytes and vertues. Oh prepare (Lorde) a delectable, and a pleafaunt habitacion for thy felfe in me. Renewe my fpirite, my foule, & my bodie, with thy excellente grace: Make me like vnto thy holy humanitie: Make me one vnto thy hartes defire: Ridde & make clere, my mind and foule and make it fyngle, and lyghten it: Graunte me free inturning vnto thee. O my Lorde God, O my very & vnchágeable goodneffe, fulfyll me with thine owne felfe. Leade me into the clere bottome of my foule, and bringe me from thens into thee my originall. Knitſe me vnto thee mofte nerely,

and

and chaung & trãsforme me altogether into thee : that thou maiest
haue thy delyte in me. Here me
gracioufely, Lorde here me gracioufely, not at my will, but at thy
bleffed pleafure. Oh Lorde teache,
illumine, directe, and helpe me in
all things, that I maye doe nothing,
I maye fpeake nothinge, I maye
thinke nothinge, nor defyre nothinge, but that, whiche maye be
acceptable before thee.

Then to haue in minde our bleffed
ladye.

O Bleffed MARIE, O mofte
fweete Virgine, haue pitye
vpon me mofte vile finner: I falute
& I honour thee. Oh bleffed ladie,
optaine for me, of thy bleffed fõne
full remiffion of all my fynnes:
optaine for me, perfect mortifica-
tion and forfakinge of my felfe,
Optaine for me, very and true humilitie

militie, patiéce, charitie, refrainyng and temperance of my tong and of my fences: Obtaine for me, puritie, fimplicitie, & freedome of minde, and that I maye bee once accordinge to the hartes defire of thy fonne.

Take in mynde all Saintes.

O All ye bleffed faintes of God, and bleffed fpirites Angelicall, whome God with his mellyfluous countenance and bleffed prefence, maketh ioyfull and euerlaftingely glad, praye ye for me: I falute and honour you. I geue lauds & thãkes vnto our Lord, which hath chofen you, and hath preuented you in his benedictions: Oh optayne for me forgeueneffe, optayne for me grace, and to be made one with God.

O Mofte benigne, & mofte mercifull I E S V, haue mercie vpon
thy

thy churche, haue mercy vpon this
place and congregacion: Graunte
that here be cōtinuallie, humilitie,
peace, charitie, chaſtitie, & puritie:
Graunt that we all maye worthily
amende and correcte our ſelues, &
that we feare thee and ſerue thee
faithfully, that we maye loue thee
and pleaſe the. I commende vnto
thy mercie all our buſineſſe & our
neceſſities. Lord haue mercie vpon
all, for whome thou haſte ſhed thy
moſte holie blood. Oh Lord, conuerte, turne, and call agayne all
miſerable ſinners: graunt vnto the
quicke, forgeueneſſe & grace, vnto
the dead reſt and light euerlaſting.
Amen.

*A prayer for ſchollares before they goe
to ſchoole. for obtayning vviſdomē, lear-
ning, and knovvledge.*

COme O holy ſpirit repleniſhe
the harts of thy faythfull: ligh-

ten

tē in vs the fyer of thy loue, which
by diuerſitie of all languages haſte
aſſembled and gathered the people in the vnitie of ſayth.

O God which by the brightnes of
the holy Ghoſt, haſt inſtructed the
hartes of the faythfull, graunte vs,
that in the ſame ſpirite we maye
knowe that whiche is ryghte and
truth, and alwaies to be ioyfull in
his conſolation. Amen.

*Holeſome Meditations vvich you may
vſe at night, before you goe to reſte.*

1 VVhen thou wouldeſt goe to
bedde, thou ſhalt yelde thankes to
God for his greate mercy, that he
hath ſo preſerued thee that daye,
wherein dyuers throughe their
ſinnes hane fallen headlonge into
hell.

2 Then after, reuolue, and call
to minde diligently all the ſinnes
whereby any way thou haſt offended

ded God, or thy neyghbour that daye, and aſke God mercye for them.

3 Fynally, thou ſhalte praye to God with thy hart, that he would vouchſafe to haue care ouer thee, and that he would not ſuffer thee to periſh in workes of darckneſſe, and by theſe (or other lyke) pray-ers folowinge, thou ſhalte call for the ayde and ſuccour of our Lord and Sauiour.

An Eueninge prayer to be ſayed as thou goeſt to bedde.

Ex viridario ſpirituali.

ALmyghtye and euerlaſtinge God, I render thee moſt har-tye thankes, for that thou haſte vouchſafed of thy greate mercye and goodnes to preſerue me this day frō all euil. And I beſeech thee more-ouer for thy bitter death and paſſion, moſte mercifully to

par-

pardone me wretched sinner aH mine offences, that this day I haue committed by thought, worde, or deede : and hereafter to preserue and keepe me from all daunger, as well of body as of soule, to the end I may rise agayne in health, to prayse the name of thy maiestie, and ioyfully serue thee in thankes gyuinge with a chaste body and a cleare harte. Amen.

Our Father. &c. *Hayle Marye.* &c.
O Mary the mother of grace,
And of mercy mother also,
Defend me from the cruell foe,
And at my death my sou'e ebrace.
I Belieue in God the Father. &c.

An other prayer for the night.

O Lord God and my heauenly Father, forasmuch as by thy diuine ordinance the night approcheth, and darknes begynneth to ouerwhealme the earth, and tyme requi-

requireth that we geue oure felues
to bodylye refte & quietnes, I render vnto thee mooft hartie thankes
for thy louynge kyndnes, whiche
hafte vouchfaued to preferue me
this day, from the daunger of mine
enemies, to geue me my healthe,
to feede mee, and to feade me all
thinges neceffarie for the cöforte
of this my poor eand nedye lyfe, I
mofte humblie befeche thee for
Iefus Chriftes fake, that thou wilte
mercyfullie forgeue me all that I
haue this daye committed againfte
thy fatherlie goodnes, eyther in
worde, deede, or thoughte, & that
thou wilt vouchfafe to fhadow me
this nyght vnder the comfortable
wynges of thy almightie power, &
defende me from Satan, and from
all his craftie affaultes, that neither
he, or anye of his minifters haue
power ouer eyther my bodye or
                                    my

my foule. But that althoughe my
body thorowe thy benefyte en-
ioyeth fweete and pleafaunt flepe,
yet my Soule maye continuallye
watche vnto thee, thinke of thee,
delight in the, and euermore praife
thee : that when the Ioyefull light
of the daye returneth accordinge
to thy godlye appointemēt, I maye
ryfe againe with a faithfull foule,
aud vndefiled bodye, and fo ifter-
warde, behaue my felfe all my life
time accordingito thy bleffed will
and commaundement, by cafting
away the workes of darkenes, and
putting on the armoures of light,
that men feeing my good workes,
may therby be prouoked to glorifie thee my heauenlye Father,
which with thy onely begotten
fonne Iefu Chrift our onely faui-
oui and the holy Ghoft, that moft
fweete comforter, lyueft and raigneft

neſt one true and euerlaſting God, world without ende   Amen.

A prayer to thy good Angell thy gar-
diane.

Ex hortulo animæ ſecū. vſum Leodienſ.

I Beſeech thee O holy Angell, to
whoſe protection and cuſtodye
I wreched ſinner am committed,
continually to defende, ayde, and
garde me, from all inuaſion and aſſaultes of the deuill where-ſoeuer
I be, both waking and ſleepinge,
dryue away from me through the
vertue of the holy Croſſe✝al the
temptations of Satan, & that which
through the deſerts of mine owne
merites I can not doe, by thy praiers obtayne at the handes of the
higheſt and dreadfull Iudge, that
he may haue no place in me,
Amen.

A prayer as thou entreſt into thy bed.

B

A MANVAL

IN the name of our Lorde Iesus Chrifte that was crucified for me, I goe into my bedde : let him bleffe me ✝, gouerne me, and defende me, and bringe me into lyfe euerlaftinge   Amen.

A prayer to be fayed as thou feitleft thy felfe to fleepe.

L. Viues in precibus general.

O Iefu Chrift our fafegarde, receaue me into thy protection, and graunt that when my body is a fleepe, my foule may watch to thee, and that it may ioyfullye and gladlye beholde that bleffed, mofte ioyfull, and heauenly lyfe, where thou art gouernour together with the Father, and the holy Ghoft, and where the Angels, with the bleffed foules are citizens for euer and euer. Amen.

An

An exhortation to watche taken
out of holy Scripture.

*The day of our Lorde shall come as a
theefe in the night. Thes. 1. v. 5.*

*VVatche ye therefore because ye
knowwe not the day, nor the houre.
Math. 25. v. 13.*

*And that vvhich I say to you I say
to all: vvatche. Marc. 13. v. 37.*

The ende of the first Chapter.

Moste holesome meditations, which we ought day and night to haue before our eyes, and alwayes to haue in remembrance.

We ought continually to remeber these three things: that is to saye: — **Tyme**

Paste.
- That we haue vnprofitably spent.
- That good which we haue left vndonne.
- That euill which we haue committed.

Present.
- Of the shortnes of mans lyfe.
- Of the difficultie to be saued.
- Of the small number that shall be saued.

To come.
- Of death moste miserable.
- Of the last Iudgement most horrible.
- Of the paynes of hell intollerable.

THE SECONDE CHAPTER CONTEYNINGE GOODly & deuout prayers, to be sayed before, at & after the holy Sacrifice of the Masse.

A prayer vvhen thou doest enter into the churche.

Ex hortulo animæ.

AH, take from me (moste mercifull Lorde) all mine iniquityes, to the ende I may with a pure and contrite harte enter into the holy of holyes. O Sauiour of the worlde which lyuest and reignest with the father and the holy ghost.

A prayer to styrre vp the minde to deuotion before Masse.

Io. Fab. ex. Aug. 33. medit.

ALmightye and moste mercifull Father, vnto thee all the

hea

heauenly companie of the celestiall citie , all the blessed orders of
saued spirites, doe incessantly with
due reuerēce sing continuall glory and euerlasting prayse. Thee O
Lord, all saintes and soules of holy
men doe laude and magnifie, with
moste worthie and condigne honour, as to whome all prayse, honour and glorie is most iustly due.
Nor there is any creature, be he
neuer so worthy , that can suffici-
ently accordinge to thy worthy-
nes , geue vnto thee worthye and
sufficiente prayse. For thou arte
that vnspeakeable vncomprehen-
sible and euerlastinge goodnes.
Thou good Lorde hast made me,
thou haste through the merites of
the bitter passion of thy moste
blessed Sonne, which he vouche-
safed, to suffer for man-kind, restored me to the state of saluation
'I o

To thee onely is due all laude and honour, if anye good thinge be found in me. Oh good Lord, I miferable wretche, a creature of thy makinge, a poore woorme of the earth, haue good will to laude and magnifie thee, with all my minde & whole intent, but without thy fpeciall grace, I finde my felfe fainte and wonderfull weake, wherfore I come to thee my God, my lyfe, & my ftrength, my hope, and onelye comforte, to craue thy mercie and grace, to geue mee power to praife thee. Graunte of thy vnfpeakeable mercy that I may worthelie prayfe & honour thee, and that what I doe therin, may be pleafing & acceptable to thee. Graunt me the light of thy grace, that my mouth maye fpeake, & my harte ftudie thy glorie, & my tounge may be occupied only in the fong of laude & praife.

D   But

But becaufe all praife in a finners mouthe is vyle, and I muft offorce confeffe my felfe manifoldelie to haue offéded with my lippes, clése thou o good Lorde my harte from all filthe and finne. Sanctifie me mofte mightie Sauioure bothe inwardlie and outwardlie, and make mee worthy to magnifie thee:receyue of thy infinite goodnes the facrifice of my lippes, and make it acceptable in thy fighte : lett the fauour therof be plefaunte & well fmelling vnto thee : Let thy holie fwetenes poffeffe wholie my mind, and feade my foule with the fulnes of inuifible thinges:lett my foule good Lorde, bee quite cutte from vifible things, & all whollie geuen to the ftudie of inuifible thinges: cleane feperat from earthlie things, and wholie addicted to heauenlie meditations, & make my foule fee

the

the wonderfull fight of thy Maie-
ftie.O almightie God,enfpire thou
my harte,that I maye continuallie
geue thankes vnto the,and honour
thee for euer.Graunt mee the grace,that in my pilgrimage, and vale
of miferie,I may fo praife thee,that
through thy mercie & grace,I may
bee affociat to their holie fellow-
fhippe, whiche fee the euerlaftin-
glie,& finge prayfe to thee worlde
without ende. Amen.

*A deuoute prayer neceffary to be fayed
euery Sunday.*

Cornel. Donters in his contemplations
of the Paffion.

MY moft louing God and Lord
and my creatour, I miferable
finner doe prefente my felfe this
day before thine eyes,befeeching
thee humblye, that through thine
infinite bountye , thou wouldefte
vouchfafe to geue me grace , that
I may

I may keepe holy this Sunday, according to thy commaundement, and the precept of our mother the holy Church, geuing me true contrition of all my sinnes that I haue committed againſt thy diuine Maieſtie, and againſt my neighbour, by thoughts, wordes and deedes, and by omiſſion of good workes which I ought to haue done: And I moſt humblie beſeech thee moſt ſweete Ieſus, that thou wouldeſt not conſider the multitude of my ſinnes, but remember thine infinit mercy, and vouchſafe to graunte me grace to ſpende this weeke folowing, without mortall ſinne: and for the honour of thy death and paſſion, to geue to al ſinners knowledge and grace to do penaunce in this worlde, and generally to haue mercy of al thoſe that our mother the holy Churche deſireth (this

day

day) to pray for, that with her we
all may be partakers of thy forowfull paſſion. Amen.

A prayer to be vſed before confeſſion,
or before Maſſe if time ſerue.

OH maker of heauen and earth,
king of kinges and Lorde of
Lords, which of nothing diddeſt
make to thine image and lykenes,
and diddeſt redeme me with thine
owne precious bloude, whom I a
ſinner am not worthye to name,
neither to call vpon, neither with
my harte to thinke vpon, humbly
I deſire thee,& mekely pray thee,
that gently thou do beholde me
thy wicked feruaunte, and haue
mercy on me, which haddeſt mercye of the woman of Canane, and
Mary Magdalene, which diddeſt
forgeue the Publicane & the thefe
hanging on the croſſe: vnto thee
I confeſſe (moſt holy Father) my
ſin-

sinnes, whiche (if I woulde) I can
not hide frō thee. Haue mercy on
me O Chrisſ,for I (wretche)haue
sore offended thee,in pryde,in co-
uetousnesse,in gluttony, in leche-
ry,in vaine-glory,in hatred,in en-
uy,in adultery in chesſe,in lyinge,
backebitinge,in ſporting, in diſſo-
lute and wanton laughing, in Idle
wordes, in hearinge, in taſtinge,in
touchinge,in thinking,in ſtepinge,
in working & all wayes in which I
frayle man and moſt wretched ſinner might ſinne, my defaulte, my
moſt greuous default.Therefore I
moſt humblye praye & beſech thy
gentlenes,which for my health de-
ſcendedſt from heauen, whiche
diddeſt holde vp Dauid, that he
ſhoulde not fall into ſinne, haue
mercy on vs(O Chriſte)the which
diddeſt forgeue Peter that did for-
ſake thee.Thou arte my creator &
my

my helper, my maker, my redemer,
my gouernour, my Father, my
Lorde my G O D, & my king. Thou
arte my hope, my trufte, my gouernour, my helpe my ftrength, my
defence, my redemption, my lyfe,
my health, & my refurrectiō. Thou
arte my ftedfaftneffe, my refuge or
fuccour, my light, and my helpe. I
mofte humblie and hartely defier
and praye thee, helpe me, defende
me, make me ftrong, & cōforte me,
make me ftedfaft, make me merye,
geue me lighte, & vifite me, reuiue
me againe whiche am dead : For I
am thy makinge and thy worke,
(oh Lorde) defpife me not. I am
thy feruaunt, thy bondeman, although euill, although vnworthy,
and a finner. But what focuer I am,
whether I be good or bad, I am
euer thine: Therefore to whome
fhall I flie, except I flie vnto thee? If
thou

thou caste me of, who shall or will receiue me? If thou despise me, and turne thy face from me, who shall looke vpon me, and recognise and knowledge me, although vnworthy cōming to thee, although I be vile and vncleane? For if I be vile and vncleane, thou canste make me cleane: If I be sick thou canst heale me: if I be dead and buried, thou canst reuiue me: For thy mercy is muche more than myne iniquitie: Thou canst forgeue me more, than I can offend. Therfore (O Lord) doe not consider nor haue respect to the number of my sinnes, but accordinge to the greatnes of thy mercy forgeue me & haue mercie on me most wretched sinner. Saye vnto my soule, I am thy healthe, which sayedst I will not the death of a sinner, but rather that he lyue, and be conuerted, & turne to thee.

O

O Lorde bee not angry with me. I
praye thee moste meeke father,
for thy greate mercie. I most humblie defeech thee, that thou bring
me to the blyffe that neuer shall
ceafe. Amen.

THESE PRAYERS FOLOVVINGE
are to be fayed at Maffe.

Confiteor Deo omnipotenti. &c.
Mifereatur tui omnipotens Deus. &c.

VVhen the Preift is at Confeffion.

O Lord God almightye, longe
fuffering and much mercifull:
I haue finned without mefure, and
ftill mine iniquities do dayly encreafe: I haue prouoked thine anger by cōmitting euill wilfully in
thy fight, as it were determininge
naughtineffe, and multiplyinge
offences: I haue finned (O Lord)
I haue finned: and I acknowledge
mine iniquitie: But thou (O God)
of

of thy greate goodnesse haſt promiſed to the penitente remiſſion
of their ſinnes : I therefore now
bow the knees of my harte, beſee-
ching mercy of thee (O Lord) and
willingly detecting and deteſting
the ſinfulnes of my conſcience. I
ſay with the penitent Publicanne,
ſaye this thriſe: [* Be mercifull (O
God) vnto me a ſinner:*] Do not
deſtroy me together with my iniquities, nor reſerue my puniſhmét
to be perpetuall, but ſaue me thy
vnworthy ſeruaunte, according to
the multitude of thy mercies, and
I ſhall prayſe thee all the dayes of
my lyfe, becauſe all the powers of
heauen prayſe thee, and to thee
belongeth honour and glorie for
euer and euer. Amen.

*VVhen the Preiſt goeth to the Alter
after Confeſſion.*

Take

TAke from vs all our iniquities
(O Lord)that we may be wor-
thy to enter into heauc:*say thisthrise*
[* Haue mercy *] on thy people
(o Chrift) whom thou hafte redemed with thy precioufe blood.
Lord haue mercy vpon vs. Chrift
&c. Lord &c. Amen.

VVhen the Prieft fayeth.
Gloria in excelfis Deo

GLorie be to God on highe,and
in earthe peace to men of good
will : we prayfe the (o Lorde) we
worfhip thee,we magntfie the,we
adore the,we glorifie the,we thäke
the for thy great glorye, o Lorde
God,heauëly king,God the father
almightie, Lorde Iefu Chrifte,the
onely begottë fonne,and the holy
ghoft,Lord God, Lambe of God,
fonne of the father, whiche takeft
away the finnes of the world haue
mercie vpon vs, who takeft awaye
the

the sinnes of the worlde heare our
prayers, who sittest on the right
hand of God the father haue mercy vpon vs, because thou only arte
holy, thou onely arte Lorde, thou
only art moste highest Iesus Christ
with the holy ghost, in the glorie
of God the father. Amen.

ALmightie and euerlasting God
I moste humbly beseche thee
vouchsafe to looke vpon this con-
gregation, & mercifuly accept the
prayers of thy churche, made vnto
thee for vs all by the ministerie of
this Priest, & therby, for thy mercies, sake geue vs remission of all
our sinnes, integretie of mynde,
healthe of bodie, necessarie susté-
tatió, peace in our daies, temperate
ayre, fruitefullnesse of the earthe,
vnitie of faithe, rootinge out of all
heresies, destruction of all wicked
councels, encrease of true religió,
                                    car-

earneſt charitie, ſincere deuotion
in prayer, patiéce in troubles, ioye
in hope, and what ſoeuer is for our
ſoules health nedeſull and moſte
belonginge to thy glorie, through
Ieſus Chriſt our Lorde. Amen.

At the Epiſtle.

O God which haſt fully accom-
pliſhed in perfecte veritie that
whiche the lawe dyd foretell, and
vnder a wounderfull Sacramét haſt
left vs the memorie of thy Paſſion:
Graunt vs we beſeche thee, ſo to
worſhipp the holy miſteries of thy
bleſſed body and bloode, that we
may alwaye feele the fruite of thy
redemption in vs who liueſt and
raigneſt with God the father and
the holy ghoſt in perfecte vnitie
for euer. Amen.

After the Epiſtle.

O Glorious Trinitie, o venerable vnitie, by the we are created

ted, to true eternitie . by the are
we redemed, to true charitie, defend, faue, deliuer: protect & clenfe
all thy people, O God almightie:
we adore thee O God the father:
we praife thee O God the fõne: we
thanke the o God the holie ghoft
to whome thre perfonnes and one
God, be all honour and glorie for
euer and euer. Amen.

O Lord deale not with vs according to our finnes, nether reward vs accordinge to our iniqui-
quities, Lorde remembre not our
former offences : but thy mercies
fpedely preuẽt vs, becaufe we haue
greate neede thereof: helpe vs O
God our fauiour, and for the glorie of thy name deliuer vs, O lord,
and be mercyfull to vs for thy
name fake.

After the Ghofpell.
Credo in Deum Patrem. &c.

Good

GOod Lord graunt that we may all continewe in the true and sincere profession of the holy Catholicke fayth, to the ende of our lyues, and that we may therin fight a good battell, exercisinge our selues in all holinesse and godlinesse, to the end that after this lyfe we may receaue of thee O Lord a crowne of righteousnesse, which thou haste layed vp for all thine electe.   Amen.

At the offertorie.

O lord holy father, who through Iesus Christ thy onely sonne, haste taught a newe oblation of a new testament, which the Church receauinge of thy holy Apostles, offereth through-out the whole world to thee O God the creator of all things, offring vnder a hidden misterie, the first fruites of thy creatures and giftes, to witt, bread and

and wyne mingled with water,
ſtreight-wayes to be conſecrated
into the fleſh and bood of thy welbeloued ſonne, that by the ſame
oblation, he may repreſente him,
whoe is the lyuely bread deſcen-
dinge from heauen, geuing lyſe to
all the worlde, who by the bloode
and water which flowed from his
ſide did waſhe vs from our ſianes:
youchſafe almighty God mercifully to accept this oblatiõ, which
thy Catholicke Church oſſreth to
thee by the Prieſte for all thy people, whom thou haſte purchaſed
with the pretiouſe bloode of thy
deare-beloued ſonne our lord Ieſus Chriſt.　　Amen.

*VVhan the Prieſt turninge deſireth the
people to pray for him.*

OVr Lord ſend thee helpe from
heauen and protect thee. Our
Lord be mindfull of this thy ſacri-
fice,

fice,and receiue it at thy handes,to
the laud and glorie of his name, &
to the healthe and comfort of our
foules,& the foules of all faichfull
liuing and dead. Amen.

O Lorde whiche Iuftyfieft the
wicked and gyueft life to the
dead,quicken and raife me o Lord:
gyue me compunction of hart and
teares to my eyes,that I maye euer
bewayle the wickedneffe of my
hart with humilytie.Let my prayer
come before thy prefece O Lord:
Yf thou be angrie with me(o god)
what helper fhall I feeke? or who
fhall haue mercie vpo mine iniquities?remeber(O Lorde)that thou
didft call the woman of Cananea &
the Publicane to repetance,& didft
receiue Peter after his teares..Re-
ceiue alfo my praiers(O God)my
Sauiour,who liueft & raigneft for
euer. Amen.

E   When

VVhen the Priest saith.
Surſum corda.

O God father moſte highe, lyfte vp our hartes and minds (I be-ſeche the) from the cogitations of earthly cares, to the meditation of heaũely Ioyes, that we may thinke, and ſpeake of thee onely, and maye in all our lyfe expreſſe thee, and af-ter may enioy thee for euer. Amen.

Then ſay vvith the Prieſt.

IT is meete and iuſt, righte and neceſſarie that we alwayes and in all places geue thee thankes (O holy Lord) Father almighty, euer-laſtinge God, through Ieſus Chriſt our Lorde: by whome the Angells praiſe thy Maieſtie, the dominatiõs adore the, the powers tremble, the vertues of heauen and the heauens, and the bleſſed Seraphin with mu-tual gladneſſe gyue praiſe vnto the

with

with whome we befeche the that
thou wilt commande our prayers
to be receiued, fayeing with humble confeffion.Holie,Holie,Holie,
Lord God of Sabaothe. The heauens & earth are full of thy glorie.
Glorie be to God on the higheft,
bleffed is he that commeth in the
name of our Lorde,O fanna in the
higheft. Amen.

At the holy Canon.

O Mofte high Prieft and true Bi-
ſhoppe Iefus Chrift, who haft
offred thy felfe to God thy father,
(vpon the alter of the Croffe,) a
pure and immaculate Hofte for vs
wretched finners,who haft left vnto vs thy flefh and bloode in a Sacrament which is made by thy diuine omnipotencie,& haft ordeyned this Sacrament, whiche thou
commaundeft to be offred in remembrance of our faluatiõ, by the
fame

fame thy almightie power, I befeche thee, that thou wilt graunte
me poore finner, worthely to remember thy bleffed Paffion, and to
refigne and confecrate my felfe,
& all that I haue, wholly to thee,
who art my Lordè and redemer, &
to be prefent at this heauenly facrifice with feare & reuerèce, with
puretie of hart, & plenty of teares,
with fpirituall gladneffe, and heauenly ioye, lett my minde tafte the
fweteneffe of thy bleffed prefence,
and perceiue the troupes of thy
faints and Angells which are about
the. Amen.

SPeake with me (o bleffed Virgin
Mary) that my prayers may take
effect before thy fonne our Lorde
and Sauiour Iefus Chrift: Entreate
for me O ye Apoftles: make interceffion for me O ye Martirs: praye
for me all ye Confeffors and all the
holy

holye companie of heauen: the
prayers of such O Lord thou def-
piseft not: Infpire thē therefore to
praye for me O Lord which liueft
and raigneft one God for euer and
euer. Amen.

*Here meditate vvith your felfe till the
Eleuation.*

ANd thinke your felfe vnworthie to be prefent amonge fo
many thowfande of Angelles and
faincts, as are there (although inui-
fiblie to vs) tending vpō him (with
all reuerence) whom we (through
our finnes) caufed to die a mofte
bitter deathe, & whome (through
our euell lyfe) we from time to time (as much as in vs lyeth) do crucifie. Thinke how great his loue is
to vs, which by this dayly oblation
woulde preferue vs in that eftate
whervnto he once brought vs.
Thefe benefittes & others (as time
will

will suffer)considered:lett vs examine our selues & our behauiour
to so gracious a Lord,and say with
the Publicane, O God be mercifull to me a sinner.

O Moste mercifull Lorde Iesùs
Christ,in the remembrance of
thy most blessed incarnatiõ,death,
Passion,wounds, sorrows,greeues,
sighes,teares and drops of thy most
precious bloode , and in remembrance of thy moste infinite loue
to mankinde, and in the vnion of
this oblation,and of that sacrifice
by the whiche thou did offer thy
selfe on the Altar of the Crosse, I
doe offer my selfe to thy laud and
glorie:humblie besechinge the to
gyue to the lyuinge grace, to the
deceassed peace and rest, and to vs
all,mercie and life euerlasting.And
I commende vnto the O Lord my
soule and body,& all that is within
me

me, moste humblie beseching thee to haue mercy vpon me, and vpon all those whome I am bounde in respect of nature or frendshippe to praye for: as N. and N. &c.

At the Eleuation of the Host.

I Adore thee, & worshipp the (O Christ) with all praise & benediction. For by thy bitter deathe & Passion, thou haste redemed my soule from endlesse afflictiō. Haue mercie vpon me deare Iesus, and graunte that thy deathe be neuer found frustrate in me, I most humblie beseche thee. Amen.

At the Eleuation of the Chalice.

AL hayle moste precious and blessed blood, flowinge out of the side of my Lorde and Sauiour Iesus Christ, washinge awaye the spottes both of the olde and new offence: clense, sanctifie, and keepe my soule I beseche thee to euerlasing laſtinge life.

VVE thanke the O Lord God mercifull father, that thou did vouchefafe to fend thine one-lye begotten fonne Iefus Chriſt, into this wretched worlde to die for vs all, the moſt fhamefull death of the Croſſe, to the end that he myght offer him felfe to thee, through the holy ghoſte, a moſte pure, cleane, holy and acceptable facrifice for our finnes: and migl.t fo purge oure wicked confcience from all fpottes of vncleaneneſſe. By this thy exceding great loue to vs, and by thefe moſte cruell tor-mentes of thy fonne our Sauiour: we moſte humblie befeche the that thou wilt preferue in vs cõtinuallie thofe moſt noble fruites of his re-demption, and make vs alfo daylie to die with him to the worlde, and to be crucified to the luſtes & de-firs

firs of the fleshe, and to liue to thee
onely all oure life : So that in the
end we raigne eternallie with him:
where thou with the same thy sonne, and the holy ghoste, liueft and
raigneft one true and lyuing God
for euer and euer. Amen.

VVhen the Prieſt ſayeth the Pater no-
ſter ſaye vvith him.

LEtt vs pray. Being admoniſhed
by holeſome preceptes, and
being taught by diuine inſtitution,
we dare be bold to ſay.

Pater noſter qui es in cælis. &c.
Aue Maria gratia plena. &c.

VVhen the Prieſt kiſſethe the pax.

O Lambe of God, that takeſt
awaye the ſinnes of the world
haue mercie vpon vs. O Lambe of
God that &c. haue mercie vpon vs.
O Lambe of God that &c. Gyue
vs peace and quietnes.

Deliuer vs we beſeech thee (O
Lord

Lord)from all our euills paste, presente, & to come : and by the intercession of thy blessed and glorious
mother the virgin Mary, & of thy
holy Apostles Peter & Paule, & of
all thy saincts, mercifully graunte
vs peace in our dayes, that we being aided hy the helpe of thy mercye, may continually be free from
sinne, and safe from all parturbati-
on of mynde and bodye. Amen.

VVhen you kisse the Pax.

GEeue peace in our dayes (O
Lorde) because their is no o-
ther that fighteth for vs, but onely
thou O Lorde God.

VVhen the Priest receyueth.

O Sacred feast wherein Christ is
receyued, the memorie of his
passion is reuiued, the minde is replenished with grace, and a pledge
is geuen vs of the glory to come.

O

O Most mercifull Lord God father of mercye, graunte I befeech thee, that this vnbloody Sacrifice of the bleſſed bodye and
blood of thy ſonne our Lord Ieſus
Chriſt, which here & euery-where
throughout thy holie Churche, is
offred, to the great benefit of vs al,
(for a cōtinuall & daylie memorie
& thankes geuing) may entreat for
vs at thy handes, mercie & remiſſiō
of all our ſinnes. Amen.

Then bleßing your ſelfe ſaye.

T He grace of our Lorde Ieſus
Chriſt, the vertue of his moſte
glorioufe Paſſion, the ſigne of the
holye Croſſe, the integritie of the
moſte bleſſed Virgin Marie, the
bleſſing of all Saints, & the prayers
of all the Elect of God, be betwene
me and all my ennemies, viſible &
inuiſible, now and in the howre of
my death.

In

A MANVAL

In nomine patris & filii & spiritus
sancti. Amen.

A prayer after the diuine Sacrifice of
the Masse.

Cornelius Donters in his contemplations of the passion.

O Moste louinge Lorde and almighty God, I beseech thee
most humbly vouchsafe to receiue
for acceptable, the diuine seruice
which I haue done this day, to thy
honour and glorie, and to the honour of thy blessed mother, and
to the honour of all saintes, whose
feasts we celebrate in remission of
our sinnes, and for all our frendes
and benefactours, aswell those that
liue, as those that be departed: most
earnestlye requestinge, that thou
wouldest louinglye receyue these
our deuotions, in this time of thy
diuine seruice, and to forgyue me
mercifully, that which I haue done
with-

without deuotion, in dedes, words, and thoughtes. Gyue vs thy grace alwayes to walke in thy holy commaundementes, and to ferue thee loyally, to the ende thou maift be honored & glorified in vs. Amen.

A prayer to recommend your selfe to God.

In Eucholo Ecclefiaft.

OLorde I recommend into the hands of thy ineftimable mercy, my foule, my body, my fenfes, my wordes and my thoughtes, my counfayle, my workes, and all the neceffities of my body and foule, my entring and goinge foorth, my fayth and my conuerfation, the courfe and end of my lyfe, the day and houre of my departinge, my death, the refte and refurrection of my foule with thy faints and thine elected. Amen.

A

A MANVAL

*A prayer to be sayed before a Catho-
licke Sermon or exhortation.*

O Lorde Iesus Chrift, open the
eyes and eares of my harte, to
the ende I may heare and vnderftand thy holy worde, and to obey
it, according to thy holy will. I am
a pylgrime vpon earth, keepe not
hidden thy cõmaundements from
me. Open myne eyes that I may
vnderftand the marueloufe things
of thy lawe.

Gyue me wifdome, to lighten my
vnderftanding, to purifie my hart,
to inflame my affection, that I
may loue thee and knowe
thee, in all and aboue
all thinges.
Amen.

The ende of the fecond Chapter.

THE THIRDE CHAP-
TER CONTEYNINGE HOL-
fome prayers for remiffion of
finnes.

*An humble bevvaylinge of finnes for a
finner that hath compunction.*

Ioan.Fab in precat. Chriftian.

Moft heauenly kinge
and mofte mercyfull
Lorde and Sauioure
Chrift Iefu, here do I
come to thee beinge
verye fainte with the infirmitie of
finne, and far from the perfection
which thou requireft to be in me.
My confciéce doth dayely accufe
me, and more and more I finde the
imperfection and fraveltie of my
flefh. I do continually offende thy
Maieftie. All the imaginations of
my harte, all my words and deedes
whatfoe

whatfoeuer I do, or leaue vndone,
whether I eate, drincke, fleepe, or
watche, all my thoughtes, all my
fenfes are wholye bent to wickednes: whether fhall I turne me O
Lorde? Thou requireft of me integritie of life, and iuftice, and that I
fhoulde walke in thy holie commaundementes, wherto thou pro-
mifeft mee thy gratioushelpe: But
O Lorde I feele my owne will fo
peruerfe & ouer-thwart that I can
not hartelie wifhe and defire thofe
thinges whiche be requifite to my
faluatiõ: I haue no will to bewayle
my finnes, ne yet repente my wickednes from the bottome of my
harte: I am fo caried awaye with the
vanitie of this life, that I doo quite
forgette the benefites of thy death
and Paffion, whiche thou of thy
bountioufe liberalitie beftowed
vpon me mofte vyle. and abhominable

nable wretche. My offences bee fo
manie in number, and fo grieuous,
O moft gracious God, (wherwith
I offend thy Diuine maieftie,) that
were not thy moft mercifull pitie,
I had bene longe agoo drowned in
the depe dongeon of euerlaftinge
tormente. VVherfore I moft humblie thåke thy vnfpeakeable goodnes & mercie, that I am not alredie
founkė into the botomles pitte of
hell. But what fhall I doo? fhall I
defpayer? fhall I faye with curfed
Cain the murtherer ofhis brother,
my offences are greater thē can be
forgyuen me? No: God forbyd
that I fhoulde haue anye fuche
thoughte: no but this will I fay, my
God is mercifull and full of pitie,
he is my comforte, my ftrengthe &
confolatiō, my refuge, & defence,
he will not defpyfe the worke of
his owne hand, nor will cafte from

F

ꝛfore him me poore wretched fin-
ner:wherfore moſte mercifull Sauiour, I come to the, openinge in
thy ſight the thoughtes of my harte,for thou neuer fayleſte me with
thy gracioufe helpe.I cōfeſſe moſt
mercifull Lorde before thee,my
weakenes , acknowledginge my
owne imperfectiō,and bewaylinge
the multitude of my offences. O
euerlaſting and endles ſwetenes, o
vnſpeakeable mercie and moſte
louinge Father, I haue ſundrie times , and manies wayes offended
againſt heauen & thee,ſo that I am
not worthie to be reputed for thy
childe. For I haue abuſed thy fatherlie clemencie & mercifull pitie to mine vtter vndoing.Accepte
me o Lorde for one of thy hyred
feruauntes,and feede mee with the
comfortable bread of thy heauenlie grace, that I beinge refreſhed
                                  ther-

therwith, maye humblie ferue the
in thy houfe, in cleanes of lyfe, and
puritie of confcience, all the dayes
of my life. O fweete Sauiour Chrift
I hnmblie befeche the for thy bitter Paffion & bleffed mothers fake,
by that Marie Magdalene, whiche
foo feruentlie loued thee, whofe
finnes all thoughe they were manie, yet thou forgaueft them, and
madeft her pertaker of thy heauenlie glorie, receyue mee vnder the
wynges of thy mercie, & take compaffion vpon mee. Take from me
the fonde loue of this tranfitorie
world, & quenfhe in me all fillthie
luftes of the flefhe, and enkindle in
my foule a burninge defire of thy
glorioufe bleffe. Graunte mee almightie God true repentaunce for
my finnes : graunt me thy grace to
lamēte in mee my wante of forowe
for my offences : make my harte
                                    pure

pure & nette that my foule beinge
cleane, maye vtterlie abhorre and
hate finne. Graunte mee reconciliation to thee, throughe the comfortable Sacramente of penaunce:
& to bee receiued into the bleffed
cōpanie of thy chofen. Gyue mee
an earnefte defire to amende my
life, that I beinge holden vp withe
thy grace, may continue in holines
of lyfe to the ende of the fame, and
laftelie may attaine to thy heauenlie tabernakle, where I maye praife
and honoure thee, world without
ende. Amen.

A prayer of a penitent finner acknovv-
leginge his vileneffe in the fight of God.
Imit: Chrift. lib. 3. ca. 9.

SHall I Lorde Iefu dare fpeake
to the that am but duft & afhes?
verelye yf I thinke my felfe any
better then afhes and dufte, thou
ftandeft againft mee, and alfo mine
owne

owne sinnes beare witnes againste
mee, that I may not with-saye it: but
yf I despyse my selfe, and set my
selfe at naught, and thinke my selfe
but dust and ashes, as I am, then thy
grace shalbe nyghe vnto mee, and
the light of true vnderstandinge
shall enter into my harte, so that all
presumption & pryde in mee, shalbe
drowned in the vale of meeknes,
throughe perfecte knowledge of
my wretchednesse. I haue lost thee,
& also my selfe by inordinate loue
that I haue had to my selfe, and in
seking of thee againe, I haue found
bothe thee and mee, and therefore
will I more depelye from hence-
fourthe sett my selfe at naughte, &
more diligently seeke thee, than I
haue done in time paste : for thou
Lord Iesu, thou doest to me aboue
all my merites, and aboue all that
I can aske or disire. But blessed bee
thou

thou in all thy workes, for though
I be vnworthye any good thinge,
yet thy goodnes neuer ceaseth to
do well to me, and also to many
other which be vnkinde to thee,
and that are turned righte far from
thee. Turne vs Lorde threfore to
thee againe, that we may hencefor-
ward be louinge, thankfull, meeke
and deuout to thee : for thou arte
our health, our vertue, and all our
strength in body and in soule, and
none but thou. To thee therefore
be ioye and glory euerlastingly in
the blisse of heauen. Amen.

*A confession of a mans owne vngrate-
fulnes towardes God, whereupon the
sinner beinge turned vnto pennaunce,
prescribeth to himselfe a certaine course
of lyfe.*

Margarita euangelica. ca. 3. li. 4.

O

O God I am the prodigall child, which hath fundrie wayes offended thee, who being created of thee, in the ftate of innocencye, haue notwithftandinge that, without all fhame moft vily gyuen my felfe ouer to all diuelifh and lewde conuerfation. Thou waft crucified and diddeft humble thy felfe for me, and I haue fwelled vppe with pryde. Thou haft fhewed thy felfe naked and nedy, and couetoufnes hath ouerwhelmed me: Thou fuffredft fmarte and payne, but I lyue in wanton delicatenes: Thou waft ferued with efyll and gall, but I lye in beftely drounkénes: Thou waft alwayes well occupied in vertuoufe exercife, but I alwayes idle and neuer well occupied: Thou dideft pray for thine enemies, and I haue bene fo far from the prayinge for mine enemies, that I care

little

little for my frendes. But alas what
shall I do? shall I fall in despayre?
No, God forbyd: Iron that is rustie
may be clensed & skowred cleane
from rust, and I will cleanse my
selfe from the ruste of conscience
with contrition, cōfession, & satif-
faction. And as I haue through
pryde lyfte vp my selfe, so will I
plucke downe my harte by humilitie, & become a mocking-stocke
and skorne to the worlde: And because I will auoyde couetousenes:
I will quite abandone all desire of
worldlie and transitorie thinges: &
againſt the wantōnes of the flefhe,
I will hamper my flefhe, with continuall fobbing and fighing for my
finnes. By the burning compaſſion
of thy brotherlie loue, and feruent
charitie and the denyinge of thine
owne will, & for thy bitter Paſſion
haue mercie vpon mee.   Amen.

An

An humble confession of sinnes with
desire of mercy and grace.

O Lorde creator of heauen and earth, king of kinges and Lord ouer all dominion & power, which haste made mee of naught euen vnto thine owne likenesse by memorie, vnderstandinge, and will, wherby I may knowe, worshippe, and loue thee, & hast also redemed mee with thy most precious bloud, whome I detestable wretche and wicked creature am not worthye once to name, muche lesse to call vpon thee: the rather, for that I do acknowllege, & confesse my selfe. I haue bene & am an horrible & greuouse sinner: & haue so haynouslie transgressed in the sight of thy Diuine maiestie, that I ã not worthy to be called thy sone, no not so much as to haue the name of thy meanest or simplest seruant, nether yet that
the

the earthe fhould beare my foote-
fteppes,but rather for my wickednes to open her mouth to deuoure
and fwallowe me vppe,to be eternallye tormented in the bottom-
leffe pyt of hell. How muche leffe
then maye I prefume to offer vppe
vnto thee anye facrifice of prayfe
or thankes geuing?For if thou haft
not fpared the naturall braunfhes
& creatures of fo great excellécie,
that is to fay,Lucifer & his wicked
fauourers, but for the offences of
one rebellioufe & proude thought
and that fcarfe of fo longe continuance as the minute of an howre,
thou hafte throwen them downe
from the high habitatió of heauen
& euerlafting ioye & felicitie,(vnto whiche they were created,)into
the vale of euerlaftinge darcknes,
there to be eternallie tormented
in the flames of vnquenfhable fire,

Alas

Alas, what shall I then moste wretched sinner saye , or what iuste
excuse may I alledge, whiche haue
not offended in one sinne onely,
but in many, and that in heapinge
sinne vpon sinne from daye to day
without anye repentaunce? But yet
most merciful father becaufe thou
arte the father of mercie, and that
it is thy propertie alwayes to take
mercie, & defpifeftnot the fighing
of fuche as are vnfeynedlie côtrite
in harte, and willefte not the death
of a sinner, but rather that he maye
be turned againe vnto thee & lyue:
therfore I cheeflie hauinge assured
confidence in thy fuperabundaunt
mercie, doo humblie proftrate my
felfe before thy mercie-feate, in-
ftantlie befeeching thee to graunt
mee pardon, and remiffion of my
wretched wickednes , and greate
offences, with which I haue fo gre-
uouflie

uouflie offéded thy eternal goodnes, wittinglye or ignorauntlie, as
thou befte knowefte, from the beginninge of my lyfe vntill this prefente, and fpeciallye with fuche a
perfon, in fuch a place, thefe manye
times, in this manner, this fuggeftion mouinge me, this longe con-
tinuing without repentaunce, and
by my euill example geuinge fuch
and fuch occafion to finne.

Here call to minde particulerly in what
thou hafte offended God: VVith whom
thou haft finned: VVhom thou hafte in-
iuryed: How often, and how longe thou
hafte continued

Of all whiche, mofte mercifull
Father, it maye pleafe thee to perdon mee mofte fillthie finner, and
abhominable lyuer, and alfo all
other finners whiche cither I haue
entifed vnto finne, or gyuen exã-
ple of finning, & likewife all thofe
whiche haue gyuen mee occafion
of

of finninge:abfoluinge and deliuering vs from the grieuous heauye
bandes thereof,throughe the mercifull merites of the mofte bitter
Paffion of thy onely fonne and our
redemer Iefus Chrifte,who fuffered mofte cruell and vyle deathe
to faue finners.For otherwife what
fhoulde become of mee in that
mofte dreadfull iudgmente daye,
when the booke of confcience
fhalbe opened,whē it fhalbe fayed
of me,beholde the perfone and his
woorkes:at which time all the iniquitie that I haue committed,from
the firft daye of my lyfe,both in
harte, worde, and woorke, fhalbe
made open to heauen and earth,&
all thofe my finnes fhalbe there
prefente to accufe mee:moreouer
the dyuell and confcience redye
to beare wittnes therevnto, allfo
thou my wratthfull iudge vppon
                                their

their iuste accufation, thy iuftice
enforcinge the fame, redy to gyue
the terrible fentence of eternall
death againfte mee, and finallie the
horrible pitte of hell continuallie
gaping and opening his vnfatiable
mowthe, defyrous to fwallow
mee, the dredfull confideration
wherof would make mee, O Lord,
to defpaire, if I didde not call to
minde the infiniteneffe of thy mercie, my mofte mercifull redeemer:
For the finnes of men, be they neuer fo manie, are to be numbred:
but thy mercie Lorde God is infinite and without numbre, and thy
mercie great aboue all thy woorkes: for thy excedinge great mercie throughe effufion of thy mofte
precious bloude and voluntarie
death, hath purchafed pardon, and
forgiuenes for vs, before wee were
futers for it, yea when wee were
thine

thyne enemies, and gonne farre
awaye frō thee, howe muche more
rather shall wee obtaine it, when
wee through thy grace now being
reconfiled vnto thee, with our vn-
feined repētante hartes inceffant'ie
doo fue, and with bytter teares
humblie craue it? VVherefore O
Lorde of mercie, deale not with
mee after my defertes, but accordinge to thy great mercie: remēbre
not, fweete Iefu, thy feuere Iuftice
againft the finner, but be mindfull
of thy longe fufferinge goodnes
towardes thy creature. Remembre
not thy wrathe againft the offen-
dour, but be mindfull of thy mercie to vardes the repentant finner.

Remembre not my difobedience whiche ath prouoked the, but
refpecte him which in great forow
and heuines of harte, for his offéces
calleth vpon thee. For what is Iefus

fus but a Sauioure : Therefore O
Iefu for thine owne fake I befeech
thee, rife vppe to helpe mee, and
fay vnto my foule, I am thy fauing
health. I prefume muche of thy
goodnes O mercifull Lord being
therevnto imboldened, forafmuch
as thou thy felfe teacheft mee to
afke, to feeke, & to knocke. VVherfore beinge admonifhed through
thy teachinge, I afke, I feeke, and I
knocke, and thou Lorde whiche
commaundeft mee to afke, graunte
me to obteine : and thou whiche
counfayleft mee to feeke, graunte
mee to finde. And thou which teacheft mee to knocke, open vnto
mee at my knockinge, & make mee
beinge ficke in foule, to be whole:
reftore mee againe beinge as one
forlorne, and a cafte-awaye: Raife
me vppe (beinge deade throughe
finne) from death, and vouchfafe

to

to gouerne and directe all my fenfes,thoughtes,woordes,and actes,
fo as they maye be pleafaunt in thy
fight, that frō henffourthe I maye
trulie ferue thee, lyue to thee, and
cōmitte my felfe wholy vnto thee,
and to delight in nothinge, but in
thee and for thee. For I knowe O
Lord, that forafmuche as thou haft
made mee, I owe vnto thee my
felfe:and becaufe thou hafte redemed mee, and waft made man for
mee, I owe vnto thee more then
my felfe,if I hadde it,by fo muche
as thou art more woorthie then I,
for whome, thou being the fonne
of God and fecond perfon in Trinitie,wouchfafeft to fuffre for my
fake moft grieuous tormentes and
fhameful deathe.Yet Lo,more thē
my felfe, I haue not to gyue, neither yet I can gyue that vnto thee
without thee, wherefore doe thou
G   re-

receiue mee, & draw mee through thy grace vnto thee, that I maye aſwell bee thine by loue and imitation, as I am thine by calling and creation. VVhich liueſt & reigneſt for euer and euer: vnto whome be all honour & glorie world without ende. Amen.

A prayer for a penitent ſinner after his relapſe or falling to ſinne agayne.
Antonius Hemert. in Speculo perfectionis.

O Lorde Ieſu Chriſt I vnhappie ſinner moſt vile and vnthankfull: Lo, now againe I haue offended thee, by this worde N. or by this ſinne N. I haue diſhonoured thy maieſtie, & haue reiected thee, which aboue all thinges ought to be to me moſt deare and agreable.

Thou knoweſt (O Lord) how muche I am yet Carnall, how litle mortyfied, how full of euell concupicupifcence, how I am flootinge in externall pleafures, how often enwrapped in vayne fanfyes, how negligent in fpirituall exercifes, how light in laughing and diffolution, how harde & difficult in wepinges and côpunction, how euell aduifed in fpeakinge, how impatient in kepinge filence, how much gyuen to eating and drinckinge, how deafe and dull in hearinge godly admonitiôs, how attêtife to babling, how fluggifh to heare dyuine feruice, how fodaynlie I am troubled and letted to doe good, how manye things I purpofe wherof I accomplifhe none.

O my Lord my God, I am full of Sorowe & grief, for that I haue finned, & alfo for that I haue tooto litle compunction: I defire with all my harte, that thou wouldefte wounde my hart with the forowe

of

of moste perfecte contrition. And
for asmuch, as perdition and offence proceedeth from me, and
grace and mercy from thee, I purpose from this time forwards (beinge assisted by thy grace) from
hence foorth to keepe my selfe,
from all misdeedes, and to auoyde
all occasions of sinne. Amen.

*A moste profitable protestation to be
made vvhyles vve are yet in healthe
and prosperitie,*
Cornelius Donters in his contemplations vpon the passion.

O Lord God almighty to whom
all thinges are manifeste and
knowne: O eternall Sapiéce which
preferueth all things, I poore wretched creature in despite of mine
enemy make protestation, whyles
I am in good health and perfecte
memory, wherein I stande at this
present

present through thy grace, that although it happen or come to paſſe that by any temptation, illuſion, deceipte or variation comming of griefe of ſicknes, or by weakenes of body, or by any other occaſion whatſoeuer, I come in daunger of my ſoule or preiudice to my ſaluation, or in errour of the Catholicke fayth in the which I am regenerated in the fountayne of Baptiſme, there promiſed to reſiſte all temptations of the deuill and all errours of fayth: And at this preſent I do reſiſte and renounce as I did then, and then as now, proteſtinge moſte feruently with all my harte to lyue and dye in the fayth of our mother the holy Church thy ſpouſe: and in witneſſe of this proteſtation and confeſſion I offer (the articles of our holy chriſtian fayth which thy holye Apoſtles

hath

hath lefte vs) in recommendinge
vnto thee my fayth, lyfe and death.
Amen.

I beleeue in God the Father &c.
The ende of the third chapter.

THE FOVRTHE CHAP-
TER CONTEYNINGE VERY
goodly prayers, for cõfort, ſtrẽgth
and deliuery (by Gods aſſiſtance)
in all ſorowes, tribulations, afflictions and aduerſities.

VVhen thou feeleſt thy ſelfe tempted,
ſaye as folovveth.
Imitatio Chriſti li.3. ca.7.

Thou Satan, the deuyll,
enemie of mankynde, I
adiure thee by the name
of our Lorde God, and
by the ſigne of the holy croſſe ✝
that thou departe and neuer hereafter

after enter into me.O thou wicked
fpirit auoide from mee,& be thou
afhamed for thou arte foule and
ouglie,that wouldeft bringe fuche
thinges into my minde.Goe from
mee thou falfe deceyuer of mankinde,thou fhalte haue noo parte
in mee for my Sauiour Iefus ftan-
deth by mee as a mightie warriour
and a ftrong champion,and thou
fhalte flye awaye to thy confufion.
I had leuer fuffer the mofte cruell
death then to confente to thy malicious ftirringes:be ftill therefore
thou curfed fyende,and ceafe thy
malice,for I fhall neuer affente to
thee,though thou vexe mee neuer
fo much,our Lorde is my lighte &
my healthe,whome fhall I dreade?
and he is the defender of my life,
what fhall I feare? Truelie though
an hofte of men aryfe againft mee,
my harte fhall not dread them,for
whie

whie? God is my helper and my redeemer. Amen.

A prayer of any captiue accordinge to the forme of Dauid, vvhen he vvas hid in the caue. Pſal. 142.

VVIth my voice I cry to thee, afore thee I open my lamentations, in thy boſome I diſcloſe the ſecrete word of my hart, my dolours and griefes I ſhew vnto thee, my harte is almoſte lyke to bruſte, ſo great is my diſcomfiture. Thou knoweſt all my dealinges O Lorde: and thou ſeeſt well ynough how the vngodly haue layed their ſnares for me. Lo I caſte mine eye on this ſide, and that ſide, aſwell on my frends as kinſſolkes, but all is in vaine, none of them al helpeth me. And againe I can not runne away, I am ſo loadē & ouercharged with irons. O Lorde my maker and father, now vnto thee I cry, thou art

mine

mine onely Shot-anker,defence &
helpe.Thou art my porciō & heritage which I poffeffe in al coūtries,
yea, I haue none other poffeffion
but thee onely:To thee therefore
I fticke altogether,knowinge certainly that nothing can goe amiffe
with me.Confider then my lamen-
table complaynte, beholde how I
am brought low: From the cruell
purfuers which be much more of
power than I am,defend me:Deli-
uer me from this prifon , and horrible feare of finne and death, that
I may fette out thy name, all thy
fainctes as well Angells as men,
make fute for me,defiring thee for
my comfort.They fhall not ceafe
vntill they obtaine their requefte,
I meane vntill thou forgyue me
my finnes, and fende me comfort
in this diftres with pacience and
lōg fuffering.This once obtayned,
the

the godly folke shal flocke aboute
me,& shall not stynt to gyue thee
thankes, when they see that thou
riddest me forth of these dangers,
to the highe prayse of thy name,
Lorde be mercyfull vnto vs, take
part with vs,then we shall for euer
lyfte vp,and magnifie thy glorious
name. Amen.

A prayer of Iob , in his moste grieuous
aduersitie and losse of goodes. Iob. 1.

Naked I came oute of my mothers womb, and naked shall I
returne agayne,our Lorde gaue, &
our Lorde hath taken awaye, as it
hath pleased our Lord,so is it done
nowe blessed be the name of our
Lorde.   Amen.

A prayer in trouble of conscience.

Psal   134.

Lorde heare my prayer,receyue
my supplicacion,harken to my
cõplaint for thy righteousnes.Try
not

not the lawe with thy feruaunt, for
trulye then fhall no lyuynge man
be founde vngyltie, yea, not one
of thy faintes fhould efcape quitte
at thy barre, vnleffe thou graunte
him thy gracious pardon, in fo-
much, euen the very ftarres be not
pure and fautles afore thee, in the
Angels thou foundeft fin. Nowe
mine enemies hunte for my foule,
they beate & dryue it downe, they
thrufte it into darcke dungeons,
where felons conuicte and con-
dempned to death, were wonte to
be kept, my fpirit is forowfull, my
hart is heauie and fadd with in my
breaft, to thee I holde vp my hädes,
requiring the of mercy. For lyke as
the dry ground lögeth for a fhow-
er of raigne, fo my foule thinketh
long till it hath thy helpe and fuccour, heare me fpedely. if thou do
not? I am in difpaire, my fpirites is
all

alwerie of this bondage.I haue bid
my life fare-well: VVherfore O
God, hide not thy face, that I be
not lyke to thofe that be hurled
into the pyt of damnatiõ:after this
night of mifery ouerpaffed,let the
pleafaunt morninge of comfort
luckyly fhyne vpõ me,that by time
I may heare and fele thy goodnes,
for in thee is all my truft : pointe
me the waye, that I fhall walke in,
for yfthou be not my guide,I muft
nedes wander and ftraye out of the
waye. To thee Lorde I lift vp my
foule,and that with all mine harte
I befech the,take me forth of mine
enemies handes. Thou onely art
my fuccour and fauegarde, teache
me to worke what foeuer fhall be
thy pleafure,for thou art my God.
Let thy good fpirite conducte me
into the land of the lyuing, encou-
rage my fpirite for thy names fake:
                                    furth

furth of all thefe troubles, for thy
righteoufnes delyuer me: côfound
mine enemies as thou art gracious
& fauourable towardes me. Thofe
that will worke me forowe and
griefe, plucke forth of the waye,
for I am thy feruaunt, and for thy
fake fuffer I all this hurlye-burlye.
As thou art God, fo helpe thou
me.   Amen.

A prayer for patience.
De Imit. Chrift. li. 3. cap. 20.

O Lorde, for as muche as thou
was founde paciente in thy
life, fulfillinge in it mofte fpeciallie
the will of thy father, it is requifite
that I moft wretched finner fhould
behaue my felfe pacientelye after
thy will in all thinges, and as longe
as thou wilt, that I for myne owne
health beare the burthen of this
corruptible life : for thoughe this
lyfe be tedioufe and as heauie a
bur-

burthen to the foule, yet neuerthe-
leſſe it is now through thy grace
made very meritoriouſe, and by
example of thee, and of thy holy
Sainctes it is now made to weake
perſons more patient, clearer, and
alſo much more comfortable then
it was in the olde Lawe, when the
gates of heauen were ſhut, and the
way thytherwarde was darke, and
ſo fewe did couet to ſeeke it. And
yet they that were then righteouſe
and were ordeyned to be ſaued,
before thy bleſſed paſſiŏ and death
mighte neuer haue come thyther.
O what thankes am I bounde therfore to yelde to thee, that ſo louingly haſte vouchſafed to ſhewe
to me, and to all faythfull people
that will folow thee, the very true
and ſtraight way to thy kingdome.
Thy holy lyfe is our way, and by
thy pacience we walke to thee that
arte

arte our heade and gouernoure.
But that thou Lord haddeſt gonne
before and ſhewed vs the waye,
who woulde haue endeuored him
ſelf to haue folowed: O how many
ſhould haue taried behynd if they
had not ſeene thy bleſſed example going before, we be yet ſlowe
and dull, although we haue ſeene
and hard thy ſignes and doctrines:
what ſhould we then haue bene if
we had ſeene no ſuch light goinge
before vs? Truely we ſhould haue
fixed our mind and our loue wholy in worldly thinges. Make therfore O Lorde that poſſible to me
by grace, which is vnpoſſible by
nature. Thou knoweſte well O
Chriſt, that I can ſuffer little, and
that I am anone caſte downe with
a little aduerſitie: wherefore I beſeech thee, that trouble and aduerſitie may hereafter for thy names
ſake,

fake, be beloued and defired of me. For truelye to fuffer and to be vexed for thee, is very good, and profitable, to the healthe of my foule.

A prayer agaynft the enemies of Chrifts trueth.   *Pfal.*   139.

DElyuer me (O Lord) from the vngodly & ftiffe necked perfones, for thou feeft howe in their hartes they imagyn mifchiefe, and haue greate pleafure to picke quarèls, their tonges bee more fharper then anie Adders ftingge, & vnder their lyppes lyeth poyfon of Adders, but O mercifull Lorde let me not fall into their handes that they handle me not after their owne luftes.

Thou onely arte my God, thou mufte heare my piteous côplainte, Lorde that ruleft all together, that arte the ftrength and power of my defence

defence,be thou as a helmet vpon
my head,whenfoeuer the vngodly
fhall affaulte mee, neither fuffer
thou not the wicked thus to pro-
fper in their matters. Suffer not
their canckarde and malicious fto-
mackes to increafe and fpitefullye
to reuile me.Looke vpõ thy poore
wretches caufe,and ryd me out of
thefe dayely greuaunces,then fhall
I with an vp right hearte and pleafaunt countenaunce extoll & magnifie thy holy name. Amen.

*A prayer vvherin is defired freedome
of the minde and auoydance of vvorld-
ly defires.*

Imitatio Chrift.li.3. ca.30.

IBefeche thee mofte meeke and
mercyfull Lorde Iefu,that thou
keepe me from the bufines and
cares of the worlde , and that I be
not taken with the voluptuoufe
H plea-

pleafure of the worlde, nor of the
flefhe, and that in lykewife thou
preferue me from all hindraunce
of the foule, that I be not broken
with ouermuch heuine s, forowe,
nor worldly dreade. And by thefe
petitions I afke not onely to be
deliuered from fuch vanities as the
world defireth, but alfo from fuch
miferies as grieue the foule of me
thy feruaunte with the common
malediction of mankinde, that is,
with corruption of the bodelye
feeling wherwith I am fo grieued
and letted, that I may not haue libertie of fpirite to beholde thee
when I would. O Lord God thou
art fweetenefle vnfpeakable: turne
into bitternefle to me all flefhely
delightes, which would drawe me
from the loue of eternall thinges,
to the loue of a fhorte and a vile
delectable pleafure: Lette not
flefh

flesh and bloud ouercome me, nor
the worlde with his shorte glorie
deceyue me, nor the fiende with
his thousand-foulde craftes sup-
plante me, but gyue me ghostly
strength in resistinge, pacience in
suffering, and constancie in perse-
uering. Gyue me also for al worldly consolations, the moste sweete
consolation, of the holy Ghoste,
and for all fleshly loue sende into
my soule the loue of thy holye
name. Loe, meate, and drinke, clo-
thinge, and all other necessaries
for the bodye are paynefull and
troublesome to a feruent spirite,
which if it mighte, would alwayes
rest in God and in ghostly things,
graunte me therefore grace to vse
such bodely necessaries tempo-
rally, and that I be not deceyued
with ouermuch desire to them. To
forsake all thinges it is not lawfull,
for

for the bodely kinde muſt be preſerued, and to ſeeke ſuperfluous
thinges more for pleaſure than for
neceſſitye, thy holy lawe prohibi-
teth, for ſo the fleſh would rebell
againſt the ſpirite: wherfore Lord
I beſeech thee that thy hande of
grace maye ſo gouerne me, and
teach me that I exceede not by a-
ny maner of ſuperfluitie.

*A prayer before vve take in hande a-
ny Iourney.*
By Arnould Sobin.

O Good God whom it pleaſed
to direct Abraham, Iacob and
young Tobias in their peregrina-
tions, and brought thē in health &
ſafety into their country: Graunt I
beſech thee to be my directour in
this Iourney, which I would in no
reſpect vndertake (much leſſe followe and finiſhe) if I knew it any
away

waye contrarye to thy holy will.
Therefore (O Lord) gyue me Ra-
phael for my conductor, to whose
custodye I may be deliuered, and
thereby be broughte with happy
successe to the accomplishinge of
that worke whereunto I prepare
and dispose my selfe.

Directe my vnderstandinge (O
Lorde) to the ende that my feete
no where straye from the obseruations of thy holye commaundementes: In the name of thy welbeloued sonne Iesus Christe our redeemer, whoe with thee in vnitie
of the holy Ghost lyueth & reig-
neth eternally.   Amen.

*Here folovveth (for the vse of those that
are desirous to rede latine prayers) certayne verses collected by Sir Thomas
Moore foorth of Dauids psalter: in the
time of his trouble and persecution for
the Catholicke faith: conteining an inuo-
ca'ion*

*cation to God for his helpe against temp-
tation, vvith an insultatio against vvic-
ked spirites, vpon hope and confidence
in God.*

IMPLORATIO DIVINI AVXILII
*contra tentationem, cum insultatione contra
Dæmones ex spe & fiducia in Deum.*

Omine quid multiplicati
sunt, qui tribulãt me? multi insurgunt aduersum me.
Multi dicunt animæ meæ,
non est salus ipsi in deo
eius.

Tu autem domine susceptor meus es,
gloria mea, & exaltans caput meum.

Ego dormiui, & soporatus sum: & exur-
rexi quia dominus suscepit me.

Non timebo millia populi circundantis
me, exurge domine, saluum me fac deus
meus.

Psa. 5. Domine deduc me in iustitia
tua, propter inimicos meos dirige in cõ-
spectu tuo viam meam.

Quoniam non est in ore eorum veritas,
cor eorum vanum est.

Sepulchrum patens est guttur eorum,
linguis suis dolose agebant iudica illos
deus

deus.

Decidant a cogitationibus fuis: fecundũ multitudinẽ impietatum eorum expell eos, quoniam irritauerunt te domine.

Et lætentur omnes qui fperant in te, in æternum exultabunt, & habitabis in eis.

Domine vt fcuto bonæ voluntatis tuæ coronafti nos.

Pfa. 7. Domine deus meus in te fperaui, faluum me fac ex omnibus perfequétibus me, & libera me.

Nequando rapiat vt leo animam meam, dum nõ eft qui redimat, neq; qui faluum faciat.

Exurge domine in ira tua, & exaltare in finibus inimicorum meorum.

Perfequatur inimicus animam meam vt comprehendat, & conculcet in terra vitã meam, & gloriam meam in puluerem deducat.

Arcum fuum tetendit, & parauit illum: & in eo parauit vafa mortis, fagittas fuas ardentibus effecit.

Ecce parturit iniuftitiam, concepit dolorem, & peperit iniquitatem.

Lacum apperuit, & effodit eum, incidit in foueam quam fecit.

Conuertetur dolor eius in caput eius, &
in

in verticem ipsius iniquitas eius descendet.

Confitebor domino secundum iusticiam eius:& psallam nomini domini altissimi.

Psa 4. In pace in idipsum dormiam & requiescam.

Quoniam tu domine singulariter in spe constituisti me.

Psa 9. Miserere mei domine, vide humilitatem meam de inimicis meis.

Et sperent in te, qui nouerunt nomen tuum domine, quoniam non dereliquisti quærentes te domine.

Et factus est dominus refugium pauperi, adiutor in oportunitatibus in tribulatione.

Vt quid domine recessisti longe, despicis in oportunitatibus in tribulatione?

Quoniam non in finem obliuio erit pauperis, patientia pauperum non peribit in finem.

Exurge domine deus, exaltetur manus tua, ne obliuiscaris pauperum.

Tibi derelictus est pauper, orphano tu eris adiutor.

Desiderium pauperum exaudiuit dominus: præparationem cordis eorum audiuit auris tua.

Domi-

Dominus in téplo sancto suo, dominus in cælo sedes eius.

Oculi eius in pauperem respiciunt:palpebre eius interrogant filios hominum.

Propter miseriam inopum & gemitum pauperum nunc exurgam, dicit dominus.

Domine deus meus in te speraui,saluum me fac ex omnibus persequentibus me & libera me.

Psa 12. Vsquequo domine obliuisceris me in finem ? vsquequo auertis faciem tuam a me?

Quandiu ponam confilia in anima mea: dolorem in corde meo per diem?

Vsquequo exaltabitur inimicus meus super me?respice, & exaudi me domine deus meus.

Illumina oculos meos,ne vnquá obdormiam in morte : nequando dicat inimicus meus,præualui aduersus eum.

Qui tribulant me, exultabunt si motus fuero : ego autem in misericordia tua speraui.

Exultabit cor meum in salutari tuo cantabo domino qui bona tribuit mihi,& psallam nomini domini altissimi.

*Psa.*15. Conserua me domine,quoniam
speꝛ

speraůi in te,dixi domino,deus meus es
tu,quoniam bonorũ meorum non eges.
*Pſa.*16. Perfice greſſus meos in ſemitis
tuis:vt non moueantur veſtigia mea.
Mirifica miſericordias tuas, qui ſaluos
facis ſperantes in te.
*Pſa.*15. Prouidebam dominum in con-
ſpectu meo ſéper,qui a dextris eſt mihi,
ne commouear.
Propter hoc lętatum eſt cor meum,& ex-
ultauit lingua mea, inſuper & caro mea
requieſcet in ſpe.
*Pſaſ.*17. Tu illuminas lucernã meam domine deus,illumina tenebras meas.
Quoniam in te eripiar à temptatione, in
deo meo tranſgrediar murum.
Deus meus impolluta via eius,eloquia
domine igne examinata, protector eſt
omnium ſperantium in ſe.
Quoniam quis deus præter dominum,
aut quis deus præter deum noſtrum.
Pſa 21. Ego auté ſum vermis & non homo, opprobrium hominum , & abiectio
plebis.
Omnes videntes me deriſerunt me, locuti ſunt labijs,& mouerunt caput.
Tu es qui extraxiſti me de ventre, ſpes
mea ab vberibus matris meæ,in te proie-
ctus

&tus sum ex vtero.

De ventre matris meæ deus meus es tu,
ne discesseris a me.

Quoniam tribulatio proxima est, quoniam non est qui adiuuet.

Tu autem domine ne elongaueris auxi-
lium tuum à me, ad defensionem meam
conspice.

Et si ambulauero in medio vmbræ mortis, non timebo mala,quoniã tu mecũ es.

Virga tua & baculus tuus ipsa me conso-
lata sunt.

Psa. 24. Ad te domine leuaui animam
meam,deus meus in te confido,non eru-
bescam.

Neque irrideant me inimici mei,etenim
vniuersi, qui sustinent te, non confundentur.

Delicta iuuentutis meæ, & ignorantias
meas ne memineris.

Secundum misericordiam tuam meméto
mei tu:propter bonitatem tuam domine.

Propter nomen tuum domine propitia-
beris peccato meo,multum est enim.

Oculi mei semper ad dominũ, quoniam
ipse euellet de laqueo pedes meos.

Tribulationes cordis mei multiplicatæ
sunt,de necessitatibus meis erue me.

Vide

Vide humilitatem meã & laborē meum,
& dimitte vniuersa delicta mea.

Psa. 26. Dominus illuminatio mea, &
salus mea,quem timebo?

Dominus protector vitæ meę,à quo tre-
pidabo?

Si consistant aduersum me castra,non ti-
mebit cor meum.

Si exurgat aduersum me prælium,in hoc
ego sperabo.

Vnam petij a domino hanc requiram,vt
inhabitem in domo domini omnibus
diebus vitę meæ.

Vt videam voluntaté domini,& visitem
templum eius.

Exaudi domine vocem meam, qua cla-
maui ad te miserere mei,& exaudi me.

Tibi dixit cor meum,exquisiuit te facies
mea,faciem tuam domine requiram.

Ne auertas faciem tuam a me : ne decli-
nes in ira a seruo tuo.

Adiutor meus esto, ne derelinquas me,
neq; despicias me deus salutaris meus.

Credo videre bona domini in terra vi-
uentium.

Expecta dominum viriliter age : confor-
tetur cor tuum,& sustine dominum.

Psa. 27. Ad te domine clamabo, deus
meus

meus ne fileas à me : nequando taceas à
me,& affimilabor defcendétibus in lacū.

Pfa 29. Pfallite domino fanƐti eius, &
confitemini memoriæ fanƐtitatis eius.

Quoniam ira in indignatione eius,& vita in voluntate eius.

Ad vefperam demorabitur fletus : & ad
matutinum læticia.

Auertifti faciem tuam à me, faƐtus fum
conturbatus.

Ad te domine clamabo,& ad deū meum
deprecabor.

Quæ vtilitas in fanguine meo,dum de-
fcendo in corruptionem.

Pfa 30. In te domine fperaui, non confundar in æternum, in iufticia tua libera me.

Inclina ad me aurem tuam, accelera vt
eruas me.

Efto mihi in deum proteƐtorem,& in
domum refugij,vt faluum me facias.

Quoniam fortitudo mea & refugium
meum es tu,& propter nomen tuum de-
duces me,& enutries me.

Educes me de laqueo,qué abfconderunt
mihi:quoniam tu es proteƐtor meus.

In manus tuas domine commendo fpi-
ritum meum,redemifti me domine deus
veri-

veritatis.

Miserere mei domine, quoniam tribulor,conturbatus est in ira oculus meus, anima mea & venter meus.

Quoniam defecit in dolore vita mea, & anni mei in gemitibus.

Infirmata est in paupertate virtus mea, & ossa mea conturbata sunt.

Super omnes inimicos meos factus sum opprobrium vicinis meis valde, & timor notis meis.

Qui videbant me foras fugerunt à me: obliuioni datus sum tanquam mortuus a corde.

Factus sum tanquam vas perditum: quoniam audiui vituperationem multorum commorantium in circuitu.

In eo dum conuenirent simul aduersum me, accipere animam meã cõsiliati sunt.

Ego autem in te speraui domine, dixi, deus meus es tu, in manibus tuis sortes meæ.

Illustra faciem tuam super seruum tuũ, saluum me fac in misericordia tua domine, non confundar, quoniam inuocaui te:

Quoniam magna multitudo dulcedinis tuę domine, quam abscondisti timentibus te.

Ecce

*Pſa.*32. Ecce oculi domini ſuper timentes eum, & in eis qui ſperant ſuper miſericordia eius.

Vt eruat à morte animas eorum, & alat eos in fame.

Anima noſtra ſuſtinet dominū, quoniam adiutor & protector noſter eſt.

Quia in eo lætabitur cor noſtrum, & in nomine ſancto eius ſperauimus.

Fiat miſericordia tua domine ſuper nos, quemadmodum ſperauimus in te.

Pſal .33. Accedite ad eum, & illuminamini ., & facies veſtræ non confundentur.

Immittet angelus domini in circuitu timentium eum, & eripiet eos.

Guſtate & videte, quoniā ſuauis eſt dominus, beatus vir, qui ſperat in eo.

Timete dominū omnes ſancti eius, quoniam non eſt inopia timentibus eum.

Diuites eguerunt & eſurierūt inquirentes autem dominum non minuentur omni bono.

Iuxta eſt dominus his, qui tribulato ſunt corde, & humiles ſpiritu ſaluabit.

*Pſa.*35. Filij hominum in tegmine alarum tuarum ſperabunt, inebriabūtur ab: vbertate domus tuæ.

Quo-

Quoniam apud te est fons vitæ, & in lumine tuo videbimus lumen.

Pfa 37. Domine ne in furore tuo arguas me neque in ira tua corripias me.

Quoniam sagittæ tuæ infixæ sunt mihi, & confirmasti super me manum tuam.

Non est sanitas in carne mea: a facie iræ tuæ, non est pax ossibus meis a facie peccatorum meorum.

Quoniam iniquitates meæ supergressæ sunt caput meu, & sicut onus graue grauatæ sunt super me.

Putruerunt & corruptæ sunt circatrices meæ a facie insipientiæ meæ

Miser factus sum & curuatus sum vsque in finem: tota die côtristatus ingrediebar.

Quoniam lumbi mei impleti sunt Illusionibus: & non est sanitas in carne mea.

Afflictus sum & humiliatus sum nimis: rugiebam a gemitu cordis mei.

Domine ante te omne desideriũ meum: & gemitus meus a te non est absconditus.

Cor meum conturbatum est, dereliquit me virtus mea: & lumen oculorum meorum, & ipsum non est mecum.

Amici mei & proximi mei aduersum me appropinquauerunt & steterunt,

Et qui iuxta me erant de longe steterunt,

& vim

& vim faciebāt,qui quærebāt animā meā.
Et quiinquirebāt mala mihi,locuti sunt
vanitates:& dolos tota die meditabantur.
Ego autem tanquam surdus, non audie-
bam:& sicut mutus non aperiens os suū.
Et factus sum sicut homo non audiens,&
non habens in ore suo redargutiones.
Quoniam in te domine speraui,tu exau-
dies me domine deus meus.
Quia dixi nequādo supergaudeant mihi
inimici mei,& dum commouentur pedes
mei,super me magna locuti sunt.
Quoniam ego in flagella paratus sum,&
dolor meus in conspectu meo semper.
Quoniam iniquitatem meā annunciabo,
& cogitabo pro peccato meo.
Inimici autem mei viuunt,& confirmati
sunt super me : & multiplicati sunt, qui
oderunt me inique.
Qui retribuunt mala pro bonis detraha-
bant mihi:quoniam sequebar bonitatem.
Ne derelinquas me domine deus meus,
ne discesseris a me.
Intende in adiutorium meum, domine
deus salutis meę.
Psa:38. Dixi, custodiam vias meas, vt
non delinquam in lingua mea.
Posui ori meo custodiam,cum cōsisteret

I   pec-

peccator aduersum me.

Obmutui, & humiliatus sum, & silui a
bonis,& dolor meus renouatus est.

Concaluit cor meum intra me,& in medi-
tatione mea:exardescet ignis.

Locutus sum in lingua mea, notum fac
mihi domine finem meum.

Et numerum dierum meorum quis est,
vt sciam quid desit mihi.

Ecce mensurabiles posuisti dies meos,&
substantia mea tanquam nihilum ante te.

Veruntamen vniuersa vanitas,omnis homo viuens.

Veruntamen in imagine pertransit homo,sed & frustra conturbatur.

Thesaurizat, & ignorat cui congrega-
bit ea.

Et nunc que est expectatio mea?nonne
dominus?& substancia mea apud te est?

Ab omnibus iniquitatibus meis erue
me,opprobrium insipienti dedisti me.

Obmutui,& non aperui os meum : quoniam tu fecisti,amoue à me plagas tuas.

A fortitudine manus tuæ ego defeci in
intrepationibus, propter iniquitatem
corripuisti hominem.

Et tabescere fecisti sicut araneam animã
eius,veruntamen vane conturbatur omnis

nis homo.

Exaudi orationem meam domine, & deprecationem meam auribus percipe, lachrimas meas.

Ne fileas: quoniā aduenā ego fum apud te, & peregrinus, ficut omnes patres mei. Remitte mihi, vt refrigerer priufquam ab eam, & amplius non ero.

Pfa. 3 9. Beatus vir cuius eft nomen domini fpes eius, & non refpexit in vanitates, & infanias falfas.

Multa fecifti tu domine mirabilia tua, & cogitationibus tuis non eft qui fimilis fit tibi.

Tu autem domine ne longe facias miferationes tuas a me, mifericordia tua & veritas tua fufceperunt me.

Quoniā circundederunt me mala quorū non eft numerus: comprehenderunt me iniquitates mee, & nō potui vt viderem. Multiplicatæ funt fuper capillos capitis mei, & cor meum dereliquit me.

Complaceat tibi domine, vt eruas me: domine ad adiuuandum me refpice.

Exultent & lętétur fuper te omnes quęrentes te, & dicant femper, magnificetur dominus qui diligunt falutare tuum.

Ego autem mendicus fum & pauper, dominus

minus solicitus est mei.

Adiutor meus & protector meus tu es, deus meus ne tardaueris.

Psa. 41. Quemadmodū desiderat ceruus ad fontes aquarum, ita desiderat anima mea ad te deus.

Sitiuit anima mea ad deum fontē viuum, quādo veniā & apparebo ante faciē dei?

Fuerunt mihi lachryme meæ panes die ac nocte, dum dicitur mihi quotidie, vbi est deus tuus?

Hæc recordatus sum, & effudi in me animam meā, quoniā transibo in locum tabernaculi admirabilis vsq; ad domū dei.

In voce exultationis & confessionis sonus epulantis.

Quare tristis es anima mea? & quare conturbas me?

Spera in deo, quoniam adhuc confitebor illi, salutare vultus mei, & deus meus.

Ad meipsum anima mea conturbata est, propterea memor ero tui de terra Iordanis, & Hermonija monte modico.

Abyssus abyssum inuocat in voce cataractarum tuarum.

Omnia excelsa tua & fluctus tui super me transierunt.

In die mādauit dominus misericordiam
suam

suam, & nocte canticum eius.

Apud me oratio deo vitæ meæ, dicã deo, susceptor meus es.

Quare oblitus es mei? & quare contristatus incedo, dum affligit me inimicus?

Dum confringuntur ossa mea, exprobrauerùnt mihi qui tribulãt me inimici mei.

Dum dicunt mihi per singulos dies, vbi est deus tuus?

Quare tristis es anima mea? & quare conturbas me?

Spera in deo quoniam adhuc confitebor illi, salutare vultus mei & deus meus.

Psa 45. Deus noster refugium & virtus: adiutor in tribulationibus quæ inuenerunt nos nimis.

Propterea non timebimus dũ turbabitur terra: & transferentur mõtes in cor maris

Sonuerunt & turbatæ sunt aquæ eorum. cõturbati sunt mõtes in fortitudine eius:

Fluminis impetus lætificat ciuitatem dei, sanctificauit tabernaculũ suũ altissimus:

Deus in medio eius non commouebitur adtuuabit eam deus mane diluculo.

Psa. 50. Miserere mei deus secundum magnam misericordiam tuam.

Et secundum multitudinẽ miserationum tuarum dele iniquitatem meam.

Am-

Amplius laua me ab iniquitate mea:& a peccato meo munda me.

Quoniã iniquitaté meã ego cognofco: & peccatum meú contra mé eſt ſemper.

Tibi ſoli peccaui,& malum coram te feci:vt iuſtificeris in ſermonibus tuis,& vincas cum iudicaris.

Ecce enim in iniquitatibus conceptus ſum:& in peccatis cõcepit me mater mea.

Ecce enim veritatem dilexiſti:incerta & occulta ſapientiæ tuę manifeſtaſti mihi.

Aſperges me domine hyſopo,& mundabor:lauabis me,& ſuper niué dealbabor.

Auditui meo dabis gaudium & lętitiam: & exultabunt oſſa humiliata.

Auerte faciem tuam a peccatis meis : & omnes iniquitates meas dele.

Cor mundum crea in me deus & ſpiritũ rectum innoua in viſceribus meis.

Ne proijcias me a facie tua : & ſpiritum ſanctum tuum ne auferas a me.

Redde mihi lætitiam ſalutaris tui:& ſpiritu principali confirma me.

Docebo iniquos vias tuas:& impij ad tê conuertentur.

Libera me de ſanguinibus deus deus ſalutis meę : &exultabit lingua mea iuſtitiam tuám.

Do-

Domine labia mea aperies: & os meum
annunciabit laudem tuam.

Quoniam si voluisses sacrificiu dedissem:
vtique holocaustis non delectaberis.

Sacrificium deo, spiritus contribulatus:
cor contritum & humiliatum, deus non
despicies.

Benigne fac domine in bona voluntate
tua Sion:vt ædificetur muri hierusalem.

Tunc acceptabis sacrificiu iustitiæ obla-
tiones & holocausta:tunc imponent super altare tuum vitulos.

*Psa.*54. Exaudi deus orationem meam,
& ne despexeris deprecationem meam,
intende mihi & exaudi me.

Cor meum conturbatum est in me,& for-
mido mortis cecidit super me.

Timor & tremor venerunt super me, &
contexerunt me tenebræ.

Et dixi,quis dabit mihi pennas sicut co-
lumbe,& volabo & requiescam?

Iacta super dominum curam tuã, & ipse
re enutriet.

Psa 61. Nonne deo subiecta erit anima
mea?ab ipso enim salutare meum.

Nam & ipse deus meus, & salutaris meus
susceptor meus,non mouebor amplius.

Quousque irruitis in hominem?interfi-
                                        citis

citis vniuerſi vos, tanquam perieti incli-
nato,& maceriæ depulſæ.

Veruntamen deo ſubiecta eſto anima
mea,quoniam ab ipſo pacientia mea.

Quia ipſe deus meus & ſaluator meus,
adiutor meus, non emigrabo:

In deo ſalutare meum,& gloria mea,deus
auxilij mei, & ſpes mea in deo eſt.

Sperate in eo omnis congregatio populi,effundite coram illo corda veſtra, adiutor deus noſter in æternum.

Semel locutus eſt dominus,duo hæc audiui,quia poteſtas dei eſt,& tibi domine
miſericordia,quia tu reddas vnicuique
iuxta opera ſua.

*Pſa.*62. Deus d eus meus ad te de luce
vigi'o.

Sitinit in te anima mea, quam multipli-
citer tibi caro mea.

In terra deſerta,inuia,& inaquoſa,ſic in
ſancto apparui tibi : vt viderem virtutem
tuam & gloriam tuam.

Quoniam melior eſt miſericordia tua ſuper vitas:labia mea laudabunt te.

Sic benedicam te in vita mea :& in nomine tuo leuabo manus meas.

Sicut adipe & pinguedine repleatur anima mea : & labijs exultationis laudabit
os

os meum.

Sic memor fui tui super stratum meum,
in matutinis meditabor in te,quia fuisti
adiutor meus.

Et in velamento alarū tuarum exultabo:
adhefit anima mea post te: me suscepit
dextera tua.

Ipsi vero in vanū quęsierunt animā meā:
introibunt in inferiora ter:æ,tradentur
in manus gladij,partes vulpium erunt.

Rex vero lætabitur in deo,laudabuntur
omnes qui iurant in eo:quia obstructuṃ
est os loquentium in iqua.

P ſ.66. Deus misereatur nostri, & benedicat nobis ,illuminet vultum suum
super nos,& misereatur nostri.

Vt cognoscamus in terra viam tuam,in
omnibus gentibus salutare tuum.

Confiteantur tibi populi deus,confiteā-
tur tibi populi omnes.

Lætentur & exultét gétes,quoniam iudi-
cas populos in æquitate,& gentes in terra dirigis.

Confiteātur tibi populi deus,cōfiteantur
tibi populi omnes,terra dedit fructū suū.
Benedicat nos deus deus noster,bñdicat
nos deus,& metuāt eū omnes fines terrę.

FINIS.

THE FYFTH CHAPTER

CONTAYNINGE DYVERS prayers verye commodiouse for obtayninge that which is profitable and holsome both to body and soule.

A prayer to obtayne fayth, hope and charitie.

Ioan. Lanspergius in diuina amoris pharetra.

I Beseech thee most mercifull Lorde Iesus for thy greate and exceedinge compassion and mercy, to power into my soule a simple, righte and pure fayth, firme hope, perfect and burning charitie, that being delyuered from all errour and sinnne, I may yeld my vnderstanding obediente to the Catholicke Church: and that I may sett all my cogitations and care vpon thee, that I may resigne

and

and commit my selfe wholy to thy
prouidence & gouernement, not
accompting of any creature in respect of thee: but perceyuing (in
all thinges) thy fatherly care and
loue towardes me, I may receyue
all thinges at thy hande, and may
praise and thanke thee for the same,
and may alwaye imploye, resigne
and offer vp my selfe, to thy moste
blyssed will and pleasure. Amen.

A deuout prayer to obtayne a feruente
loue tovvardes God, our neighboures,
and our enemies.

Ioan. Lanspergius Ibidem.

O Moste louinge sauyour Iesu
Christ, which haste loued and
washt vs, with thy precious blood,
& gyuen thy soule to death for vs,
haste bene reputed with the wicked and impious, thou was moste
cruelly wounded, for our iniquities

ties, brufed and crufhed for our
offences, and by thy ftrypes, we
were made whole.

I befeech thee (O Lord) for this
thy ineffable & vnfpeakable mercy and charitie, to power into my
harte the vnquenfhable lighte of
thy heauenlye grace, fo that the
fire of thy charitie, may perpetually burne and worke within me, and
that their may alwayes growe in
me, fuch a continuall chaft and ne-
uer-fayling affectiō, of pitie, bene-
uolence, and pietie, as extendeth
it felfe to all creatures through the
loue and contemplation of thee.

Fill O Lorde I befeech thee, my
foule, my fenfes and defires, with
feruent and perpetuall charity, that
in all thinges, and aboue all, I may
mofte hartely loue thee, and that
accordinge to thy good will and
pleafure, I may loue my neyghbour

bour in thee and for thee.

Graunt me grace(I humblie befeech thee) that with all my harte
I may to thy glory loue, fearche,
and aduaunce, the faluation, profit
and commoditie of euery one.

Graunte me O Lorde to loue
mine enemies moft perfectlye, not
in worde or fhowe onelye, but in
deede and trueth: take from me all
bitterneffe of minde, wrath, euill
anger, rancour, difdayne, fufpition,
enuie, and whatfoeuer is againft or
contrarie to pure and fincere charitie : fo that in all fimplicitie of
harte, I may haue a good opinion
of all men: that I may iudge no
man rafhly, but may loue euery
one in thee with mofte holy and
hartye affection, and that I may
fhewe them both in wordes and
workes all fweetnes, clemency and
loue. Amen.

                                    For

A prayer for obtayninge of heauenlye vvisdome.

GRaunte me O almyghtye and moste mercifull Lorde hartely to thirst after all such thinges as are pleasaút and acceptable vnto thee, wisely to search them out, truely and vnfaynedly to acknowledge them, and throughly in deede and worde to accomplish them. Direct me in the path of thy glorye, and gyue me knowledge to wil and do such thinges as thou commaundest me to doe: with due execution to fulfil all things belonging to salua-tion. Graunt that my way towards thee be certayne, safe, and stedfast, neither waueringe through aduer-sitie, or prosperitie, lest by the one I be puffed vp with to much pride, or dryuen with the other into des-peration. Gyue me grace to yelde thee thanks for my prosperitie, and

to

to take aduerſitie patiently, to reioyce or take pleaſure in nothing,
but onely in ſuch thinges that be
furthering to thee, deſire to pleaſe,
or feare to diſpleaſe none but thee
onely. Graunt me good Lord charitie in all my doinges, and to ac-
compte as vile and abhomynable
all thinges not partayninge to the
true worſhiping of thee. Directe
my deedes not accordinge to cuſtome, but in thy feare and deuotion. Graunt that al tranſitory things
may grow lothſome vnto me, thy
glorie and honour to be of moſte
pryce with me, and ſpecially aboue
all thinges that I may loue and honour thee, my moſt ſweete ſauiour
Chriſt. Make all things vnpleaſaunt
vnto me that are not pleaſaunt vnto thee. Cut of from me all deſire
of any thinge that towcheth not
thee, make me to delighte in euery
la-

labour that concerneth thee, and
earneſtly to hate all reſte and quy-
et but in thee onely. Graunte mē
ſweete Ieſu often to delight in the
ſweete and comfortable thoughts
of thy diuine Maieſtie, beſīde my
whole affection towardes thee, and
gyue me grace erneſtly to bewaile
my ſinnes, with ful intent to amend
my lyfe. Graunte me O mercifull
Ieſu, true contrition without diſſi-
mulation, myrth without wanton-
nes, heuines of my ſinnes without
abiection of minde, ripe iudgemēt
without coūterfait grauitie, quicknes without vnſeemely lightnes,
truethe without doublenes, true
feare of thee without deſperation,
a perfect hope and affiance in thee
voyde of all preſumption, chaſtitie
and cleanes of lyfe free from all
laſciuious luſtes, to finde faulte and
rebuke others without malice, to
loue

loue hartelye without diffimula-
tion, yea and to helpe all men both
with counfayle and good example
without pryde or vayne glory, to
be obediente without grudginge,
and patiente withot fpurninge at
aduerfitie. Graunt fweete fauiour
Chrift vnto me a vigilāt and wake-
full mind, that no fonde fancy may
cary me away from thee : ftedfaft-
nes that no wauering affection may
fhake: conftancie that no paine, forowe, or tribulation may daunte,
that freedome of mynde that no
violence of feruile pleafure maye
pearfe: a ftraight and true harte towardes thee that no peruerfe or fi-
nifter thoughte haue power to
make me fwarue from thee. Gyue
me fweete Iefu an vnderftandinge
minde in the knowledge of thee:
diligence to fearch thee : wifdome
to fynde thee: conuerfation accep-
K   table

table and pleasinge vnto thee: perfeuerance in the fweetenes of thy
holy fayth: a fure confidence and
trufte in thee: to be faftened to thy
holy paffion by penaunce : to enioy the merites of thy bleffed benifites through grace. And laftlye
of all to be partaker of thy heauenly manfion in the euerlaftinge
bliffe and felicitie. Amen.

A prayer mofte godlye and deuoute
vvhich S. Thomas of Aquin vfed day-
ly to praye.

GRaunt me moft mercifull God
feruentlie to defire fuch things
as may be acceptable and pleafing
vnto thee, with wifdom to fearche
after them, not to be deceyued in
the knowledge of them, and vn-
faynedlie to accoplifhe the dooing
of them, to the prayfe and glorie
of thy holie name. Directe fo my
life

lyfe, and graunte mee that I maye
both haue knowlege,wil & power
to doo,that whiche thou requie-
reſt I ſhoulde doo, in ſuch ſorte,as
is behoueable and moſt expedient
for my foule. Let my waye vnto
thee O Lorde be ſure,ſtraight,and
perfect,that I maye neither fainte,
nor fall from thee:either thorough
aduerſitie or proſperitie,that I be
not puffed vppe in pride thorough
the one,nor yet dryuē downe into
diſpaire thorough the other : But
that I maye for the one gyue thankes,& be in the other armed with
pacience.Alſo that I maye reioyſe
in nothinge,but in that which may
allure mee vnto thee:nor ſorrowe
ought but that whiche doth with-
drawe me from thee, that I deſire
to pleaſe or diſpleaſe none , but
thee,or for thee:& that all thinges
tranſitorie maye for thy ſake Lord,
be

be of no reputation with mee, and
that all thinges lykinge vnto thee
maye be delectable vnto mee, and
thou God more then all other
thinges : and that I maye haue no
reioyſinge beſides thee, let all labour delight mee that is taken for
thee, and all eaſe be vnpleaſant th·t
is without thee. Make me to lifte
vp my heart often vnto thee; and
when I fall from thee, graunte mee
to call it ſorowfullye to mynde
with full purpoſe of amendemente.
Graunte mee that I maye bee obedient without repinyng, or geuing
of froward language : and poore
without fallinge from thee: patient
without murmuring or grudging,
pure and cleane without defiling,
or corruptiō. Make mee alſo lowe-
lye without counterfeiting, merry
without looſnes, ſad without lum-
piſhnes, ſobre without dullenes,
nimble

nimble and quick without lightnes
of behauior, trew without doublenes, fearinge thee, but not to difpaire, to doe good workes, but not
to prefume, tellyng my neighbour
his faulte without flatering, inftru-
cting him bothe by woorde and
exāple without fcorning, or taun-
tinge. Graunte mee mofte louynge
Lorde and my God, that my harte
maye alwayes foo wake vnto thee
that no vaine worldlye thought
with-drawe mee from thee, gyue
me that conftancye that no euyll
affectiō or wicked fuggeftion doo
plucke mee away from the, and a
harte foo ftable, that no troubles
maye ouercome mee, fo free from
all vice, that finne maye chalenge
nothinge in me. Graunt mee O my
Lord God vnderftanding to know
thee, diligēce to feke thee, wifdom
to finde thee, conuerfatiō to pleafe
thee

thee, faithfullie to perseuere, loo-
king after thee, & finallie thorough
hope to imbrace thee, & in respect
of thy most grieuouse paines suffered vpon the Crosse for mee, that
I maye willingly suffre penaunce
and all tribulation for thee. Also
through thy grace to enioye the
graciouse benefittes here in this
transitorye lyfe, and in the world
to come to be partaker of thy rewarde & heuenlye ioyes, throughe
the precious bloude of that imma-
culat lambe our onelye Sauiour
Iesus Christ: to whome with the father and the holy ghost three personnes and one God, be al honour
and glorie worlde without end.
Amen.

*A prayer to God that he vvill vouch-
safe to preserue the fruttes of the earth.*

Ioan Ferus. in lib. prec.

O

O Omnipotent, euerlasting, and mercifull God, we beseeche thee consider our daylye needes: shewe vs thy mercy, and gyue vs a sufficiente harueste for our dayly necessities, graunt that corne, trees, and other fruites of the earth, may (by thy holy benediction) growe, encrease and multyplye : Turne backe and with-drawe from the fruites of the earth, all that may be dammageable, as tempestes, ouer-flowing of waters, coldnesse, hayle and other lyke thinges, which are anye waye hurtfull: Through our Lorde Iesus Christ thy sonne the euerlasting lyfe. Amen.

A prayer to desire that vve may vse all temporall thinges, for the health of our soules onely.
Thomas de Camp. in lib. de Imit. Christ.

I be-

IBeseeche thee moste mercyfull God, vouchsafe to preserue me, from excessiue cares of this lyfe, that I be not to much encombred with many thinges concerning the necessitie of my body, and that I be not ouertaken with any voluptuousnes of these thinges.

O my God, my ineffable sweetenes, chaunge and turne into bitternesse all my carnall consolations, which withdraw me from the loue of celestiall thinges. Suffer me not (my God) to be conquered, not to be ouercome of flesshe and of blood. Suffer me not to be deceyued of the worlde, and of the transitorie glory thereof, nor that the deuill through his subtiltie ouerthrow me to the grounde. Gyue me strengthe to resist: pacience to endure : and cõstancie to perseuer: for, meate drincke, clothes, and all

ne-

neceſſayrie things to vpholde the
bodie, are painfull & troubleſome
for that perſon, that hathe a deuout ſpirite. Therefore graunt me
Lorde to vſe theſe thinges mode-
ratly, and that my harte be not to
much encombred with the deſyre
of them. The holy law forbiddeth
vs to require ſuperfluous thinges,
and ſuche as are more delectable
than profitable : for otherwyſe the
fleſhe ſhould be ouer burdenouſe
to the ſpirit. And alwayes I requeſt
that thy holy hande may gouuerne
& inſtruct me, that I doe nothinge
exceſſyuelie. Amen.

The ende of the fiſth Chapter.

THE

THE SIXTE CHAPTER

CONTEYNINGE HOLESOME
prayers of the lyfe and paſſion of
our Sauiour and redeemer Ieſus
Chriſt.

A prayer to be ſayed before the Cru-
cyſix.

Cuthbertus Tunſtall in lib. bell. prec.

Mercyfull crucifix,
the redeemer of all
people, whoſe heade
was filthely lacerat &
torne with a croune
of thorne, whoſe hands & feete extended vpõ a croſſe were through-
bored with nayles, whoſe whole
feble bodye was hanged on highe
and twoo theues to his ignomie &
ſhame, faſtened on his righte and
lefte hande, of the whych the one
diſpiſed thee, the other knowleged
thee to be a kinge, whoſe ſpirit cõ-
mẽded vnto the father, was gven
vppe

vppe to redeme vs withall. And
being deade thy fide thorwe-pear-
ced, gufhed & poured outewater
and bloude.VVhat toung can worthely expreffe,what minde can cō-
ceyue thofe innumerable paynes,
the which thou an innocente hafte
fuffered? VVee befeeche thee,for
thefe fo exceding great tormentes
to illuminate our foules with the
lyghte of thy knowledg,to mode-
rat our vnderftāding to ftrengthen
our handes too good workes, to
conuerte our feetefteppes and go-
inges to thy wayes,to directe our
thoughtes,wordes,and deedes,and
lafte of all to bringe vs wretches
vnto thy kingedome : where that
wee with thy holye Angells,maye
haue thy fruition:the which doeft
liue and raigne God with God the
father & the holy ghofte through
all worldes. So be it.

ℒ

A prayer acknovvledginge that man vvas the cauſe of Chriſts ſuffering.

Io. Fab. ex 7. Medit. B Auguſtin.

VVHat haſt thou done ſweet chylde, that thou ſhouldeſt haue this iudgement? VVhat haſte thou done, that thou ſhouldeſt be thus ſtreitly delte-with? what is thy offéce, what is thy gilte? what cauſe of thy death? what occaſion of thy condemnation? I truly, I am cauſe of thy trouble, my fault hath made thee to be ſlaine : my deſert hathe brought thee vnto this deathe: vḡgeance is taken of thee for my hay-nouſe gilte: thou art thus torméted for me, and I the occaſion of all thy ſmart. O maruelous ſorte of iudgement, & order of the vnſpekeable diuine miſterie. The wicked ſinneth, and the iuſte is puniſhed. The gilty offendeth, and the innocente is beaten. The ſinner tranſgreſſeth, and

and the godly is condemned. That
whiche the bad hath deserued, the
good suffreth: for that wherin the
seruaunt hath done euill, the maister maketh recompence: for that
the man hath committed, the sonne
of God is plagued: how farfurthe
thou sonne of God, how farfurth
hathe thine humilytie descended?
what hathe seruente loue enfor-
ced the to doo? Howfarfurthe is
thy mercye extended? how doth
thy bountie encrease? howfarfurth
hath thy loue reached? Vnto what
passe is thy compassion come? For
I haue done wickedlie, and thou art
punished: I haue committed a greuous faulte, and it is layed to thy
charge: I am the offender, and thou
arte put to the torture: I was puffe
vp in pryde, and thou imbaced and
made of no reputation: I was dis-
obedient, & thou sufferest the paine
of

of my difobedience. I haue pam-
pered my felfe with delicat fare, &
thou therfore redie to perifhe tho-
row hunger. My affectió through
concupifcence had made mee to
doo thinges vnlawfull,and perfect
charitie in thee hath brought thee
to fuffer vpon the croffe : I prefu-
med to doo that I was forbidden,
and thou fubmitteft thy felfe to
receyue rebukes and punifheméts
therefore:I delight in all banquet-
tinge and pleafure,and thou art put
vnto miferable paynes vppon the
Croffe.I lyue at eafe,and thy hádes
and feete are perfed with nayles : I
taft the plefaunt aple,and thou the
bytter gaule:Eua laugheth and re-
ioyfeth with mee, bleffed Marye
lamenteth & foroweth with thee.
Beholde,O Kinge of glorie,Loo
what myne iniquitye is, and howe
abundant thie mercie is:Loo what
myne

myne vngodlines is,and how meruailoufe thy rightuoufnes is. O my
King and my God,with what maye
I poffible recompence thee for the
greate goodnes fhewed towardes
me. Mannes harte is not able to
thinke what maye be worthelye
gyuen in recompence for fo great
benefites.For is ther any fuch fines
of witte in man,that is able to make
it felfe equalle with the mercie and
compaffion of God? Or can man
imagine whiche waye to doo fuch
dewtifull feruice,as might iuftlye
requite his readie fuccoure & pro-
uident care continuallie hadde for
man? There is trewlie fweet Soone
of God,there is thorough this thy
meruailoufe difpenfacion, wherin
manos fraylie maye in fome thing
do that,which maye be acceptable
vnto the,tꝉ at is to faye,if thorough
compunction of harte ftirred vp.
by

by thy visitacion, he doo crucifie
his fleash with her concupiscences,
and vices, whiche thoroughe thy
grace being brought to passe, then
beginneth he to be a sufferer with
thee, for whose offences thou
vouchsauedst a vile deathe to dye.
So by the victorie of the inwarde
man throughe thee, beinge his ca-
paine, he shalbe armed vnto the
outwarde victorie, that after con-
queste made of the spirituall enemie, he shall not feare for thee likewise to dye, and for thy sake to
offer his bodye to be hewed in
peeces by the matteriall sworde.
Thus the smalnes and simplicitye
of mans condition and state, yf it
maye so please thy godlines, shalbe
able accordinge to his litle power
in some parte to be aunswerable
to the greatnes of the creators
goodnes. This sweet Iesu is the

hea-

heauenlie medicine and a preserua-
tiue of thy loue. I beseeche thee
therefore, for thy noble mercies
sake, powre that into my festred
woundes, that may clense me from
the corruption of the Serpentes
venemouse poyson, & restore mee
againe to my former healthe, that
tasting the pleasaunte liquour of
thy sweetnes, it maye cause me to
sett at naughte all the wanton in-
tisements, & pleasaunt allurements
of the worlde, and for the loue of
thee, not to feare anye aduersities
threatnede by it and that hauinge
in remembrance the perpetuall
blessednes, I make none accept of
the raginge stormes of this transitorie tyme. Let nothinge like me,
lett nothinge be preciouse in my
sight, but that whiche is pleasinge
vnto thee. Also I praye thee, let all
thinges besides thee, seeme fylthie

L   vnto

vnto mee and of no reputacion,
cause me likewise to abhorre all
thinges whiche is offensiue vnto
thee, and my desire neuer to be sa-
tisfied in seking to do those things
whiche are pleasing vnto thee. Let
no ioye delight mee that is without
thee, and lett mee reioyce in all
troubles I suffer for thee. Lett the
remembraunce of thee, bee my
solace, and thy blessed name my
consolation, let my teares be nou-
rishment vnto mee both daye and
night, in seking after thy righteousnes. Lett the lawe of thy mouth be
more precious vnto mee, then
thousandes of golde or siluer, lett
it be delectable vnto mee to obey
thee, and detestable to committ
ought against thy diuine pleasure:
I humblie beseeche thee (my onely hope) for all thy mercyes sake,
thou wilt be mercyfull vnto mee,
and

and pardonne all mine iniquitie.
From the bottome of my harte I
defire thee to open mine eares to
heare that thou commandeft, and
fuffre not my harte to decline frõ
thee, nor through woordes of wickednes to feke excufes for my finne. Finallie I befeeche thee, for thy
meruailoufe humilitie, let no pride
raigne in mee : nor the power of
the finner feare mee. But that I may
all waye kepe my felfe vndefiled
for thee, which lyueft and raigneft
for euer, and euer. Amen.

*A prayer vvherein man doth offer (to
God the Father) the paffion of his fonne
our Lorde and fauiour Chrift.*
B. Auguft. cap 6. Medit.

BEholde O holye Father thy
derely beloued fonne fo cruelly tormented for me, beholde
mofte mercifull kiug who it is that
fuf-

suffreth, and remember for whom
he suffereth: Is it not O Lorde thy
moste innocent sonne whom thou
haste gyuen to death that he might
redeeme thy seruaunt? is it not the
Authour of lyfe who being ledde
as a sheepe to the slaughter, and
made obediente vnto thee, euen
vnto death, spared not the moste
cruell kynde of death?

Call to minde O distributor and
gyuer of al goodnes, that this is he
whom although thou haste begotten of thy diuine powre and vertue, yet notwithstanding hast made
him partaker of my infirmitie and
weaknes: verely this is thy deytie,
which being clothed with my nature, ascended the gybbet of the
crosse, vpon the which he suffered
moste dolorous death.

O Lorde caste the eyes of thy
Maiestie vpon the worke of thy in-
cffa-

effable bountie, beholde thy moſt
ſweete ſonne with his whole body
ſtretched out: beholde his innocent hands beſprinkled with moſte
precyous blood, and mercyfully
pardon thoſe faults which with my
handes I haue committed: looke
vppon his naked ſide pearced with
a ſpeare, and renewe me with that
ſacred fountayne which I beleeue
did iſſue from thence: Conſider
his vndefiled footeſteps, which neuer ſtood in the way of ſinners, but
alwayes walked in thy lawe, howe
with ſharpe, and longe nayles they
are faſtened to the croſſe, & guyde
my ſtepps in thy path, and make me
hate the wayes of iniquitye, and
chuſe euermore the way of trueth.

O Kinge of Angels and ſaints,
I beſeech thee for this holy of holyes, for this my redeemer to make
me runne in the waye of thy com-
maun-

maundementes, that I may be vnited and ioyned to him, whoe hath not difdayned to be cladde with my flefhe.

O bleffed Father wilte thou not behold the head of thy dere fonne, with his necke as whyte as fnowe refolued to dye, beholde mofte meeke creator the humanitye of thy beloued fonne, and haue mercy vpon the frayltie of thy frayle creature: his whyte breaft is naked, his blody fide is read, his ftretched bowels dryed vppe, his fayre and bewtiful eyes waxt dimme, his roiall and princely vifage is pale, his marble-white leggs hange downe: the ftreames of his precious blood, doe water his feete quyte perced thorowe.

Beholde O glorious Father, the rente and torne members of thy welbeloued fonne, and benignely re-

remember what my fubftance is:
beholde the paine of God and man
and releafe the myferyes of man
thy creature: beholde the punifhment of the redeemer, and forgyue
the offence of the redeemed : this
is he (O my Lorde) whom thou
hafte fmytten for the finnes of the
people, although he was thy beloued in whom thou wafte well pleafed, this was that innocét in whom
their was foũd no guyle, & yet was
he reputed amongſt the wicked.

*A deuoute prayer, vvith the remem-
braunce of the paſſion of our ſauiour Ieſus Chriſt, to obtayne ſuccour and fauour of him.*

Io. Fab. in preca. Chriſt.

O Mofte fweete Lorde and my
redeemer whiche was by the
heauenly Father fente downe into
this worlde, and hafte willingly of
thine

thine owne accord suffered moste
cruel bitter paines vpon the crosse,
and haste carried the same Crosse
vpon thy blessed shoulders, to the
ende that this thy patience mighte
be vnto vs saluation and a myr-
rour: and finally thou diddest con-
sente vpon that tree to dye and redeeme vs.

I moste poore miserable and
wretched sinner, most humbly beseech thee, for the incredible pacience which thou didst show in the
course of thy whole lyfe: and then
especiallye, when the vngracious
Iewes did so rage against thee with
villanous & spitefull words : when
they did mocke thee, and all be-
spytte thy vvsage : when they did
hoode-winke thine eyes, and with
their most filthy and impure hands
did smyte thee vpon the most blessed face: when they did moste cruelly

elly whippe and scourge thee faste
bounde to a piller: when they did
thruste vpon thy most sacred head
a pricking crowne of thorne: when
with yron nayles they did pearce
thy blessed armes stretched alonge
vpon the crosse : when thy blessed
syde was thruste throughe with a
speare: when in thy great thirst and
extreame agony they offered thee
a sponge full of vinager and galk
whē with thy head inclined downe
thou sayed *It is consummate* , when
thou diddest commend thy spirite
into the handes of God the Father:
and all this ended for the redemption and saluation of mankinde, in
thy graue thou was buried.

For all these paynes, and passions,
O most meeke Lorde Iesus Christ,
I poore and wretched sinner doe
humbly beseech thy infinite maiestie, not to forsake, nor suffer me
to

to be accufed, and condemned
in thy terrible iudgement: but let
thy dolorous paffion fo helpe and
ayde me, that I may be brought to
euerlaftinge felicitye: let thy holy
Angells alway be in my company,
and fpecially at the houre of death,
that they may protect, defend,
& keepe me, fo that the cruell
infernall enimy may haue
no powre or parte
in me.

The ende of the fixt Chapter

THE SEVENTH CHAP-

TER CONTAYNINGE DE-
uoute and holesome prayers to be
sayed before and after the receyuinge of the B. Sacrament.

*Aduertismentes for more wworthelye
receyuinge the holye Eucharisle.*

I. Cor. cap. II.

Verse. 26.

*Or as often as you shall
eate this breade, and
drincke the chalice, you
shall shewve the death
of our Lorde vntyll he
come.*

Verse. 27.

*Therefore wwhoe soeuer shall eate this
breade, and drincke the chalice of our
Lorde vnvworthily, he shall be giltye of
the body and bloode of our Lorde.*

Verse. 28.

But lett a man proue him selfe: and so,
let

let him eate of that breade, and drincke
of the chalice.

Verſe 29.

For he that eatethe and drinckethe vn-
vvorthyly: eateth and drinketh iudgemente to him ſelfe, not deſcerninge the
body of our Lorde.

This probation according to the
wordes of the Apoſtle (Lett a man
proue him ſelfe) conſiſteth principally in fower poyntes.

1. Fayth, before all thinges is neceſſarye to him that ſhall receyue the bleſſed
Sacrament of the Aultar, that is to ſay
he muſt firſte beleeue the preſence
of the true body and blood of our
ſauiour Ieſus Chriſte in the Sacramente of the Aultar: for they that
denye it, doe aſmuch as thy can, to
denye the omnipotencye of God,
and doe accuſe God with lyinge:
for he hath ſayed: (This is my body:
and this is my blood. Alſo you muſt
of

of neceſſitie beleeue that the body of Ieſus chriſt is deliuered to death: and his blood truely ſhedd for the remiſſion of your ſinnes.

2. *Penaunce*, or repentaunce, to the ende you may acknowledge your ſinnes with all your harte, and haue true repentaunce for the ſame, and truely to confeſſe thē to the prieſt your ghoſtly father: And after you haue obtayned abſolution, you muſt firmely purpoſe not to commit any deadly ſinne hereafter: and hauinge forſaken all rancour and malice you muſte be reconciled to them, whom you haue offended or that haue offended you.

3 *Honeſt and decente behauiour, and countenaunce apparteyning to a chriſtian man*, whereby is required that none goe to this moſte bleſſed Sacramente, and greate miſterie, but faſting, and with modeſtie, humilitie

tie and feruente zeale : & not with
any difhoneft or vncomely behauiour.

4. *Deuotion and a harte not occupied
in other bufines or affaires*, that fo you
may imploy your felfe wholly by
meditations and deuout prayers to
receyue fuch an excellente facra-
mente, in confidering and wonde-
ringe at the incomprehenfible humilitie of almightie God : I meane
hereby: that he being a Lord of fo
greate and infinite maieftye, hath
bene obediente vnto his heauenly
father euen vnto death, to gyue vs
lyfe. And with all, that by fuch deuout meditations and prayers, you
maye be ftirred and prouoked to
loue almighty god aboue al things,
and to gyue him moft harty thanks
for his fo great benifites: defiringe
him mofte humbly, that the merits
of his moft bitter paffion and death
may

maye be applied to the comforte and profit of your soule.

A prayer to be sayde before the recey-uinge of the Blessed Sacrament.

I Adore and worshippe thee, and gyue thākes vnto thee (my most louing Lorde Iesu Christe) for thy innumerable benefites and giftes gyuen vnto me moste vnwhorthy. All those I yeeld and offer vnto thee, into an euerlastinge laude and prayse. I gyue vnto thee thankes for all the goodnes, that euer thou diddest shew, or euer wilt shew vnto any reasonable creature. I gyue thee thāks for al the mercies of thy moste swete goodnes. I gyue thee thankes for thy holy Incarnation, Natiuitie, Infancie, Childhod, Man-state, labours, sorowfull cares, Pas-sion, Death, Resurrection, & thine Ascension. I moste humbly thanke thee, that thou haste vouchsafed, to
ad-

admitte me most vile sinner to the
noble and liuelie feaste of this thy
holy table. O gracious Iesu I beseche thee, for that loue that in maner constreigned thee to be incar-
nated, to suffre and to die for me,
that thou wilt make me fully cleane from all sinne, and make me to
please thee in all thing. Adorne and
garnish my beggarlye and poore
soule, with thy mercies & vertues.

Graunte mercifull Iesu, that I
may with moste humble reueréce,
with burninge desire and chaste
affection, receiue the moste venerable Sacrament of thy blessed Bodie, in memorie of all those things,
that thou haste vouchsafed to doe,
to speake, and to suffre for my saluation. Graunt, good Lorde, that I
maye performe this thinge moste
purely, to the euerlasting glorie of
thy name, to the honour of thy
moste

moste sweet Mother and Virgin
Marie, and to the honour of thy
blessed Saint N.

(Here name the Sainte of that daye.)
to the honour of all thy blessed
Saintes and Angells of heauen, to
the foule-health of me, and N. and
to the foules health of all Christen
people, quicke and dead.

Haue mercy, good Lord, haue
mercy vppon thy Churche, haue
mercy, good Lord vpon this place
and this compagnie. Grauntē that
here be alwaye humilitye, peace,
charitye, chastitye, and cleanesse.
Graunt, that we all maye worthily
amende and correct our selues, and
that we feare thee and serue thee
faithfullye: and that we maye loue
thee, and pleafe thee: I commend
vnto thy mercy all our busines, and
all our necessities: be mercifull vnto all those, for whome thou hafte
M shed

shed thy precious blood. Graunte
vnto the quicke forgyuenesse and
grace, graunt vnto the faithfull departed, rest and light euerlastinge.
*Another Prayer before the receyuinge
of the holy Sacrament.*
By Sir Thomas Moore.

O Benigne Iesu that wouldest
suffer so many greuous paines,
yea death it selfe for the loue of
mankind: greate and meruailous is
thy charitie. O good God for that
thy charitie, and that thou vouche-
safedst with thy precious bloud to
wash awaye our sinnes, I praye thee
gracious Lorde, that thou forgyue
me all the sinnes that I haue done,
thought, or said, in pride, in wrath,
in enuie, in couetousnes, in gloutonie, in slouth in lecherie, in vn-
cleanes of body, 'and of soule, in
mispendinge of my fiue wittes, in
breaking thy commaundementes,
in

in waſtinge the tyme of my lyſe
in vice, in that I haue not folowed
vertue, nor done thoſe ghoſtlye
deedes that I myghte hauedone.
O mercyfull Ieſu with that precious bloud that thou diddeſt ſhed
on the Roode for our ſaluation,
waſh all the ſinnes away that I haue
done ſince my birth, comfort and
make me whole with the holy Sacrament, which thou haſt ordeined
and left here on earth to be our
medicine, and life, through whiche
we ſhould liue after thee, and with
thee, & thou in vs. For, good Lord,
thou ſaydſt at that holye worke
when thou madeſt it & gaueſt it to
thy Diſciples: (*Iohan. 6.*) *Panis quem
ego dabo, caro mea eſt, pro mundi vita:
qui manducat me, ipſe viuit propter me,
ipſe manet in me, & ego in eo.* O thou
holy mightfull Prieſte and Biſhop,
that by thy diuine might madeſt
the

the worthy Sacrament of thy precious Body in fourme of breade,
gyue me grace to receyue it this
day with puritie of heart, & cleanes
of soule, with loue, dread & stedfast
beleefe. O benigne god, I acknow-
lege & confesse to thy high goodnes, that I am not worthy to come
vnto thy boorde to be fed with so
royall meate as is thy blessed Body.
But gracious Lord, I beleeue verily, that thou maiest make me worthy who haste made all thinge of
nought, and of sinfull, haste made
righteous and holy. O almighty
God, for this thy greate might I
praye thee, that thou make me
worthy and able to receyue the
precious Bodie deuoutly with all
reuerence, with perfect mekenes,
and holines, with full contrition, &
teares of deuotion, with spirituall
comfort & gladnes, of thy presen-
ce

&c. O bleſſed Bodie in fourme of
bread, come and entre into my
mouth and hart, that by thy diuine
preſence my ſoule bee fed, yea and
faſtened to thee with perfect charitie. O Lord, fill me with grace, &
ſtrégthen me, that I may euer hereafter lyue after thy will, and that
I may lyue in thee, and thou in me.
Ieſu for thy great bountie ſaue me
from all perils, teache and comfort
my ſoule in all doubtes and dreads,
clenſe me from all vices, ſuffer nothing to abide in my hart, but onely thy ſelfe whiche arte my ſoules
lyfe & leach. O heauenly meate, O
ioye of Angels, O ſoules ſtrégth, O
precious Bodie that gyueth en-
dleſſe helpe, mercifull Lorde Ieſus,
thus didſt thy ſelfe ſaye, (*Iohan. 6.*)
Ego ſum panis viuus qui de cœlo deſcē-
di: ſi quis manducauerit ex hoc pane, vi-
uet in æternum. O thou Bread of life
that

that diddest descēde from heauen,
who that eateth this bread, shall
lyue euerlastingly : O blessed Iesu,
make me nowe at this time worthy
to receyue this Sacrament, that is
thy precious Body, that I maye liue
euerlastingly with thee in thy pre-
sence, & see thee face to face, euer
to ioye in thy goodnes in blisse
euerlasting. Amen.

A deuoute prayer to be sayed at the E-
leuation of the moste blessed and Sacred
Hoost.

Anselm. cap. 2. in specu. sermo. euangel.

WE adore and worship thee
O Iesu Christ king of Isra-
ell, light of the Gentils, and prince
of the kinges of the earth: Lord of
Sabaoth, and moste stronge power
and puissance of the omnipotente
and almightie God, we worshippe
thee O precious pryce of our redemption, O peaceable Hooste,
which

which by thy smellinge sweetnes
onely, diddest inclyne thy Father
which reygneth in heauen to beholde our poore estate, and diddest
reconcyle him to vs , his children.

O sauiour Iesus Christ we prayse
the multitude of thy mercies : we
plentifully founde out the memorie of thy sweetnes, we offer vnto
thee O sauiour Christ the sacrifice
of laude and praise, for the greatnes
of thy bountye which thou haste
shewed vnto vs sinners, beinge a
wicked seede and vngracious children of perdition.

*A prayer to be sayed before the blessed
Sacramente of the Aulter.*

Io. Fab. ex cap. 2. soliloq. B. Augustini.

OMnipotent and most mercifull
God, thou art truely good, and
in deede I am euill, thou arte holy,
I am wretched, thou art iuste, I am
vniuste: thou arte the lighte , I am
blind,

blinde,thou art the lyfe,I am dead:
thou arte a conuenient medicine, I
am weake and ficklye : thou arte
ioy,I am heuines : thou art the foueraigne veritie , I am the vniuerfall vanitie, and fo is euery liuinge
man.

VVhat fhall I faye then my creator? heare me my maker,I am thy
creature and the worke of thy
handes, but O Lorde , I am nowe
brought to nothing,and I am dye-
ing dayly, thy handes haue made
and framed me : euen thofe handes
I faye which were nayled to the
Croffe for my fake.

Moft benigne redeemer difpife
not the worke of thy handes, but
looke vpon the woundes of thine
owne handes : loe my Lorde God
thou hafte written me in thy hands,
reade the wrytinge and heale me,
beholde I thy creature doe fighe
vnto

vnto thee , thou arte my creator
comfort me: I cry vnto thee, thou
arte the lyfe, quicken me, and gyue
me lyfe: to thee I lift vp my voyce
helpe me and reſtore me.

Spare me O God for my dayes
are nothinge , what is man that he
can thus ſpeake to God his creator ? pardonne me thy ſeruaunte
which preſumeth to ſpeake to ſo
great a Lorde, neede hath no lawe,
griefe and ſorowe compell me to
ſpeake , the calamitie and miſerye
which I indure, enforce me to crye
out : I am ſicke, therefore I call to
the phiſition: I am blind therefore
I haſten vnto the light, I am deade
therefore I ſigh after lyfe.

To thee O Ieſus of Nazareth I
haſten, thou arte the fountayne of
lyfe : O Ieſu ſonne of Dauid haue
mercy vpon me, haue mercy vpon
me O fountayne of mercy , thou
haſte

hafte hard me being ficke callinge
vpon thee, reach me thy hande O
mofte gentle Father: bring me to
thee, that I may come to thee, and
in thy lighte, may fee that euerlafting light: fpare and pardonne me
O Lorde, I am the vnhappie man
borne of a woman, lyuinge but a
fhorte time, and yet replenifhed
with much mifery: I am earth and
afhes, and by and by in griefe and
anguifhe I mufte dye, and then I
fhall be but wormes meate.

VVhat other thing is my lyfe O
my Lorde God, then a fhadowe
which foudenly vanifheth awaye,
lyke as the flower which doth flo-
rifhe and is greene, & by& by doth
wither: euen fo my frayle and de-
ceiptfull lyfe paffeth away, and yet
notwithftanding, it is on euery fide
hedged in with the fnares of death,
I knowe affuredly that I muft dye,
but

but when or howe I can not tell.

I therefore beseeche thee O
meeke and mercifull God to helpe
me:holde me vppe and staye me in
thy power and strength : appeare
vnto me O euerlasting lighte, and
shine in my hart that I may reioyse
in thee : come vnto me O my lyfe
moste noble, and most sweecte, that
through thee I maye lyue in thee,
and with thee in thy kingdome for
euer: heare me O Lorde God to
the glory of thy name, and the felicity and blisse of my soule. Amen.
A prayer to be sayd after the receiuing
of the Blessed Sacrament.
By Sir Thomas Moore.

I Adore and worshippe thee, and
gyue my humble and heartie
thankes vnto thee, moste mercifull
Lorde Iesu Christe, whiche haste
vouchsafed to admit me moste vile
sinner, vnto the noble and liuely
feast

feaſt of thy moſte holy table. Alas
poore wretch that I am. For I haue
receyued this moſte venerable Sacrament to-to vnworthily.

Lorde, haue mercy on me, Lord
forgyue me. I commãd that which
I haue done, vnto thy Diuine hart,
thereto be amended, & to be made
perfeĉt. Receyue (I beſeeche thee
Lorde) theſe moſte holy myſteries
of thy bleſſed Body, whiche I haue
receyued to the euerlaſting glorie
of thy holy name, to the honour
of thy moſt ſwete Mother the Virgin Marie, & to the honour of thy
bleſſed Saint N.

(Here name the Sainte of that daye.)

to the honour of all thy bleſſed &
holy Saints and Angels of heauen,
for my ſoule healthe, and for the
ſoule health of all Chriſten people
quicke and dead. Receyue (good
Lorde) this moſte excellent Sacrament

ment,in full amendment,purgatiõ
and fatiffaction for all my finnes &
negligences, and for the finnes of
all the worlde. Reftore by it,and
make vp againe all my ghoftly rui-
nes and decayes, and fupplie my
needy pouertie. Mortifie,by it in
me, what foeuer doth difpleafe
thee:and make me one accordinge
to thy heartes defire. By it, make
my fpirite,my foule and my body,
conformable to the fpirite, foule
and body of thy holy Humanitie:
and lighten me altogyther with the
light of thy Diuinitie.

Graunt by it,that I may be fta-
blifhed in thee,that I perfytly with
perfeuerance loue thee,that I may
be incorporate vnto thee, & moft
nerely vnited vnto thee:and that I
maye be chaunged all whole into
thee, to the laude of thy bleffed
name. Amen.

Con-

COnuert(Lorde) miferable finners, call againe heretikes and
fchifmatikes. Lighten the infidels
that knowe not thee,helpe all that
be in anye neceffitye and trouble,
helpe all them that haue commended them felues or defired to be
cõmended vnto my prayers. Haue
mercy vpon my parentes & bene-
factours.Haue mercy vpon all thẽ,
for whome I am bound to praye,&
that thou wouldeft be intreated
for.Haue mercy on this place and
companie.

Graunte,that here bee alwaye
humilitie, peace, charitie, chaftie,
and puritie.

Graunt,that we all may worthily
amend and correct our felues,that
we may feare the, and ferue thee
faithfully,& that we may loue thee,
and pleafe thee. I commend vnto
thy mercy all our bufineffes,and all
                                    our

our neceſſities. Lorde, be mercifull vnto all people, for whome thou haſt ſhedde thy precious bloude.

Graunt vnto the quicke forgy-uenes and grace, & vnto the faith-full departed, reaſt and lyfe euer-laſting. Amen.

Another Prayer after receyuing of the Sacrament.

By Sir Thomas Moore.

THankes' be vnto thee, O holy Father, God almightie, that thou diddeſt voucheſafe of thy great pitie to ſende thy only Sōne from thy high Throne into this vale of wo & miſerie, here to take our nature and ſhape, & in the ſame to ſuffer moſte ſharp paines & bit-ter death to bring our ſoules to thy kingdome, and to leaue that pre-cious Body here to be our ſtrēgth, and comfort: I thanke thee moſte mercifull Lorde Ieſu with all the might mighte and ftrength that thou haft gyuen me : I offer to thee thankes: that thou this daye hafte fed me with thine owne precious Body, by whiche I hope to haue healthe of foule, and euerlafting lyfe, with ioye when I depart hence. O holy Ghoft come good Lorde and enflame my hart with thy brenninge beames of loue, and make me with vertuous fwetenes continually to yelde acceptable thankes to the holy and glorious Trinitie. O ye three Perfons & one God, glorie, laude, and honor, with all reuerence be offered to you of all creatures without ende. Amen.

The ende of the feuenth Chapter.

THE

THE EIGHT CHAPTER

CONTEYNING LAVDES, PRAI-
ses and thankes-gyuing, for the benefites that God hathe beftowed
vpon vs.

A pſalme in vvhich a ſinner yeldeth
thankes to God that his enemyes haue
not preuayled agaynſte him , nor gotten
the vpper-hand of him.

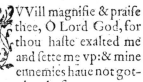 VVill magnifie & praiſe
thee, O Lord God, for
thou haſte exalted me
and ſette me vp:& mine
ennemies haue not got-
ten the ouerhand of me.

O Lorde of hoaſtes,I haue cried
vnto thee,and thou haſte ſaued me.

Thou haſte broughte my foule
out of hell: thou haſte holden me
vp from fallynge into thee deepe
lake,from whence no man retour-
neth.

N Thou

Thou haste not closed me vp, in the handes of myne ennemies : but thou haste sette my feete in a place both wyde and broade.

I haue sought thee, and thou hast hearde me, thou haste brought me into libertie oute of great distresse.

Thou haste turned my sorowe into gladnes, thou haste ceased my mourning, & compassed me round aboute with myrth.

Thou haste declared thy great magnificence in helpinge thy seruaunt.

I hou haste done meruaylouslie with me in my miseries.

Thou haste regarded the paine of the poore : thou haste turned awaye thy face from me.

I will be synging and speakyng of thy mercyes: and I will publishe to other thy fidelitie and truthe, so long as I shall lyue.

My

My mouthe shall neuer cease to speake of thy rytghteousnes, & of thy benefites:which be so manye, that I can not number them.

But I will gyue thee thankes tyll death take me awaye, I wyll syng in the prayse of thee so longe as I shall continue.

I will triumphe and reioyce in thy mercy, for thou haste looked vpon my necessityes,and regarded my soule in great dystresse.

Thou haste bene my sure refuge,and the strength of my truste and hope.

I thanke thee Lorde for thy goodnes alwaye:and for thy excedinge mercie.

Thou haste bene my comfort in the time of my trouble,thou hast bene mercifull vnto me. O Lorde, and haste reuenged the wronges that myne enemyes haue done to
me

me.

Accordinge to the multitude of the heauy thoughtes that I had in my minde, thy cōfortes haue cheared and lyghtned my hart.

Thou haft fente me nowe ioyes, for the dayes wherein I was in forowe: and for the yeares in whiche I fuffred many a painfull ftorme.

Thou hafte called to remembraunce the rebuke that thy feruaunt hathe bene put to, and howe furioufly myne enemies haue perfecuted me.

O Lorde God of hoftes, who may be compared vnto thee? thou arte great, & greatly to be prayfed.

Thou arte hyghe vpon all the earth, thou art exalted farre aboue all goddes.

Glory and honour before thy face: holynes and magnificence in thy fanctuary.

VVith

VVith iuſtice and iudgement thy royall throne is ſtabliſhed:mercye and truthe go before thy face.

Bleſſed arte thou(O Lorde) which haſte not holden backe thy mercy from thy ſeruaunt.

After that I had longe looked for thee O Lorde,at the laſte thou diddeſt attende vpon me,and heardeſt my crye.

Thou haſte taken me oute of the lake of miſerie,and ſet my fete vpon a rocke,& made my ſteppes ſure.

Thou haſte gyuen me my deſyer,I haue ſeene thy ioyfull countenaunce.

Thou haſte ſtricken all my aduerſaryes, and haſte abated their ſtrength.

Thou haſte rebuked the rablemente of them that vexed me, and haſte plucked me forthe of their
handes

handes.

Thou haſt caſt them heádelong into their owne pytte, their feete be wrapped in the net whiche they layed priuilye for me.

Myne enemyes are retyred backe, they are fallen downe and deſtroyed from thy ſyght.

Thou haſte bene the poore mannes defence, and his helper in tribulacion, when moſt neede was.

Thou haſte done iudgemente for me: thou haſt deſéded my cauſe againſt my accuſers.

And although thou was verye angrye with me a litle whyle, yet nowe I lyue throughe thy mercye and goodneſſe.

Verely I ſuppoſed with my ſelfe that I was cleane caſte oute of thy fauour.

But thou haſte harde my pray-ers: and according to thy greate
mercie

mercye haſte taken me agayne into thy fauour.

O Lord of thyne owne minde and will thou haſte gyuen ſtrength vnto my ſoule:but when thou hiddeſt thy face from me, O Lorde, howe greatly aſtonyed was I?

VVhen I was in aduerſitie,then I cried vnto thee,and thou diddeſt aunſwere me : when my ſoule was in great anguiſhe and trouble,then O Lorde I remembred thee.

I haue taſted and ſeene howe ſweete thou art:truly bleſſed is the man that truſteth in thee.

Accordinge to thy name ſo is thy commendation and praiſe,but thy counſayles touchynge vs be without example,and greater then with wordes can be expreſſed.

Dominion, power, and glorie be thyne,for thou haſte made all thynges,and becauſe thy will is ſo, they

they do ftyll continue.

Thy name be bleſſed, prayſed, and magnifyed, bothe nowe and euer:and worlde withoure ende. Amen.

A Pſalme in vvhiche the goodneſſe of God is prayſed.

O Lorde oure gouernoure how wounderfull is thy Maieſtye through oute the whole worlde: whiche haſte ſet thy glorye aboue all the heauens.

VVhat is man, that thou magnifeſt him ſo greatlyc?or the ſonne of man that thou doeſt viſite him?

O Lorde thou arte great and muche to be prayſed in thy holye hyll.

Prayſe be vnto thee O Lorde God, lett our vowes made to thee be alwayes perfourmed.

Confeſſion and magnificence are thy worke : and thy righteouſ-
neſſe

neſſe continueth for euermore.

Thou haſte done many thinges (O Lord God)both maruailous & greate : and there is none that can bee lyke vnto thee in thy woɪkes.

Thy wayes be iuſte and true, who will not feare and dread thee, and magnifie thy name.

I thanke thee(O Lorde God,) with all my harte, and I will ſanctifie thy name for euer.

O Lorde thou aɪt my ſtrength and my prayſe.

Thou haſte broughte downe myne enemyes which arte a iudge euen from the begynning.

Thy righte hande is exceding ſtronge:thy righte hande worketh manye great actes.

Thyne arme is myghtye and ſtrong:and becauſe it hath pleaſed thee,thou haſt ſtrengthened myne infirmitye.

I wil

I will prayse thy greate and
dreadfull name, for it is holy.

Although I haue fallen, yet I am
not crushed in pieces: for thou hast
suftayned my hande.

I haue opened and shewed my
waye vnto thee, and in thee I haue
trusted, and thou at length haste ac-
complished my desires.

Thou haste broken the heades
of myne ennemies, and haste made
them to stoupe : whiche walked
proudely in their sinnes.

Thou haste dominion ouer their
power, and when they be exalted
and set alofte in their wayes, thou
abatest their courage, and destroi-
est them with thy mighty arme.

In thy name I wil euer reioice,
and in thy mercy is all my glory.

Thou louest righteousnes and
iudgement, the earth is replenished
with thy mercy.

Thy

Thy eye looketh fauourably vpon them that dreade thee, and trust in thy mercy.

There shall no good thing be lackinge to them that seeke thee, and they that feare thee shall not be helpelesse.

For thou directeft their wayes, and heareft them when they crye vnto thee.

That thou mayeft deliuer their foules from death, and swage their paynes, when they be grieued.

For thou helpeft them, whose hartes be broken with forowe, and beareft vp with thy hand them that be contrite in spirite.

Thou saueft the foules of thy seruauntes : and all they that trufte in thee, shall not be dyftroyed.

VVherfore my toung shall sing thy prayse: O Lord God, I will alwayes magnifie thee.

I will

I will loue thee(O Lord)which
art my ftrength,my ftay,my might,
my Sauiour,and my refuge.

My God, my defendour and,
my buckler,the ftrength of my faluation, and my fupporter.

After that I had called vpon thee
with due laude and prayfe , thou
haft faued me from myne enemies.

VVhen I was in trouble I called
vpõ the,thou haft hearde my voice
oute of thy holy temple,& my crie
hathe entred vp into thine eares.

Thou haft faued me from mine
aduerfaries , that rofe vp agaynft
me, thou hafte deliuered me from
wicked enemies.

Thou hafte taken me from the
compagnie of euell men, and mine
eye hath feene vpon mine enemies
the thinges that I defired.

And therfore if it fhould fortune
me to paffe through the darke vale
of

of miserie: I will goe without feare,
for thou wilte be with me, thy rod-
de and thy staffe shall comfort me.

Thou shalt deliuer me from
tribulation, thou shalt kepe me frō
them whiche feeke to destroy me.

Myne eyes be vpon thee (O
Lord,) for thou shalt bring my fete
forth of the snare.

Vnto thee O Lord God I will
perfourme my vowes, I will gyue
thee thankes bothe nowe & euermore, and world without ende.
Amen.

*A Pfalme of the benefytes of God,
with thankes for the fame.*

MY foule prayfeth thee O Lord,
and all that is within me, prayfeth thy holye name.

My foule gyueth thee humble
thankes, and thy benefites I will
neuer forget.

VVhiche forgyueſt all my finnes
and

and healeſt all mine infirmities.

VVhiche haſte ſaued my lyfe from deſtruction, & ſhewed in me thy grace and mercye.

VVhich haſte ſatiſſyed my deſier with good thinges : and ſhalte once reſtore my youth agayne.

Thou haſte entreated me mercifully at all times, and haſte reuenged me of myne enemyes,

Thou haſte bene a defence to me (O Lorde) and a ſure foundation of my wealth.

Thou haſte guyded me with thy counſaile, & taken me to thee, through thy mercie.

Thou haſte manye wayes declared in me thy greate myght and power, and after thine anger hathe bene paſte, thou haſte turned agayne and comforted me.

Thou haſte ſente me many grieuous troubles, but at the lengthe
thou

thou hafte brought me oute of the
bottomles depeneffe.

Thou hafte made me preuye to
thy wayes, and hafte not hydde thy
counfayles from me.

Thou arte full of mercye and
grace(O Lorde)flowe to wrathe
and ready to goodnes.

Thy difpleafure lafteth not alwaye, & thou kepeftnot backe thy
mercies in thine anger for euer.

Thou rewardeft vs not accordinge to our finnes, nor punifheft
vs accordinge to our defertes.

Loke howe high the heauen is
in coparyfon of the earth, fo greate
is thy mercye towardes vs.

How farre as the earth is diftaunt
from the weft: fo farre(O Lorde)
remoue our finnes from vs.

Like as a naturall father hath
pity vpon his children, euen fo (O
Lorde God thou hafte had compaffion

passion vpon vs.

Thou haste not forgotten thy creature, thou remembredst that we are fleshe, yea all men liuinge.

And that the age of men is lyke vnto grasse, and may be compared to the floures in the fielde.

VVhich as soone as the sharpe winde hathe blowen vppon them with his blastes, wither away and dye, so that no man can tell where they dyd growe.

But thy mercie O Lorde, and louyng kyndenesse is alwayes vpon them that feare thee, and thy ryghteousnes endureth for euer.

So that we kepe our promyse and conuenaunt with thee : and so remember thy commaundementes that we doe them in deede.

O Lorde thou haste stablished thy throne in heauen : and thou gouernest all thinges by thine imperyall

peryall power.

I will magnifie thee O Lorde, and prayfe thy name worlde withoute ende.

I will gyue thankes alwaye and make thy name glorious fo euer.

O Lorde thou arte puiſſant and greate, and thy magnyſicence is vnſearcheable.

One generation ſhall ſhewe to another thy workes, and they ſhall declare thine auncient noble actes.

They ſhall euer prayſe the magnificence of the glorie of thy holynes, & the memorie of thy great goodnes.

For thou arte good and gracious to all men, and thy mercye excedeth all thy workes.

The eyes of all men beholde & wayte vpon thee, that thou ſhouldeſt gyue them their ſuſtenaunce in time conuenient.

     O   Thou

Thou openest thyne hande, and filleſt euery lyuinge creature, with neceſſary foode.

O Lorde thou art ryghtfull in al thy wayes, & holy in thy deedes.

Thou kepeſt all them that loue thee, and the tourmente of malice, ſhall not touche them.

My mouthe ſhall ſpeake thy glorie and prayſe, and all lyuinge creatures ſhall honour thy holye name for euer.

Prayſe our Lorde, oh ye his Angels mightie in power, whiche doe his commaundementes, and obeye the voyce of his worde.

Prayſe ye altogyther God, O all ye hoſtes, you his miniſters that do his will and pleaſure.

Prayſe our Lorde as I do, and let vs magnifie his name togyther.

Prayſe our Lorde, oh all ye his Saintes, for his name is glorious and

and his prayſe goeth aboute heauen and earth.

Prayſe our Lorde togyther, O
all ye his workes:euerye thing that
liueth prayſe our Lorde. Amen.

A thankſ-giuinge to God for his innu-
merable benefits beſtowved on man from
his infancie.

B. Auguſt. cap. 18. Soliloq.

I The ſonne of thy hand-mayd in
theſe my poore confeſſions doe
confeſſe to thee my redeemer,with
all my hart,and will call to mynde
all the benefites whiche thou haſte
beſtowed vpon me all the time of
my lyſe euen from mine infancye,
for I knowe well (O Sauiour)that
thou art greatlye diſpleaſed withe
ingratitude:for it is the roote of all
ſpirituall euill:and a certaine wynd
dryenge and burninge all good,
ſtopping the fountaine of thy dyuine

uine mercy towardes man.

But I O Lorde will gyue thee
thankes, leaſt I be ingratefull to
thee my redeemer, becauſe thou
haſt delyuered me: howe oft had
that dragon ſwallowed me vppe, if
thou haddeſt not taken me from his
mouth? how oft haue I ſinned, and
he was redy to haue deuoured me?
but thou my Lorde God haſte defended me: when I wrought wic-
kedly agaynſt thee and did breake
thy commaundementes he would
haue drawen me to hell, if thou
haddeſt not letted him: I did offend thee, and thou diddeſt defend
me: I did not feare thee, and thou
diddeſt preſerue me: I departed from
thee, and offered my ſelfe to mine
enemie: but thou diddeſt affraye
him that he durſt not take me: thou
diddeſt beſtowe theſe great benefites vpon me (O my God,) yet I
poore

poore wretch did not know it.

Thou haft often times deliuered
me from the iawes of the diuell,
thou haft takē me out of the mouth
of the lyon, and hafte brought me
many tymes from hell I not know-
inge it: for I wente downe to the
gates of hell, but thou hafte ftayed
them that I entred not in: I did haf-
ten to the portes of death, but thou
diddeft not fuffer them to inclofe
me in, thou hafte alfo often deliuered me from bodyly death O my
fauiour.

VVhen I haue bene fore vexed
with ficknes, and in greate danuger
by lande, and fea, by fier and fword,
thou hafte ftoode by me, and mercifully deliuered me from all: for
thou diddeft knowe (O Lorde,) if
death had then ouertaken me, hell
had receyued my foule, and I had
bene damned for euer: but thy
mer-

mercye and grace preuented me,
and deliuered me from death both
of bodye and foule O my Lorde
God.

These and many other benefites
thou hafte heaped vpon me, but I
being blind did not perceiue it vntill thou dyddeft illumynate me.
Now therefore O the light of my
foule, O my Lorde God; O my life
by whom I lyue, O the lighte of
mine eyes by the which I fee: loe
thou hafte illuminated me, and I
know thee, for by thee I lyue. And
I gyue thee thankes, although in-
fufficient and nothing correfpon-
dente to thy benefites, yet fuch as
my frayltie is able to afford, I offer
vnto thee: I confeffe and acknowledge thy goodnes, for thou hafte
broughte me from the lower hell
once, twyfe, thryfe, yea a hundred
and a thoufand tymes: I was euery
day

day going downe to hell, but thou
diddeſt bringe me backe agayne:
and iuſtly thou might a thouſande
tymes haue condemned me, if it
had bene thy pleaſure: but thou
wouldeſt not becauſe thou louedſt
ſoules, and diſſembleſt the ſinnes
of men expectinge their repentance.

O my God, my ſauiour, in all
thy wayes their is great mercy, now
I ſee and manifeſtly know through
the light of thy grace, and my ſoule
doth faynte in the contemplation
of thy greate mercy towardes me,
becauſe thou haſte pluckt me from
the lower hell, and haſte brought
me backe againe to lyfe. It is then
by thee wholy that I liue, and therfore I wholy offer my whole ſelfe
to thee, my whole ſoule, my whole
harte, my whole body, my whole
life, let it liue vnto thee O my ſweet
lyfe

lyfe: for thou haste wholy delyuered me, that thou mighte wholye
possesse me: thou hast wholy made
me : that thou mighte wholy haue
me agayne : Therefore I will loue
thee O Lord, which art my strēgth,
I will loue thee O my ineffable ioy
and comforte, so that my wholle
life shall liue no more but for thee,
which lyfe was loste in my misery,
and nowe reuyued agayne in thy
mercy : for thou art a God mercyfull to thowsands that loue thy holy name. Amen.

*A prayse and thankes- gyuinge to God
for his great benefites.*
Io. Roffo. psal. 13. lib preca.

MY soule doth praise thee O my
God, and all that is within me
doth laude thy holy name: my soul
doth render thee hūble thankes, &
I wil neuer be vnmindful of thy benefites, for thou doest pardonne all
my

my sinnes, & hast healed all my infirmities: thou haste redeemed my
lyfe from death, and haste shewed
vnto me mercy and grace.

Thou haste multiplied in me thy
magnificéce, after thine anger thou
haste comforted me: thou haste
shewed me many tribulations and
aduersities, but in the end thou hast
brought me backe againe from the
depth of deapnes: thou haste made
knowen to me thy wayes, and from
me thou haste not hid thy counsels.

Thou arte mercyfull and full
of grace O Lorde, slowe to anger,
prone and redy to goodnes: thou
wilt not alwaie be angrie, and thou
doest not for euer holde backe thy
mercie: thou rewardest vs not according to our sinnes, nether doest
thou punishe vs accordinge to our
iniquities.

As the father doth pitie his children

dren: so thou haste compassion of vs O God our Lord: thou forgettest not thy handy-worke, thou remembrest that euery liuinge man is fleshe, and that the daies of man are as grasse, and as the flowers of the fielde, which with a blaste of colde winde vanishe away, so as none can fynde the place where they grewe.

But thy mercy is euerlastinge to those that feare thee, and thy iustice remayneth alwayes, so that we keepe thy law and fulfill thy commaundementes.

I will extoll thee my God, and prayse thy name for euer and euer: I will render thee thankes at all seasons, and I will make thy name famous for euer, and longer if longer may be: for thou arte good to all, and thy mercye exceedeth all thy workes.

The eyes of all thinges looke
vp

vppe vnto thee that thou wouldeſt
gyue them meate in due time: thou
openeſt thy hand & filleſt with thy
bleſſinge euery liuinge thing :thou
preſerueſt all that loue thee,& no
tormente of malyce ſhall touche
them: my mouth ſhall ſhew foorth
thy prayſe, and euery liuing thing
ſhall celebrate thy holy name for
euer and euer.

Prayſe our Lorde O ye Angels
mightye in power, which doe his
commaundementes, and are obediente to the voyce of his worde:
prayſe our Lorde O all ye Armies
which doe his will : magnifie our
Lorde and lett vs extoll his name
in it ſelfe.

Prayſe our Lord all ye his Saints,
whoſe onely name is moſte highe:
whoſe onely prayſe doth exceede
heauen and earth: Prayſe our Lord
all ye his workes, through all his
do-

dominion in euerye place : euerie
thinge that liueth praise our Lorde.

The ende of the eyghte Chapter.

THE NYNTH CHAPTER

CONTAYNINGE NECESSA-
rie prayers for the prosperitie of
our bretheren friends and neyghbours.

Timoth. 2. & Iacob. 5.

A prayer for the Churche afflicted.
Franc. Tittel in para. Psal. 78.

God the gentiles, bar-
barous Nations, and
Infidelles which haue
no fayth in thee, nor
knowleadge of thy
name, are entred into thy heritage,
they haue taken thy people by
force of armes, and as vanquishers
they

they occupie our cyties, they haue
defyled with their abhominations
thy temple dedicated to thy honor
and feruice, they haue polluted the
veffels confecrated for the feruice
of the temple, and vfed them pro-
phanely.

VVe are become a reproch and
laughing-ftocke to our neighbors,
in fuch forte that they fcorne, difpife, and make a iefte of vs, reioy-
fing at our afflictions, and in their
mirth they vpbrayd vs : but thou
O Lord vpon whofe will we wholy depend, how long wilt thou be
angry with vs.

And wherfore doeft thou fo deliuer vs into the hāds of our enemies,
as though thou haddeft fhaked vs
of, &hereafter would haue no more
care ouer vs: wherefore doeft thou
fhewe the furye of thy wrathe towardes thy people, which are the
fheepe

sheepe of thy holy pasture, where-
of thou art the ruler, sheppard, defender and protector.

Be myndfull O Lorde of thy
holy Churche, and leaue it not in
the hands of thy enemyes, but delyuer it by thy stronge powre beholde, and consider, the league and
testament made with the elect. Remembre thy promise made vnto
thē, that thou woldest not forsake
them that were contrite in hart, but
woldest saue them that were humble in spirite.

For in trueth we are kepte vnder, afflicted and broughte to nothing, we are contemptible, abiect
and miserable, in such sorte that we
are a gasing-stocke and ignominie
to all nations: wherefore O Lorde
doest thou not turne thy face to
vs thy poore seruantes? why doest
thou turne thy face from them, and
                                    suffer

suffer thy enemies so cruellye to rage against them? why doest thou not beholde the misery and affliction wherin we thy seruantes (destitute and desolate of all helpe, and hauing no comfort but in thee) are afflicted and tormented of our enemies;

Awake O Lorde God, dissemble no longer but come to succour thy people, and make hast to helpe thy faythfull seruants, and saue vs from the hands of our enemies(we humbly beseech thee) for thy moste glorious names sake, for thine own selfe, and for thy infinite mercye: that we the posteritie may a little taste the sweetnes of thy promises, which our forfathers haue so abundantly felte.

But we that are thy people, and the sheepe of thy pasture, which worshippe no other God, which

seeke

seeke no other sheppard & gouernour besides thee, whiche put our
whole trust & cōfidence in thee, &
desire to be fedd, ruled and gouer-
ned, by thee onely, we will render
thee moste humble thankes, and
sett foorth thy glorye for euer and
euer.

VVe will declare and shewe thy
prayses from generation to generation, for thou of thy mere good-
will, haste restored vs to the liber-
tye which we haue requyred: we
therefore (in aduersitie as well as in
prosperitie, or how soeuer it shall
please thee to dispose of vs) will
serue thee with ioye and gladnes:
we will continewe still in thankes
gyuinge, attendinge patientiye thy
ayde and helpe. Amen.

A prayer for our parentes.
Io.Ferus in lib. precat.

O

OAlmightye and omnipotente God, which haste strictly commaunded vs, next vnto thee to honour our father and mother, and to pray for their happy and good successe: graunt vnto my parentes, and the whole familye, health, & peace: keepe them in the piety and trueth of thy fayth: defend them from all daungers bodily and ghostly: gyue them grace (I humblye beseeche thee) that they offende not thee in any thinge, but that they may alwaye find thee, a louing, gentle, and mercyfull father and God. Amen.

A prayer to be sayed for them that are fallen from the Church.
Io. Fabius in preca. christ.

OMnipotent benigne and moste mercifull father, we moste entierly besech thee, that it wil please thee to visitt with thy fatherlye af-
P   fection

fection, all thofe that are fallen, and
departed from the pure Catholike
and chriftian Church : or doubt in
any article thereof:and are feduced
or deceiued through any falfe per-
fwafion, to illuminate their hartes
O Lorde, with the beames of thy
diuine light : ftaye them and bring
them backe to acknowledge their
errour, that being in fuch fort conuerted, they maye with the whole
vniuerfall Church, confeffe with
mouth, and fhewe in workes, one
true, catholicke and chriftian faith,
and remayninge in it, they maye
worke their owne faluation:fo that
they and we beinge of one minde
and will, in one foolde may heare
and followe thee our fhepparde,
through Iefus Chrift our Lorde.

Amen.

*A prayer that chilldren may be inftru-
Eted in vertue and in the feare of God.*

Io.

Ioan. Ferus in lib. precat.

O God graunt that not onely we our felues cleaue to thy holye worde and doctrine, but alfo that we may inftruct and bringe vp our children in thine honor, in thy feare and difcipline, in vertue and obedience, and that they may encreafe and growe in comelynes, fayth and piety, that we may haue perfect ioy without any forrowe, and that we may laude and prayfe thee all the dayes of our lyfe. Amen.

A prayer for a friende and generallye for anye that is commended vnto our prayers.

O Mofte fweete fauiour Iefus, I mofte humbly befeech thee to vouchfafe to illuminate with the lighte of thy grace, the harte of N. thy feruaunte and my harte alfo: and to comfort and replenifhe our
hartes

hartes, with thy moste louing charitie, to the ende that we may wholy seeke thine honour and blessed
will, and thee alone with all our
hartes to serch and loue: and wholy & altogyther to leaue our selues
and our owne wills, and to resigne
them wholy to thee, so that alwaies,
and at all times, we may lyue accordinge to thy holy pleasure, in obseruing and sulfilling thy holy wil.

Iesus for thy holy name and for
thy bitter passiō, saue vs from sinne
and shame and endlesse damnation,
and bring vs to the blisse which neuer shall haue ending. Amen.

*A generall prayer for the lyuinge and
the departed in the Catholicke fayth.*
Ex lib. veterum orat. grœcerum.

O Sweete sauiour Iesu forgyue
those that hate vs, and handle
vs outragiousłye, render good to
them

them that doe vs good: graunt vnto our brethren thofe neceffaries
which they doe afke,and lyfe euerlafting: comforte the ficke: directe
faylers : and keepe the paffengers
in their righte waye.

O Lord according to thy great
mercy , haue pitye vpon thofe that
are recommeded vnto our vnworthy prayers: remember our fathers
and bretheren departed this lyfe,
bringe them to that place where
they may beholde the light of thy
countenaunce : call to minde our
brethren which are in captiuitie,and
delyuer them from their affliction.
Affifte all thofe that doe good and
labour in rulinge of the Churche,
graunt them their iuft requefts, and
gyue them euerlaftinge bliffe : be
not vnmindful O lord of vs poore
wretched finners thy vnworthye
feruaunts,powre into our harts the
lighte

A MANVAL
lighte of thy knowlege, and keepe
vs in the path of thy commaundementes, by the intercession of the
moste holy, sacred and blessed
virgin Mary, and of all the
saintes of heauen, for
thou arte blessed for
euer and euer.
Amen.

The end of the ninth Chapter.

THE TENTH CHAPTER
CONTEYNINGE HOLESOME prayers to the holy Trinitie.

A prayer or thankes geuynge vnto the holy Trinitie.

Blessed Lorde Father, Sonne, and Holy Ghoste, three personnes and one God, my Lorde, my God, my maker, my redemer, my nourisher, my defender, my swetenes, my mercie, my refuge, my strēgthe, my victorie, my ioye, & my glorie eternal, I laude thee, I glorifie thee. I honor and worshippe thee, O blessed Trinitie for that thou arte in thy selfe, for thou arte the hiest good, from whome floweth all goodnes, thou arte gracious eternitie, thou art eternall felicitie, thou arte onely God, and there is none without thee. I laude and honour
thee

thee o blessed Trinitie that might-
fully haste made of nought heauen
and earth, sonne and moone, and al
thinges that be in them: and for that
it pleased thee to make the holye
Angels to laude, & to prayse thee
eternally, and that they might assiste
vs faithfully in this exile and ban-
nishement, with there good coun-
sayles and helpings, and to declare
thy ineffable goodnes, thou madest
all thinges for man, and moreouer
thou madest man, with thy propre
handes to thine owne ymage and
similitude, onely for thee: and thou
formedst in him vnderstanding, &
adornedst him with free wil. I laude
& glorifie thee for that great gifte.
Thou didest set him in paradise
flowing with delites, that he might
haue the thinges that are aboue to
enioye, and gouuerné the thinges
inferioure, & to possesse all things,
and

and to worshippe thee for euermore. And thou made not thefe
noble creatures Angels & men for
any neceffity thou hadeft of them,
for truly all thinge was fufficient in
thee to thine eternall ioye & glo-
rie:but of the feruoure of thy charitye thou waft moued to create
them,that fuche creatures fhoulde
bee partakers of thy ineffable ioye
and glorie.I laude and honour thee
good Lorde for that it pleafed thee
among all thy bleffed workes to
make mee a reafonable man, and
haft gyuen mee wifedome,reafon,
vnderftanding,and free libertie, &
hafte fourmed mee with all right
lymmes,and features of bodie, and
hafte gyuen mee manye bleffed
giftes fpirituall and temporall,and
alfo meate,drincke, clothe, and all
thinges neceffarie, whiche manie a
good creature that hath ferued the
bet-

better than I haue done hathe
wanted, and for that thou haft vifi-
ted my harte many times with many graces, and fpirituall motions,
deliuering mee oft from many pe-
rilles both of bodie and foule, and
from flaunders, fhames, and rebuks
of this worlde, into the whiche for
my finnes I myght haue fallen: and
for that alfo thou haft fuffered mee
in all mine iniquitie, and all myne
horrible and abhominable finnes,
pacientlye alwaye abydinge for
my conuerfion, and amendemente,
whereas at innumerable times thou
myghteft haue flayne mee, and of
righte haue putt mee to eternall
paines and dampnation. I laude and
glorifie thee O Lorde God for all
thy mercie, whiche alwayes thou
hafte fhewed to finners. pacientlie
abyding for them, mercyfully callinge them, beninglye receyuinge
them

them,abundantlye geuing grace to them,& to such familiaritie admittinge them,as though they had neuer sinned. O mercyfull Lord and paciente God, what shall I saye to thee for all these benefites? VVhat laudes and thankes shall I yelde to thee? VVhat and all my sinnes were cleane taken awaye from mee, trulie yet were not I worthy for the leaste of thy benefites and mercies to gyue thee condigne lande. But as a wretched sinner can, with all my hart I laude thee, I prayse thee. I thanke thee, I honoure and worshippe thee, yea all honor, laude, & prayse be gyuen to thee, nowe and euermore. Amen.

A prayer to God the father
S.Cyprianus author esse scribitur

O God father of our Lorde Iesus Christ thy sonne, God of Patryarckes, God of Prophetes, God
of

of Apoftles, God of Martyrs, God
of Virgins, God of all beleeuers:
I befeech thee O father of maiefty,
which without limitation of tyme
hafte taken pitie vpon vs, fendinge
vnto vs Iefus Chrift thy fonne our
Lorde and fauiour, borne of the
virgin Marye by the operation of
the holy ghoft, by the annunciati-
on of the Angel Gabriel:by whom
thou hafte delyuered vs from imi-
nente and prefent death.

I befeech thee O Lorde to fuccour and helpe me, and iudge me
not accordinge to my workes, for
I haue not bene obediente to thy
commaundements,but thou which
loueft repentance haue mercy vpon me,which before thy face make
confeffion of all my finnes : and as
Dauid prayed: O Lord for the loue
of thy holy name wype awaye my
finnes: fo I befeech thy diuine Maieftie

ieſtie to blotte out all my ofiences·

Make me to abyde in thy holy
Catholike Church,with an vndefiled faith,a pure hart,firme deuotiõ,
continuall loue, and to perſeuer in
good workes : deliuer me from the
eternall fyre & euerlaſting payne,&
from all torment which thou haſte
prepared for the wicked : graunte
this,for our good and bleſſed Sauí-
ours ſake,by whom to thee al laud,
honour, power and glorye be for
euer and euer. Amen.

A prayer to God the Sonne called,
O bone Ieſu.

OBountifull Ieſu,O ſwete Ieſu,
O Ieſu the ſonne of the pure
Virgin Marie full of mercy and
trueth,O ſwete Ieſu,after thy great
mercy haue pitie on me.O bening
Ieſu I praye thee,by the ſame precious bloude,which for vs miſerable ſinners, thou waſt contente to
ſhed

ſhed on the aulter of the croſſe, that
thou wouldeſt vouchſafe to auoid
clene all my wickednes and not to
deſpiſe me, hūbly aſking pardō, &
callingvpō thy moſt holy name Ieſus. This name Ieſus is the name of
health: what is Ieſus but a Sauiour?
O good Ieſus that haſt created me
& with thy precious bloude rede-
mied me, ſuffer me not to be dāned
whom of nought thou haſt created.
O good Ieſu let not my wickednes
deſtroye that which thy almightie
goodnes hath made and formed in
me. O good Ieſu, reknowlege that
which is thine in me, & wipe cleane
away that which is not thine in me:
O good Ieſu, while time of mercy
is, haue mercy on me, and cōfound
me not in time of thy terrible iudg-
ment. O good Ieſu if I wretched
ſinner, for my moſte grieuous offē-
ces haue by thy verye iuſtice de-

ſer-

serued eternall paine, yet I appeale
from thy verye righteousnes, and
stedfastlye trust in thine ineffable
mercy: so as a mylde father & mercyfull Lorde oughte, take pitie on
me. O good Iesu, what profit is in
my bloud since I muste discende
into eternall corruption? they that
be dead shal not magnifie thee, nor
lykewyse all they that descende to
hell. O moste mercyfull Iesu haue
mercy on me, O most sweete Iesu
deliuer me, O moste meke Iesu be
vnto me comfortable, O Iesu ac-
cepte me a wretched sinner into
the number of them, that shalbe
saued. O Iesu the health of all them
that truste in thee, haue mercy vpõ
me. O Iesu the sweete forgyuenes
of all my sinnes, O Iesu the sonne
of the pure Virgin Marie, endue
me with thy grace, wisdome, charitie, chastitie, and humilitie : yea &
in

in all myne aduersities with stedfast
pacience, so that I maye perfectlye
loue thee, and in thee to be glorified, and haue myne onely delight
in thee, worlde without ende.
Amen.

A prayer to the holy ghoste.
Io.Fab.cap.9.medita.

COme O holy spirite the moste
sweete comforter of the sor-
rowfull and desolate, the loue of
the diuine puissance, the holy com-
munication of the almightie and
omnipotent father, and of his most
blessed sonne, descende with thy
mightie power into the entralls of
my harte : lighten and bewtifie the
darke closetts of my desolate harte
with thy cleare brightnes, and that
which with continuall filth of my
vnfruitfull lyfe is dryed vppe, visit
thou and make fruitfull with the a-
boundaut dewe of thy grace.

Touch

Touche and wounde my harte
with the darte of thy loue, inflame
my dull and slouthfull harte : lighten the inner partes of my soule
withe the heate of thy holye fyre :
make me to drincke of the riuer of
thy sweetnes , that hereafter I may
feele no taste in any worldly delyte which is venimous.

O holye spirite, O excellente
workman, whomsoeuer thou doest
inhabite, thou buildest a lodginge
for the father and the sonne : come
therfore O moste sweete comforter of my sorowfull soule, defende
me in all tribulation: come O puri-
fier of our sinnes, and saluer of our
deadly sores: come O strength and
fortitude of the weake, and guide
of the humble : come meeke father
of the fatherlesse, and sweete Iudge
of the widowes : Come O soue-
raigne hope of the poore, and com-

Q   for

forter of the weake: come O bright
starre of saylers, and sure porte of
the shippwracte : come O singuler
bewtie and ornament of the liuing,
and onelye saluation of the deade:
come moste holy spirite, come and
haue mercy vpon me, make fitt and
accomodate me to thee : condes-
cend benignely to me accordinge
to the multitude of thy mercy, that
my littlenes may be agreeable
to thy greatnes, and my imbe-
cillitye and weakenes to
thy diuyne puissance:
through Iesus Christ
our Sauiour.
Amen.

The ende of the tenth Chapter.

All

THE ELEVENTH CHAP-
TER CONTAYNINGE CHRI-
ſtian Catholicke prayers to Saintes
& citizens of the glorie of heauen.

A prayer vnto the holy virgin Mary.
Cuth. Tunſtall in lib. prec.   Luke. 1.

ALl hayle vndefiled Vir-
gin Marye mother of
the ſonne of God, ele-
cted and choſen aboue
all other Virgins, the
whiche euen from the wombe of
thy mother Anna (a woman moſte
holy) haſt bene of the holy Ghoſt
ſo ſanctified, illuminated, and ſo
greatly defended with the grace of
God almightie, that vnto the conception of oure Lord Ieſus Chriſt
thy ſonne, and whileſt thou dideſt
conceyue hym, and vnto the tyme
of his birthe, & whyleſt thou dideſt
beare

beare him , and continuallye after
his byrth,thou continuedst,and re-
maynedst a Virgin of all other that
be borne moste chaft,most vncor-
rupte, and of bodie and foule all
thy lyfe moste immaculate and vn-
spotted. For truely thou hafte far
passed all other Virgins,how many
foeuer haue bene hetherto fyns
the beginninge of the worlde, or
euer shalbe to the later ende therof,in a fincere confcience of an
impolluted minde. By thefe thy
most excellent gyftes of heauenly
grace , infused into thee, by God
very fingulerly, O Virgin and mother Marie,aboue all other women
and Virgins,wee praye thee which
art vnto vs(miferable mortal men)
a mercyfull patroneffe, that thou
wilt voutchefafe to make interceffion to God the Father omnipotente,and to his fonne Iefus Chrift,
                                    bego-

(begoté certenly as cócerning his
Diuinitie of the Father before all
worlds,& borne of thee,cócerning
his humanity, & to the holy Ghoſt
proceding from the father and the
ſonne) that our ſinnes may be forgeuen vs, and that wee, throughe
thy interceſſion maye meryte continuallye to reioyce with thee O
holye Virgin, and to prayſe thee
in the kindome of heauen,without
ende. Amen.

*A prayer to our Ladye the bleſſed vir-
gin Mary and S.Iohn Euangeliſt.*

S. Edmundus Arch.Cantuarienſis author
ſcribitur

O intemerata.

OVndefiled & for euer bleſſed,
ſingular and incóparable Virgin Marie mother of God,his moſt
pleaſaunt Téple,the noble Shryne
of the holy Ghoſt, the Entree and
Gate of the kyngdome of heauen:
by

by whome next after God all the world lyueth. Bowe downe thyne eares (O mother of pitye and mercy) vnto my poore prayers, and be to me (wretched sinner) a pitiouse helper in all thinge.

O most Blessed Ihon Euangelist the famyliar frend of Christ, which of the same Iesu Christ our Lorde was a chosen Virgin, amonge all others muche beloued, and aboue all others instructed and learned in heauenly Secrettes and mysteries: thou was made his Apostle and Euangelist moste excellent: therefore I call vpon the and Marie the mother of the same Lorde Iesu Christ our Sauiour, that thou and shee would vouchsaf to help me. O ye two heauēly Gemmes Marie and Ihon. O two diuine Lampes, euer shyninge before God, dryue away with your blessed beames the
darke

darke cloudes of my sinnes: for ye
are the two in whom the onely begotten sonne of God, for the me-
rit of pure virginitie, confirmed the
priuilege of his singuler loue, while
he was hanging on the crosse, saying thus to the one of you: *VVoman
beholde thy sonne* : and after to the o-
ther: *Beholde thy mother* : Therefore
(in this sweetenes of such sacred
loue, wherin ye were then conioy-
ned (by the mouth of our Lorde)
as Mother and Sonne) to you two
I moste wretched sinner commend
this day my body and soule, that
in euery houre and momente, inwardly and outwardly, ye woulde
vouchsafe to be my suer keepers
and pitifull intercessors to God for
me. Aske I beseech you health of
body and soule for me: Helpe I
praye you, helpe with your glori-
ouse prayers, that the holy Ghost

the

the noble gyuer of graces, woulde wouchſafe to viſite, adorne and inhabite my harte, to purge me from all filthe of ſinne : to bewtifye me with all holy vertues, and make me ſtand perfectly and perſeuer in the loue of God and my neyghbour: And after the courſe of this lyfe, I may be ledde to the ioyes of the elect by the ſame holy Ghoſt; who with the father and the ſonne, eternally lyueth and raigneth one God almightye worlde without ende.

Amen.

A prayer to all the holy Angelles.
Victor. Vticenſis. libr. de perſecutione Vandalica.

HEare vs O holy Angells of our God, whoſe ayde neuer faileth, for you are conſtituted (in your ſeruice)for them that ſhal be heires of euerlaſting ſaluation: watch and take heede, and behold howe Sion
the

the Citie of our God is become of
litle eftimation, and as it were polluted with infection amongeft her
enemyes: the enemy hathe abu-
fed and waftfully occupyed all her
pleafaunt & beautyfull ornamétes,
for he hathe feene infidelles and
vnworthy perfones affaile & enter
within the gates whoe our Lorde
had commaunded fhould not enter into his Churche.

Saye vnto God our protector,
(euen as thofe whiche haue a fure
truft to obteyne that whiche you
require) that his Church is afflicted & trauelled, & her wombe fore
troubled with her outcries, for fhe
is fet amongeft infidels & doth find
no reft, & not any to comfort her.
She hathe foughte who woulde
mourne with her, but coulde finde
none; fhe hath fought who woulde
gyue her comforte but no perfon
was

was to be founde, euen when shee
dyd eate Gaule in her meate, and
in her thirst tooke vynager for her
drincke folowinge the Passion of
her spouse and Lorde who suffred
for hyr, to the end, that shee might
followe his steppes.

A prayer to S. Iohn Baptist.
Ludo. carthusianus li. de vita Christi.

O Moste blessed Iohn the fore-
runner of Christe, the crier of
the Iudg, frend of the spouse, voice
of the diuine word which haste deserued to declare & fortell the ioy
and comfort of our redemption:
obtaine for me poore and miserable sinner of the same Lord Iesus,
by thy most holy prayers, that my
harte, being clensed from vice and
adorned with vertues, I may according to thy hoolsome admonitiōs
prepare the way of our Lord, and
make streyght his pathes in suche
sort

ſort,as in the laſte and finall Iudge-
mét,when he ſhall clenſe the floore
of his Church,& ſhall ſeperate the
good corne from the chaffe,I may
deſerue to be found amongeſt the
wheate,& his elect,& with thé may
be layde vpp in the barne of his
heauenly manſion.   Amen.

A prayer to any of the Apoſtles.

O Lord God which amongeſt al
and aboue al thy other ſaintes,
haſte moſte maruelouſlye chóſen
thy moſte bleſſed Apoſtles, to be
the firſte pillers and foundation of
thy Church , and before all other
haſte firſte ſent them to preach thy
Ghoſpel through the whole world,
confirminge and eſtabliſhing their
doctryne , by maruelous workes,
wounders and miracles : and thou
more-ouer by the ſame Apoſtles
haſte

haste fought, allured and inuited vs
Gentyles; to the knowledge and
prayſe of thy holy name.

VVe humblye beſeech thee O
Lorde, mercyfully to graunte, that
we beinge by thee founded vpon
the rocke of the Apoſtolicke confeſſion, and in the vnion of the ſame
fayth, are choſen and called to o-
beye & prayſe thee perpetually, be
neuer ſeperated from thee, through
any errour or temptation: make vs
pertakers of the interceſſion of S.
N. and of the twelue Apoſtles in
the ſtrength and fortification of a
true fayth, amendment of our lyſe,
and auoyding and eſchueing of all
euil, through Ieſus Chriſt our Lord
Amen.

A prayer to any of the holy Martyres.
Hora B. virgi. ſecund. vſ. ord. D. Bene.

O God which haſte ſo ſtrengh-
thned in thy fayth and loue thy
bleſſed

blessed Martyr S. N. as no fleshlye
delites, no threatninges of tyrantes,
no sworde or torture of tormen-
tors could withdraw him from the
worshipping of thee: graunte vnto
vs miserable sinners, by his worthy
merites and intercessions, helpe in
tribulation, comforte in persecution, that we may manfully fighte a-
gainst all the deceites of the deuill,
despise the worlde and all that is in
it, that we may feare no aduersitie,
but may obtaine that, which by thy
holye inspiration we doe desire,
through Christ our Lorde. Amen.

A prayer to any Confessor.
Petrus Canisius li catho. prec.

Almightye and euerlasting God
which art the wounderful light
of thy beloued saintes, and principally thou haste appoynted for vs
blessed bishopps, pastors, doctors
and

and confeſſors as burninge lightes
in thy houſe:and by their doctrine,
exhortations, writinges and teſti-
monies, recalleſt and reduceſt ſinners from euill to good.

VVe humbly beſeech thee, that
thou wilte vndoe & loſe the bonds
of our ſinnes , and although we be
vnworthie, yet make vs partakers
of that interceſſiõ of bleſſed S.N. &
all thy holy confeſſors,that we for-
ſakinge our ſinnes , and walking in
true fayth and charitie , folowinge
them in good workes, may at laſte
enioy their companie in the eternal
beatitude,through Ieſus Chriſt our
Lorde. Amen.

A prayer to any holy Virgin.
Idem in eodem lib.

O God which amongeſt the o-
ther miracles of thy power and
might, doeſt gyue and graunte in a
fraile ſex to all virgins,wydowes &
matro-

matrones, the victorie of martyr-
dome, and immaculate chaſtitiye:
mercyfully graunte that we which
amongeſt thy other holye virgins
and widowes, do celebrate the memory of thy bleſſed ſainte N. may
by her example and interceſſion,
deſpiſe the allurements of the fleſh,
the pleaſures of the worlde, and in
true fayth to paſſe all perrils of ſoul
and body, and exercyſe our ſelues
daily more and more in thy ſeruice
in ſuch ſorte, that with them after-
wards we may haue the fruition of
ioye and ſolace eternall. Amen.

A prayer to any of the holy Sayntes.
Ex tabella quadam Coloniæ in templo
S. Vrſul.

OHoly and bleſſed S. N. I humbly beſeech thee that thou wilt
haue me (poore and wretched ſinner in remembraunce, before the
face

face of my God and fauiour, that by
thy merites and interceſſions I may
be preſerued from all daungers bodyly and ghoſtly, that I may dayly
more and more increaſe in vertue
and good workes: and at the houre
of my death and departure out of
this worlde, vouchſafe to ſuccour
and defend me, againſt the aſſaultes
and deceites of mine ennemies, and
bring my ſoule deliuered and made
free from all tribulatiõ, to the ioyes
of the heauenly paradyſe. Amen.

Pray for vs O holy S. N. that
we maye be made worthye of the
promiſſes of Chriſt.

VVe humblye beſeech thee O
Lorde God father omnipotente to
receiue the prayers of thy ſeruants,
that we worſhipping the memorye
of thy bleſſed S. N. by his merites
and interceſſions may be delyuered
from al bodyly aduerſities: and that
our

our hartes may be clenfed from all
euill and idle thoughtes, through
Iefus Chrifte our fauiour. Amen.

*A prayer to all the blyffed Saintes in
heauen.*

Ex heræ B. M. ad vfum Sarum.

O All yee holy & electe of God,
vnto whome almightie God
hathe prepared his eternall kingedome from the beginninge: I befeech you through the charitie, by
the which God dyd loue you, that
you doe fucker mee mofte miferable finner, before death doe take
mee awaye oute of this wretched
world: and reconcile mee vnto my
creator before that hell deuoure
mee. O bleffed Marie mother of
God, the mediatrix for finners vnto Chrift, heare mee, kepe mee, faue
mee: O thou fweete Lady obtaine
to mee righte faithe, firme hope,

R   per-

perfecte charitie, true humylitie,
chaftitie, and fobrietie, & after the
courfe of this lyfe the felowfhippe
of the euerlafting blyffednes. Thou
alfo holye Michaell, with all the
thoufandes of Angells praye for
mee, that thou mayeft take & keepe
mee from the power of my aduerfaries, helpe mee, obtaine for mee
the loue of God, purenes of hart,
ftrength of faith, and the pleafure
of heauenlie glorie. Alfo yee holy
Patriarkes and Prophetes, procure
for mee of God pardon, penaunce,
continencie, and godlye perfeuerance, and alfo lyfe euerlaftinge. O
yee bleffed Apoft'es of God vn-
lofe mee from my finnes, defende
mee from the paynes of hell, and
take mee from the power of darkenes, & bringe me vnto the euerlaftinge kyngdome. I befeche you
alfo yee holy Martyrs of God, that

perfect

perfecte charitie, syncere loue, a
pure minde, a chaste lyfe, and remission of my sinnes be gyuen of
almightie God vnto mee.

O yee glorious Confessours of
God, praye for mee, that through
you the desire of heauenly thinges,
and reuerence of maners & washinge away of my misdeedes bee of
God graunted vnto mee. Likewise
I praye you all holy Virgines of
God, that you doe ayde mee, to
thintent I may haue a good minde,
and health of bodie and soule, humilitie, chastitie, & after the course
of this my miserable lyfe fellow-
shipe of the perpetuall blessednes.
O all yee Saints of God I do pray,
and also do make humble supplication, that you will woutchsafe to
helpe mee, and haue compassion
vpon me most pytyfully, and pray
for mee instatly, that through your
inter-

interceſſion, a pure conſcience bee
ingraſted within mee, with compunction of harte for my ſinnes,
and laudable endinge of my lyfe,
ſo that through your merites
I maye bee able to come
vnto the countrye of
eternall bleſſednes,
almyghtie God
graunte it.
Amen.

The end of the eleuenth Chapter.

THE TVVELFTH CHAP-
TER CONTEYNING ADVER-
tiſments & conſolations with prayers and ſuffrages for the ſicke.

*An aduertiſment for the ſicke, diligent-
ly to prepare him ſilfe to dye vvell.*
Lud. Bioſius cap. 1. poſterioris li. Ench.
paruulorum.

Vhoe ſoeuer doethe
loue God dutifullye,
being at anye time o-
uertaken with ſicknes,
whereby deathe is feared to be at
hand: let good heede be taken that
with diligēce thou prepare thy ſelfe
to end well: diſcharge thy harte of
the cares & troubles of this world:
receiue deuoutly the Sacramentes
of the Church, to the ende thou
maieſt purchaſſe ſuccour & ſtrēgth
to paſſe through thy iourney: and
wholly recommende thy ſoule to
God.

Cod.

Remember the paſſion of our ſweete Sauiour and redeemer: embrace in thy hart his holſome croſſe kiſſe his ruddy woundes, and thruſt thy ſelfe with all thy power into them, that beinge hidden in them thou maieſt be ſafe, and happely eſcape from all the ſnares and entyſmentes of the deuill: humblye beſeech our Sauiour Ieſus Chriſt, that he would wouchſafe to waſhe thee with his precious blood, and that he woulde whollye abandonne all thy ſinnes.

And for wante of meritoriouſe good workes, offer to God the father the merites of Ieſus Chriſt: offer him his moſte holy and ſacred conuerſation, death and paſſion: offer him the merites of his moſte ſweete mother the wirgin Mary, & of all Saintes: for ſo it ſhall come to
paſſe

paſſe that thou which art poore, naked and miſerable of thy ſelfe, ſhalt
appeare marueloufly adorned with
ſpirituall ornaments: recommende
thy ſelfe alſo to our bleſſed Ladye
the glorious virgin and mother of
God, and to the other Cytizens of
heauen, and principally to that ſaint
which thou haſte accuſtomed moſt
to pray vnto, hoping and beleeuing
certainly that they heare thy prayers, and that if thou call vpon the
bleſſed virgin with all thy hart, and
turne moſte humbly and aſſuredly
thy ſelfe to her, ſhe will without
doubt make thy entraunce into the
kingdome of heauen, where other-
wiſe it may be (through the diuine
iuſtice of God) that thou canſt not
enter, becauſe of thine iniquitie, for
ſhe is the mother of mercy, and the
Porte of of heauen.

Then

Then folovveth this proteſtation or ſuch lyke, very profitable to be made by the ſicke.

Lud. Bloſius cap. 3. lib. ſup.

I wicked ſinner moſte vnworthy, (redeemed with the precioufe bloode of our Lorde Ieſus Chriſt) doe confeſſe openlye, that with an entyer and pure harte I forgyue all thoſe that haue at any time euer offended me, or done me iniurye, in what maner ſoeuer: deſiring moſte humblye all and euerye one that I haue offended, iniuried, grieued, or any way angred (whyther they be preſent or abſent) that they would vouchſafe alſo to forgyue me.

Here let the ſicke call to minde his ſinnes in particular, and aſke God forgynenes, purpoſing firmely by God his grace neuer to commit ſinne agayne: and though his ſinnes be neuer ſo many, and the maner of his offences neuer ſo horrible and grieuouſe, yet he is to truſt in the omni-

po-

potency of God whose mercyes are innumerable, and to take hope and comfort in the passion of Christe our redeemer: Saveng.

I beleue in God the father almighty. &c.

A prayer for the sicke person to saye after his beleefe.

O Holy Trinitie I beseech thee. keepe and preserue this pure religion of my fayth, and graunte that it may euer be sounding in my conscience vntill my spirit departe.

O almightie and mercysull Iesu, I protest before thee and before all the courte of heauen, that I haue a will and desire to finishe my lyfe in this fayth, wherein of necessitie euery childe (obediente to our Mother the holye Church) ought to dye.

Further my sweete Sauiour I protest to beleeue wholly and vniuersally all that which is conteined

in

in the Catholicke fayth, and that
which a true faithful chriſtiā ought
to beleeue: that if it happen by the
aſſaults of the deuil, or by violence
of ſicknes, I come to thinke, ſay, or
doe any thing contrary to this purpoſe, I doe reuoke it at this preſent,
& proteſt that I gyue no conſent to
any ſuch thought, word, or worke.

I reioyce and render thankes to
my louinge creator and redeemer,
through the maruelouſe goodnes
of his bounty, by the which I hope
vndoubtedlye to dye in the holye
Catholicke fayth : and ſo I recommende my ſoule and body into his
moſte holy handes nowe and at the
houre of my death. Amen.

Prayers in ſickneſſe.

Dionyſ.Cart.in dial.de part.iudicio
animarum.

O Swet Ieſu, I deſire nether lyſe,
nor deathe, but thy moſt holy
will

wil'.Thee O Lorde I loke for, be
it vnto mee according to thy pleasure. Yf thou wilt sweete Iesu, that
I dye, receyue my soule. And albeit
I come to thee euen at the verye
eueninge, as one of the laste, yet
graunt that with thee, and in thee,
I may receyue euerlasting rest. Yf
thou wilt sweete Iesu that I lyue
longer on earthe, I purpose to a-
mende the rest of my lyfe, and offer
all into a burnt sacrifice vnto thee,
for thy honour and glorie, accordinge to thy blessed will : and for
the perfoorminge of this I desire
the assistance of thy holy grace.

Another prayer.
Hieron. in Agone mortis, auctore
Eusebio.

O Mercyfull Iesu, my vertue and
power, my comforte and ease,
my receyuer, and my redemer, in
whom

whome I haue hoped, in whome I
haue belyeued, and whome I haue
loued, my fwete delight. my tower
of ftrength , my hope from my
youthe, the guide of my lyfe, call
mee, and I will anfwer thee. O creator of heauen and earthe, ftretche
foorth the power of thy mercye,
vnto the worke of thy hãds, which
thou createdft of the flyme of the
earth, and tiedft together with bones and fynowes. Commaund O
Lorde, ftaye not, for it is time, that
duft may returne into duft, and my
foule maye returne to thee his Sauiour, who diddeft fende it downe
into this worlde.

Open vnto me the gates of
lyfe : for thou diddeft hange vpon
the Croffe for my fake, and madeft
mee promife to receyue mee.

Come my fweete Lorde, lett
mee embrace thee, lett mee not
leefe

leefe thee. Bring mee into thy heauenlie palace. Thou arte my receyuer, my glorie, mine aduauncer, my habitation, and my benedictiō. Receyue me moſte mercyfull Lorde, accordinge to thee multitude of thy mercies. For thou dyinge on the Croſſe receyuedſt the theefe, returninge vnto thee.

Another prayer.

Ibid.

I Am fycke: my lyfe is weake in this poore ſtate, and therfore to thee O Lorde I runne, as to my onely phiſitiō. Heale mee O Lord, and I ſhalbe healed. And for that I haue mine affiance repoſed in thee, lett mee not be confounded. But what am I, O moſt mercifull God, that ſpeake ſo boldly to thee? I am a ſinner, begottē, borne, & brought vp in ſinne: I am a rotten carkas, a ſtinckinge veſſell, and meate for

woor-

woormes. VVhat victorie O Lord
shall it be, yf in conflict thou ouerthrow mee, who am lesse than a
litle strawe before the face of the
wynde? Forgyue O Lord forgyue
all my sinnes, and lyst vpp a poore
man from this durty dounghill of
earthe. Certes good Lord, this will
I saye, yf it please thee, thou mayest
not refuse him that hathe his recourse to thee. For thou arte my
Lord God, flesh of my flesh, bones
of my bones. For to this intent,
thou not leauing the right hand of
thy father, diddest assumpte my hu-
maine nature, and becamst God &
man, remayning in one person the
selfe same, whiche thou wast from
thee beginninge. And why diddest
thou woorke this so hard & wounderfull misterie, but that I should
boldlye haue recourse to thee, as
vnto my brother, & thou wouldest
                                    mer-

mercifully so couer thy diuinitie,
that I should not be affraid of thy
heauenlie power. VVherfore arise,
O Lorde, and helpe me, arise, and
put mee not backe for euer.

Another prayer.
Ibid.

Ett my request entre into thy
sight, O Lord, and let thy hande
bee made to make me whole. Beholde I am the man that cominge
downe from Hiericho, was taken
and wounded of theeues, and left
half dead. Doo thou receyue mee
O mercyfull Samaritan. I haue sinned excessiuelie in my lyfe, and
wrought muche iniquitie in thy
syght. From the sole of my foote,
euen to the toppe of my head, there
is no sounde health in mee. Verely
onlesse thou dying on the Crosse
hadst assisted mee, my soule had
bene worthy to dwell in hell. I am,
                                sweete

(sweete Iesu,) a parte of that deare
price: for me, thou diddest shed thy
precious bloud, cast me not away. I
am the sheepe that wēt a stray, seeke
that sheepe, O good shepheard, &
put hym in thy folde, that thou
mayst be iustified in thy woorde.
For thou diddest make mee promise, that at whatsoeuer houre a
sinner did repēt him of his sinnes &
returne to thee, he shoulde be saued. I lament O Lord and moorne
for my sinnes, I acknowledg myne
iniquities, my wickednesse is in my
sight, I am not woorthy to be called thy sonne. For I haue sinned
against heauen & before thee, thou
shalt make mee heare that, whiche
shalbe great ioy & gladnes vnto my
heart. Turne away thy face O Lord
from my sinnes: blotte out myne
iniquities accordinge to thy great
mercie. Cast me not away out from

t' y

thy fig:t. Deale not with mee accordinge to my finnes, nor reward mee after the defert of myne iniquities. But helpe me O Lorde, my God aud my Sauiour, and for the glorye of thy holy name delyuer mee. Deale mercifully, as it femeth beft to thy holy will, that I maye dwell in thy howfe all the dayes of my lyfe, that I may prayfe thee for euer more, as they doe that dwell there, worlde without ende. Amen.

Prayers and fuffrages to be fayd for one lynge in death bedde.

L Orde haue mercie vpon vs.
Chrift haue mercy vpon vs.
Lorde haue mercy vpon vs.
Holy Marie praye for him.
All holy Angelles, and Archangels praye for him.
Holy Abell praye for him.
All the companye of the iufte pray

for him.

Holy Abraham praye for him.

Holy Iohn Baptiſte praye for him.

All yee holye Patriarkes and prophetes praye for him.

Saint Peter praye for him.

Saint Paule praye for him.

Saint Andrewe praye for him.

Saint Iohn praye for him.

All yee holy Apoſtelles and Euan-
geliſtes praye for him.

All ye holy Diſciples of our Lord
praye for him.

All yee holie Innocentes praye for
him.

Saint Stephen praye for him.

Saint Laurence praye for him.

All yee holy Martyrs pray for him.

Saint Silueſter praye for him.

Saint Auguſtine praye for him.

All yee holy Biſhoppes and Confeſſors praye for him.

Saint Benet praye for him.

Saint

Saint Francis praye for him.

All ye holy Monkes and Eremites
praye for him.

Saint Mary Magdalen pray for him.

Saint Lucie praye for him.

All ye holye virgins and wydowes
pray for him.

All ye holy Saintes of God make
interceffion for him.

Haue mercy,& fpare him O Lord.

Haue mercy:& heare him O Lord.

Haue mercy : and deliuer hym O
Lorde.

From thy anger, delyuer hym O
Lorde.

From an euill deathe delyuer him
O Lorde.

From the daunger of deathe, deliuer him O Lorde.

From the paines of hell, delyuer
him O Lorde.

From all euil,deliuer him O Lord.

From the power of the deuill,de-
liuer

liuer him O Lorde.

By thy Natiuitie, deliuer him O Lorde.

By thy Croſſe and Paſſion, deliuer him O Lorde.

By thy death and buriall, delyuer him O Lorde.

By thy glorious reſurrection deliuer him O Lorde.

By thy wounderfull aſcenſion deliuer him O Lorde.

By the grace of the holy ghoſt the comforter, deliuer him O Lorde.

In the day of iudgemente, deliuer him O Lorde.

VVe ſinners doe beſeech thee to heare vs.

That thou wouldéſt ſpare him, we beſeeche thee to here vs.

Lorde haue mercie vpon vs.

Chriſt haue mercie vpon vs.

Lorde haue mercie vpon vs.

O thou Chriſtian ſoule, departe thou

thou out of this world in the name
of God the father almightie, who
hath created thee, In the name of
Chrift Iefus the fonne of the liuing
God, who hath fuffered for thee,
In the name of the holy ghoft, who
was powred into thee, In the name
of the holy Angelles and Archan-
gelles, In the name of the Thrones
and dominations, In the name of
the Powers and Poteftates, In the
name of Cherubin and Seraphin,
In the name of the Patriarches and
Prophetes, In the name of the holy
Apoftelles and Euangeliftes, In the
name of the holie Martyrs & Confeffours, In the name of the holye
Monkes and Eremites, In the name
of the holie Virgins, and of all the
Saintes of God. Lett thy place be
this daye in peace, and thy habitation in holye Sion, through Chrift
our Lorde. Amen.

$\mathcal{A}$

A prayer.

O Mercyfull God, O benigne God, O God who accordinge to the multitude of thy mercyes doeſt blott out the ſinnes of ſuche as are penitent, and with thy remiſſion and pardon doeſt cleane purge the blame of offences paſte, mercifully looke vpon this thy ſeruant. N. and for our prayers graunt him his requeſt, who with all his harte confeſſynge thy name, doeth moſt earneſtlye craue for pardon of all his ſinnes. Renew in him, O moſte mercyſull father, what ſoeuer is corrupte through the frayeltie of the fleſh, or that whiche hath bene deſyled by the crafte of the deuill: and ioyne agayne vnto the vnitie of thy bodie the church, the member whiche thou haſte redeemed. Haue mercye O Lorde vppon his ſighes: haue mercy vpon his teares, and

and admitte agayne vnto the Sacrament of thy reconciliation hym,
who hath no hope but in thy mercie, through Chriſt our Lorde.
Amen.

Another prayer.

DEarely beloued brother I cō-
mende thee vnto almyghtie
God, and to his protection I commit thee, whoſe creature thou art,
to the ende, thou hauing payed by
the meanes of thy death, the debte
of all man-kinde, mayeſt returne
againe vnto thy maker, who hath
framed thee of a piece of claye.
Lett therfore the noble compainie
of Angels meete thy ſoule departinge out of thy bodie. Lett the
whole Senate of the Apoſtles, iud-
ges of the worlde, come vnto thee.
Lett the triumphant armye of the
gloriouſſe Martyrs come againſt
thee. Lett the floriſhing companie
of

of the shining Confessours cōpasse thee aboute. Lett the whole quire of the singinge Virgines receyue thee, & with embracing, settle thee faste in the bosome of the Patriarches, which is the place of blessed reste and quietnes. Let Christ Iesus appeare vnto thee with a milde and chereful, countenāce, and adiudge thee to bee emonge those, who alwayes attend vpon hym. Be thou ignorant of all that quaketh in darkenes, that crashed in fire, and houleth in tormentes. Lett the moste cruell fiend Satan, with all his souldiars gyue place vnto thee : lett him tremble at thy comming, thou being accompaigned with the holie Angells, and lett him flye into the huge pitte of euerlastinge darkenes. Lett God arise, and lett his enemyes be dispersed, and lett all that hate him, flye awaye from his

face

face.Lett them vanish awaye as the
smoke vadeth:as the waxe melteth
before the face of the fire,so lett
all sinners perish from the face of
God:and lett the iuste make merie
and reioyse in the sight of God.
Therefore lett all the legions of
hell be confounded and ashamed,
and lett not the ministres of Satan,
be so bolde as to stop thy iourney.
Christe deliuer thee from all torments,who was crucified for thee.
Christ deliuer thee frō death,who
hath vouchsafed to dye for thee.
Christ the sonne of the liuing God,
place thee in the garden of his paradise,whiche alwayes is pleasaunt
& flourishinge:& he that is the true
shepeherd, agnise thee emong his
sheepe.Lett him absolue thee from
all thy sinnes,and place thee at his
right hande,in the inheritaunce of
his electe.God graunt thou maiest
see

see thy redeemer, face to face, and
that thou maist be alwayes present
at hande, and with thy blessed eyes
beholde the moste manifest trueth.
God graunt therfore, that thou being placed emonge the compagnie
of the blessed soules, maiest enioye
the swetenes of the countenaunce
of the diuine maiestie, for euer and
euer. Amen.

Receyue O Lorde thy seruant
into the place of Saluation, whiche
he muste hope to haue of thy mercie. R. Amen.

Deliuer O Lorde the soule of
thy seruant from all daungers of
hell, and from all snares that maye
entrappe him to paine, and from all
tribulation. R. Amen.

Deliuer O Lorde the soule of
thy seruaunt, as thou haste deliured
Enoch and Elias from the cōmon
death of the world. R. Amen.

De-

Deliuer O Lorde the foule of thy feruaunt, as thou deliueredft Noe, from drowninge in the generall fludde. R. Amen.

Deliuer O Lorde the foule of thy feruaunt, as thou deliueredft Abraham out from Vr of the Chaldees. R. Amen.

Deliuer O Lorde the foule of thy feruaunt, as thou deliueredft Iob from his paffions and paines. R. Amen.

Deliuer O Lorde the foule of thy feruaunt, as thou deliueredft Ifaac from beinge offerd in Sacrifice, and out from the handes of his father. R. Amen.

Deliuer O Lorde the foule of thy feruaunt, as thou deliueredft Loth from Sodom, and from the flame of fier. R. Amen.

Deliuer O Lorde the foule of thy feruaunt, as thou deliueredft
Moyfes

Moyſes out from the handes of
Pharao, Kynge of the Egyptians.
R. Amen.

Deliuer O Lorde the ſoule of
thy ſeruaunt, as thou deliueredſt
Daniel out from the denne of the
Lyons. R. Amen.

Deliuer O Lorde the ſoule of
thy ſeruaunt, as thou deliueredſt
the three Children out from the
fiery fournace, and from the hands
of the cruell & vnmercyfull Kyng.
R. Amen.

Deliuer O Lorde the ſoule of
thy ſeruaunt, as thou deliueredſt
Suſanna frō the crime with which
ſhe was falſely charged. R. Amen.

Deliuer O Lorde the ſoule of
thy ſeruaunt, as thou deliueredſt
Dauid, from the handes of kinge
Saul, and Golias. R. Amen.

Deliuer O Lorde the ſoule of
thy ſeruaunt, as thou deliueredſt
S.

S.Peter and Paule out of pryson.
R. Amen.

And as thou deliueredst that
blessed Virgin, and Martyr Tecla,
from her moste cruell toiments, so
vouchesafe to deliuer the soule of
this thy seruant, and make him partaker of the euerlastinge ioyes in
heauen with thee. R. Amen.

Lett vs praye.

VVE commend vnto thee O
Lord the soule of thy seruant, & beseeche thee sweete Lord
Iesu Christ, Sauiour of the worlde,
that thou doe not refuse to place
hym in the bosome of thy Patriarches, for whom thou descededst
mercifully into the earth. Acknowledg O Lord thy creature, created
not of any straung gods but of thee
alone, the true and lyuinge God,
for there is no other God, but
thou

thou O Lorde, and there is none
according to thy woorkes. O Lord
make his soule reioyse in thy sight:
and remembre not his olde iniquitie, and drunckenesse, whiche inordinate concupiscence and raginge
lustes dyd rayse in hym. Albeit he
sinned, yet he denied not the father,
the sonne, and the holy Ghost, but
belyeued stedfastly in them: and he
had the zeale of God in his harte,
and adored the God, that created
all of nought. R. Amen.

Lett vs praye.

REmembre not, we beseech the
O Lorde, the sinnes and igno-
raunces of his wylfull youth, but
according to thy great mercie bee
myndefull of him in the glorye of
thy eternall deytie. Let the heauens
bee opened vnto hym. Lett thy
Angels reioyse of hym. O Lorde
re-

receyue thy seruant into thy kyngdome. Lett holy Michaell the high
messenger of God, that hath deserued to bee the chiefe all the holye
cõpany of Angels, receiue him. Let
all the holy Angels of God, come
forth and meete him, & conducte
him into the heauēlie Citie Hieru-
salē. Lett blessed Peter the Apostle,
who had the keyes of the kyndom
of God delyuered vnto hym, receyue hym. Lett the holy Apostle
S. Paule, who was woorthy to bee
a chosen vessell, receyue hym. Lett
S. Iohn the elect Apostle of God,
to whome the heauenly secret mysteries were reuealed, receyue him.
Lett all the holy Apostles who receyued of Christ power to loose
and bynd, praye for hym. Lett all
holye Saincts who haue sustained
tormentes for the name of Christ,
pray for him, that after he is loosed
out

out of the pryſon of this mortall
fleſh, he may be founde woorthy
to come to the glorie of the heauenly kyngdome, by the aſſiſtance
of our Lord Ieſus Chriſt, who with
the father and the holy Ghoſt, lyueth and raigneth, worlde without
ende. Amen.

Into thy handes O Lorde we cō-
men his ſoule. O Lorde God of
truth, thou haſte redeemed hym
Lett that ſweete voyce of thyne
O Lorde Ieſu, founde in his
eares. This daye thou
ſhalt bee, vvith me
in Paradiſe.
Amen.

The ende of the tvvelfth Chapter.

THE THYRTIENTH CHAP-
TER CONTAYNING DEVOVT
praiers, healthfull for the departed
soules.

An exhortation by the vvhich vve are
shevved and admonysshed to praye for
soules, departed in the Catholicque
Church.

Clemens 1. Ponti. Max. Ca. 47. lib. 8.
constit. Apostol.

Y brethren, lett vs praye
for our brother that res-
teth in Iesu Christ, to the
ende that our good God
which hath recieued his soule, may
forgyue him all his sinnes willingly or vnwillingly committed, and
that he obteining forgyuenes may
be receyued into the kingdome of
the blessed: in the bosome of A-
braham, Isaac and Iacobe, with all
those that from the begining haue
pleased God, and haue done his

T   will

will: from whom all sorow, griefe
and payne is secluded.

Commendations of the soule that is late-
ly departed.

Albertus Castella. Sacer. Rom. part. 1.

OLorde we commend the soule
of thy seruant that being late-
lye departed this lyfe, he may lyue
in thee, and according to thy mercye, pardone him his sinnes which
he hath committed throughe hu-
mayne frayeltie.

VVe commende O Lorde the
soule of this thy seruante, into the
handes of the holy and moste glo-
riouse virgin Mary, the mother of
mercye and clemency, Also into
the handes of all the holy Archangels, Angels, and celestiall courte
of heauen, into the handes of the
holy Patriarches and prophets: into the handes of the blessed Apostles,

tles, Euangeliftes and difciples : into the handes of the martyrs and confeffors: into the handes of the virgins, widowes and all votaryes who-foeuer.

And finally we commend the foule of this thy feruaunt into the hands of all fuch thy bleffed faynts and feruaunts, as haue pleafed thee from the firft creatiō of the world, that by their interceffion and fuccour, he may be deliuered from the prince of darknes, and from all dreadfull torments: graunt this O God almightye, omnipotente and full of mercy, through the bitter paffion of thy fweet fonne our fauiour Iefu, to whom with thee and the holy Ghoft, be all honour and glorye for euer and euer.   Amen.

A prayer for the faythfull foule departed.

Precat.

Precat. Ecclef. in Miſſa.

OEternall and almightye God, to whom we neuer pray with-out hope of mercy : Haue mercy of the ſoule of thy ſeruaunt N. and make him to bee vnyted to that companye of Saintes, which is de-ceaſed from this life, in the confeſ-ſion of thy name : through Ieſus Chriſte our Lorde. Amen.

Another prayer.
Pontifical. Rom. part 3.

OGod by whom all thinges ly-ueth, and through whom our bodies diminiſheth not in dyeng, but are chaunged into better : we moſte humblye beſeech thee, to commaunde the ſoule of thy ſer-uant to be receyued by the handes of thy holy Angels, to bring him vnto the boſome of thy friend the Patriarch Abraham, to ryſe againe at the laſte greate iudgement day,

par-

pardonning him mercyfully all his finnes which he hath committed, throughe the falfe deceiptes and fuggeftion of the deuill: through Iefus Chrifte our Lorde. Amen.

Another prayer.

Clemens Apofto. difcip. lib. 8. cap. 47. conftit. Apoftol.

O God of Abraham, God of I-faac, God of Iacob, which art God of the liuinge and not of the deade, for as much as all foules of the righteoufe lyueth with thee, and are in thy handes: they fhall not be touched with any payne or torment.

Looke bountifully vpon this thy feruaunt, which thou hafte re-ceyued into another lyfe, pardone him that, which he hath committed through the frayeltye of his will: Appoynt him thy louing Angels, to carye him into the bofomes of

Pa-

Patriarches, Prophetes and Apoſt-
tles, and of all thoſe that hath pleaſed thee from the begining of the
worlde, where is neither ſorowe,
griefe, nor horrour, but an aſſem-
blye of Saintes whiche are reioy-
ſing in the countrye of the happye
and iuſte, ſeeing the glory of thy
Chriſt: through whom be to thee
glory, honour, ſeruice and adora-
tion in the holy Ghoſt eternallye.
Amen.

A prayer for the ſoule of thy father.
Io. Damaſe in hiſtoria bar l. & Ioſa.

O Lorde God of inſearcheable,
and ineffable bountye, bringe
my father to the place of reſt and
refreſhing : where the light of thy
countenaunce dothe gloryouſlye
ſhine: do not remembre his former
offences, but accordinge to thy
great mercy, blotte out & cancell
the obligations of his ſinnes, teare
and

and rent them afunder, for thou art
worthy of all glorye, for euer and
euer. Amen.

A prayer for the foule of thy mother.
B. Aguſtinus ca. vlti. li. 9. confeſſionum.

O The God of my hart, my life
and my prayſe, I humbly deſire thee to pardone the ſinnes of
my mother: gracioufly heare me
for his ſake, which is the medicyne
of our woundes, whiche did hange
vpõ the tree, & now ſitting on thy
righte hande maketh interceſſion
for vs ſinners: I know that ſhe hath
delt charitably, & frõ her hart hath
forgyuen all her debtors: releaſe
alſo vnto her all thoſe ſinnes what
foeuer, ſince her baptiſme, ſhe hath
fallen into.

Releaſe them O Lorde, releaſe
them I befeech thee, and enter not
into iudgemente with her: let thy
mercy exceede thy iudgement, for
thy

thy wordes are true, and thou hàste
promiſed mercy to the mercyfull.

For my mother (when the day
of her death approched) did requeſt and deſire this, that we wolde
remember her ſoule, at thy holye
Aultar where ſhe had ſerued thee:
wherby ſhe did know and beleeue,
that the holy oblation of the body and precious bloode of our ſauiour Ieſus Chriſt, was made: wherby the obligation made againſt vs,
was cancelled : whereby the enemie was vanquiſhed, counting our
ſinnes, & ſearchinge what he might
obiecte againſt vs, and finding nothinge in vs by the meanes of Ieſus
Chriſt in whom we haue victorye:
whoe ſhall render to Ieſus Chriſte
his innocent bloode? who ſhall requite the pryce wherwith he hath
bought vs, that he might pull and
draw vs, from our enemye.

To

To the misterye of the which price, thy seruaunt hath vnited and bounde her soule by the bonde of fayth: let no man withdrawe her furth of thy protection: let not the dragon nor lyon intrude him selfe neither by force nor deceipt: neither as yet, will thy hand-mayd answere that she is not in debte, leste she be conuinced and possessed of that crafty accuser: but she will answere, that her debtes are released by him, whom none cã repay that, which he owinge nothinge hath payed for vs: let her therefore rest in peace with her husband, before whom and after whom, she was neuer maried to any other, whom she hath serued, and broughte foorth fruite to thee with great patience, to the ende she mighte gayne him to thee.

Inspire O my Lord God, inspire thy

thy feruauntes my brethren, thy
childrē my fuperiours, whom with
voyce, harte & penne I doe ferue:
that, who foeuer fhall reade thefe,
they may remember at thy Aultar
thy feruant Monica, with Patricius
her late hufband: by whofe flefhe
thou hafte broughte me into this
worlde, by what meanes I knowe
not how: let them remember with
deuoute zeale my parentes in this
tranfitorye lyfe, and my brethren
vnder thee their Father, in the lapp
of their Catholicke Mother, and
my countrye-men in the eternall
Ierufalem, which thy people in
their pilgrymage, from their departure vntill their returne, defire
to attayne vnto, that-fhee may attaine by the prayers of many, thofe
thinges which fhe requyred at my
handes when fhe departed.

Amen.

A pray-

A prayer for the soule of thy parentes.

O God which haste commanded vs, to honour and reuerence our father and mother, haue mercy I beseeche the on the soules of my father and mother : and of all my other parentes, forgyue them their offences, and graunt that I may see them in the ioye of thy euerlasting blysse. Amen.

A prayer for thy friend departed.

O God the gyuer of pardon and louer of mans saluatiō, we beseeche thy clemency, through the intercession of the glorious Virgin Marie, and of all the holy Saints of heauen : that thou wilt graunt, that the brethrē sisters & friends departed (in the vnitie of the Catholicke Church) with all our benefactours, maye come to the blysse of thy euerlastinge kyngdome, throughe Iesus Christ our Lorde. Amen.

A prayer

A MANVAL

A prayer for the lyuing & the deade.

ALmighty and euerlafting God,
Lorde of the lyuinge and the
dead thou fheweſt mercye to all
thoſe, whome by faythe and good
worcks, thou knoweſt to be thine:
we humbly befeech the, that thoſe
for whome we haue determined to
pray, whom ether this preſẽt world
yet retayneth in fleſhe : or the
worlde to come hath alredie receyued, maye through the clemencye of thy bountye, & interceſſion
of all thy bleſſed Saints, obtayne
full remiſſion of their ſinnes. Amẽ.

*A prayer for the departed to be ſayd at
maſſe.*

B. Ambr. præcatio. 1. præpa.

VVE humbly befeech thee O
holy father for the ſoules of
the faythfull departed this life, that
the holy Sacrifice of the maſſe may
be

be to them eternall saluatiō:perpe-
tuall health,ioy & rest euerlastiⁿg.
O my Lorde God,lett this wounderfull and excellent mysterye of
pyetie,and bountie,be vnto them
this day,full & perfect ioye:graunt
that they maye bee replenished
with thee,the lyuing & true bread,
which descēdest from heauen,and
gyuest lyfe to the world : and with
that holy and blessed flesh of thee,
the immaculate Lambe, which ta-
kest awaye the sinnes of the world:
and make them to drinke of that
fontaine of thy pyetie, whiche by
force of the souldiars lance issued
from the syde of our Lorde Iesus
Christ crucified,that so beinge cō-
forted they may reioyce in thy
holy laude and glorie.
Amen.
The ende of the thyrtienth Chapter.
FINIS.

This is the Iuſtice of man in this
life, Faſting, Almeſ-deedes, Prayer.

Ibidem in ſerm. 59.

He that wyll haue his prayer to
flye to heauen, muſte make it two
wynges, Almeſ-deedes, & Faſting,
and it ſhail ſpedelye aſcende and
bee harde.

A TABLE OF PRAYERS

MEDITATIONS, EXHORTAtions and aduertiſmentes, contayned in this preſente Manuall of prayers.

An

V   After

*The thirde Chapter contayning hole
fome prayers for remiffion of finnes.*

          A i.

The fourth Chapter contayning verye goodly prayers for comforte, ſtrength, and delyuery (by God his aſſiſtaunce) in all ſorovves, tribulátions, afflictions and aduerſities.

A pray-

The fifthe Chapter contayninge dyuers prayers, very commodious for obtaining that which is profitable both for bodye aud soule.

Apray-

*The fixte Chapter contayninge holefome
praiers of the life and paffion of our Sauiour and redeemer Iefus Chrift.*

Sonne our Lorde and Sauyour Iefu-Chrift. folio 82.

A deuoute prayer with the remembrance of the paffion of our fauiour Iefus Chrifte, to obtayne fuccour and fauour of him. folio 84.

The feuenth Chapter contayninge deuout and holefome prayers to be fayed, before and after the receyuing of the B. Sacrament.

The

The eyght chapter contayning laudes, prayeses, & thankesgyuing, for the benefytes that God hath bestowved vpon vs.

The nynthe chapter contayning neceſſarye prayers for the proſperitye of our brethren frendes and neyghbours.

A prayer

*The tenthe chapter contayninge hole-
some prayers to the holy Trinitie.*

*The eleuenth Chapter conteyning Chri-
stian Catholicque prayers to Saints and
Cytyzens of the glorie of heauen.*

10

The twelfth chapter contayninge aduertismentes and consolations with the prayers and suffrages for the sicke.

AN aduertisment for the sicke, diligently to prepare hym selfe to dye
well. folio. 131.

X

The thyrtienth chapter contayning de-
uout prayers, healthfull for the depar-
ted soules.

AN exhortation by the which we are
shewed and admonyshed to praye
for the soules departed in the Catholicque Churche.   folio.145.

The ende of the Table.

Certaine differences betvvene loue to-
vvardes God and loue tovvards crea-
tures, & vvhat loue God hath, & vvill
haue, to thofe that vvill perfectlye loue
and ferue him.

1. IF I loue a creature, it can not
knowhow much nor in what
maner my loue is : but yf I loue
God, he knoweth better the loue
of my harte then my felfe.

2. If I loue a creature, oftentimes
I receyue no rewarde or recompence: but if I loue God, he rewar-
deth a hundreth folde.

3. If I loue a creature, I finde it not
at al times, nor fo often as I would,
and I can not fpeake to it fo often
as I defire, and as neede requireth,
neither doeth it harkē to my wordes as I wiſhe: but yf I loue God, I
haue hym at all times with me : I
maye fpeake with hym as often as
I pleafe, and at all times he harke-
neth

neth to my wordes, yea and to the
defires of my harte.

4. If I loue a creature, often times
it putteth me to trouble, & is hin-
drance to me in my praiers, for that
I think of it: but yf I loue God, he
bringeth peace into my harte and
confcience, & if I thinke on him as
I ought in my praiers, he gyueth to
me hymfelfe whiche is foueraigne
fanctitye.

5. If I loue a creature, oftentymes
I haue care of it: but if I loue God,
he hathe a care ouer me.

6. If I loue creatures I knowe not
their fecrets: but yf I loue God, he
openeth often to me the trueth of
all hydden and fecret things.

7. If I loue a creature, it yeldeth
not my hartes defire: but yf I loue
God, he will gyue me wholy all
my defires.

8. If I loue a creature, it is out of
me:

me : but yf I loue God, he dwelleth in me and I in hym.

9. If I loue a creature,it knoweth
not all my affaires nor the thinges
to me appartaining : but yf I loue
God,he knoweth the better then
I doe my felfe.

10. If I loue a creature,fometimes
it deceiueth me:but if I loue God,
he will truely affure me.

11. If I loue a creature oftentimes it
moueth me to heauineffe & greife:
but yf I loue God,he gyueth me
ioy and confolation.

12. If I loue a creature , it feeketh
at my hand a profit and gayne to it
felfe:but yf I loue God,he wifheth
my profit and commodytie.

13. If I loue a creature often it departeth from me,and for that caufe
I haue fhort ioy and pleafure of it:
but yf I loue God, he remaineth
with me(fo long as I am without
deadly

deadly finne) from whome I haue
all ioye and pleafure.

14. If I loue a creature, I knowe
not yf I be loued of it:but yf I loue
God, I am affured of his loue.

15. If I loue a creature, it perifheth
or decayeth:but yf I loue God, he
dwelleth withe me euerlaftingly.

16. If I loue a creature, I finde it
often a lyar, variable and incon-
ftant:but yf I loue God, I finde him
mofte trew, and his will firme and
conftant.

17. If I loue a creature, I fee often
in it that difpleafeth me:but yf I
loue God, nothinge that I fee in
hym can difpleafe me.

18. Therefore I take and choofe
for my Louer & Spoufe our Lord
Iefu Chrift, who through his owne
pleafure is myne, and fo am I his,
& none is to me fo good, fo faire,
fo fweete, fo riche, fo noble, fo
mighty

myghty, fo wife, fo piteoufe, fo
benigne, nor fo amyable, as is my
harty louer Iefus. VVho liueth and
raigneth with the father and
the holy ghoft worlde
without ende.
Amen.

CERTAINE DE-
VOVT AND GODLY
Petitions, commonly called.

IESVS PSALTER.

Nomen datum

*There is none other name vnder hea-
uen geuen vnto men, in vvhiche
vve must be saued. Act. 4.*

CVM PRIVILEGIO,

Anno. 1583.

Miserere mei, Iesu, fili Dauid.

*The VVoman of Chanane ceassed
not to crie. Matth. 15.*

Haue mercie on me, Iesu, the
Sonne of Dauid.
O Lord, helpe me.

CERTAYNE DEVOVT AND
Godly Petitions Commonly
Called.

IESVS PSALTER.

T is to vnderstand, that there be three maner of Psalters. The Fyrste is called Dauids Psalter, which conteineth thrise Fifty Psalmes. The second is called the Psalter of our Lady, conteining thrise Fifty Aues. The third is called the Psalter of Iesu, or the inuocation of Iesu, conteininge fiftine principal petitions, which ten times repeted, make also thrise Fyfty. In the which Psalter & inuocation, is the glorious name of our Sauiour Iesu called vppon foure hundred and Fifty times VVhosoeuer vseth to say it, let thé trust verily, that they shall finde thereby speciall helpe to resist temptation, & haue encreafe of grace and vertue by the singuler helpe of Iesu. Of this blessed name S. Peter in the Actes of the Apos-

A 2   tles

tles sayeth : There is none other name
vnder heauen geué to men, in the which
it behoueth vs to be saued.

And our Sauiour sayeth in the Ghos-
pell of S.Iohn, that we should make our
petitions in his name , which is the Me-
diator of our saluation, whose glorious
vision , and most amorous fruition in
the celestiall glory, shall be our perpetuall ioy and incomprehensible consolation.

Here is to be noted (as it is sayed before) that the fiftiene principall petitions must be sayed ech one by them selfe,
ten times, like as they shall be sett furth
in this booke by order. And you may
say them vpon your ten fingers , or vpon ten beades, or els reade them as they
be writen , and it is good for them that
can not reade, to learne these inuocati-
ons without booke.

Beginne your Psalter with deuoute
genuflexion , or at leastwise with incli-
nation to Iesu : and saye thus, as foloweth.

Philippe. 2.

In nomine Iefu omne genu flecta-
tur, celeftium, terreftrium, & inferno-
rum. Et omnis lingua confteatur, quia
Dominus Iefus Chriftus in gloria eft
Dei Patris.

The firft petition.

i	Iefu. Iefu. Iefu.	mercy.
ii	Iefu. Iefu. Iefu.	mercy.
iii	Iefu. Iefu. Iefu.	mercy.
iiii	Iefu. Iefu. Iefu.	mercy.
v	Iefu, Iefu. Iefu.	mercy.
vi	Iefu. Iefu. Iefu.	mercy.
vii	Iefu. Iefu. Iefu.	mercy.
viii	Iefu. Iefu. Iefu.	mercy.
ix	Iefu. Iefu: Iefu.	mercy.
x	Iefu. Iefu. Iefu.	mercy.

IEfu haue mercy on me, and forgiue me the great offeces which
I haue done in the fight of thee.

Craunte me grace, Iefu, for the
loue of thee, to defpife finne and
all worldly vanitie.

A 2   haue

Haue mercy on all sinners, Iesu,
I beseche thee : turne their vices
into vertues, and make them true
obseruers of thy lawe and louers
of thee, bringe them to blisse in e-
uerlasting glory.

Haue mercy also on the soules
in Purgatory for thy bitter Passiõ,
I beseche thee, and for thy glorious name Iesu.

The holy Trinitie , one very
God, haue mercy on me.
Pater noster. Aue Maria.

The second Petition.

i	Iesu. Iesu. Iesu.	helpe me.
ii	Iesu. Iesu. Iesu.	helpe me.
iii	Iesu. Iesu. Iesu.	helpe me.
iiii	Iesu. Iesu. Iesu.	helpe me.
v	Iesu. Iesu. Iesu.	helpe me.
vi	Iesu. Iesu. Iesu.	helpe me.
vii	Iesu. Iesu. Iesu.	helpe me.
viii	Iesu. Iesu. Iesu.	helpe me.
ix	Iesu. Iesu. Iesu.	helpe me.

Iesu

x. Iefu.Iefu.Iefu.   helpe me.

IEfu helpe me,to ouercome all
tentations to finne, and the malice of my ghoftly enemie.

To fpend my tyme in vertue
and labour acceptable to thee, to
repreffe the motiõs of my flefh in
flouth,glotony,and leacherie.
To haue myne heart enamored of
vertue & the glorious prefence of
thee, to haue good name & fame,
Iefu to thyne honour,and to the
comforte of me.

Haue mercy on all finners,Ie-
fu,I befeche thee:turne their vices
into vertues , and make them true
obferuers of thy lawe,and louers
of thee : bring them to bliffe in
uerlafting glorie.

Haue mercy alfo on the fouls
in Purgatory for thy bitter paffion,I befeche thee, & for thy glorious name Iefu.

A 4   The

IESVS

The holy Trinitie, one verye
God haue mercy on me.
Pater noster.   *Aue Maria.*

The third petition.

i   Iesu. Iesu. Iesu.   strength me.
ii   Iesu. Iesu. Iesu.   strength me.
iii   Iesu. Iesu. Iesu.   strength me.
iiii   Iesu. Iesu. Iesu.   strength me.
v   Iesu. Iesu.Iesu.   strength me.
vi   Iesu. Iesu. Iesu.   strength me.
vii   Iesu. Iesu. Iesu.   strength me.
viii   Iesu. Iesu. Iesu.   strength me.
ix   Iesu. Iesu. Iesu.   strength me.
x   Iesu.Iesu.Iesu.   strength me.

IEsu strengthe me in soule and
body, to execute the workes of
vertue, to the pleasure of thee,
wherby I may come to thy euerlasting ioye and felicitie.

Graunt me firme purpose, most
merciful Iesu, to amende my lyfe,
& to recompése for those yeares,
whiche I haue mispent to the dis-
pleasure

pleasure of thee in euill thoughts, delectations, consentings, words, workes and euill custome.

Also in breaking thy commaundementes, whereby I haue deserued damnation, and thine enmitie.

Make mine harte obedient to fulfill thy will, and redy to doe for thy loue the workes of pitie.

Graunt me the seuen giftes of the Holy Ghost, the eyght beatitudes, the foure cardinall vertues, & in receauing of the Sacraments deuoutly to dispose me.

Haue mercy on all sinners, Iesu, I beseche thee : turne their vices into vertues, and make them true obseruers of thy law, and louers of thee : bring them to blisse in euerlasting glory.

Haue mercy also on the soules in Purgatorye for thy bitter Passion, I beseche thee, and for thy

glo-

glorious name, Iefu.

The holy Trinitie, one very God, haue mercy on me.
Pater nofter. Aue Maria.

       The fourth petition.
i   Iefu. Iefu. Iefu. comforte me.
ii   Iefu. Iefu. Iefu. comforte me.
iii   Iefu. Iefu. Iefu. comforte me.
iiii Iefu. Iefu. Iefu. comforte me.
v   Iefu. Iefu. Iefu. comforte me.
vi   Iefu. Iefu. Iefu. comforte me.
vii   Iefu. Iefu. Iefu. comforte me.
viii Iefu. Iefu. Iefu. comforte me.
ix   Iefu. Iefu. Iefu. comforte me.
x   Iefu. Iefu. Iefu. comforte me.

IEfu comforte me, and gyue me grace, to haue my mofte ioye & pleafure in thee.

Sende me heauenly meditations gooftly fwetnes and feruour of thy glorie.

Rauyfh my foule with brennyng defire to the heauenly ioye, where

where I fhall euerlaftingly dwell
with thee.

Graunt me, fweete Sauiour
Iefu, contempte of all damnable
pleafure full of finne and miferie.

Graunt me remembrance of
my faluation, with feare of damnation.

Alfo remembrance of thy good·
nes,thy gyftes and great kyndenes
fhewed to me.

Reduce into my minde my
finnes and vnkindenes,whereby I
haue offended thee.

Graunt me the fpirit of perfite
penance,contrition, confeffion,&
fatiffaction,to obteyne thy grace:
& from filthy finne to purge me.

Haue mercy on al finners, Iefu,
I befeche thee, turne their vices
into ver tues, and make them true
obferuers of thy law and louers of
thee: bring them to bliffe in euerlaftinge

laftinge glorye.

Haue mercy alfo on the foules in Purgatorye for thy bitter paffi-on, I befeche thee: and for thy glorious name, Iefu.

The holy Trinitie, one very God, haue mercy on me.

Pater nofter.   *Aue Maria.*

The fyfth Petition.

i   Iefu. Iefu. Iefu.   make me conftant and ftable.

ii   Iefu. Iefu. Iefu.   make me conftant and ftable.

iii   Iefu. Iefu. Iefu.   make me conftant and ftable.

iiii   Iefu. Iefu. Iefu.   make me conftant and ftable.

v   Iefu. Iefu. Iefu.   make me conftant and ftable.

vi   Iefu. Iefu. Iefu.   make me conftant and ftable.

vii   Iefu. Iefu. Iefu.   make me conftant and ftable.

Iefu

viii Iefu Iefu.Iefu.   make me
    conftant and ftable.

ix Iefu.Iefu.Iefu.   make me
    conftant and ftable.

x. Iefu.Iefu.Iefu.   make me
    conftant and ftable.

IEfu make me conftant & ftable in faith, hope, and charitie with continuance in vertue, and will not to offende thee.

Make me oft to remember thy paffion and bitter paines, which thou fuffredft for me.

Sende me perfect patience in all tribulation and aduerfitie.

Preferue me from Pryde, Ire, Enuie, Couityfe, and from all offences to thy lawes contrary.

The Catholicke obferuances of the Church make me to keepe truely.

Make my foule to holy doctrine obedient, and to things perteininge

teininge to my ghoſtly weale for the loue of thee.

Suffer no falſe delight of this deceauable lyfe, by fleſhly temptation and fraude of the fiende, for to blynde me.

To the houre of my death, my fiue wittes, Ieſu, kepe I beſeche thee.

From exceſſe in ſpeaking, in feeding, and workinge, preſerue my frailtie.

Haue mercy on all ſinners, Ieſu, I beſeche thee, turne their vices into vertues, and make them true obſeruers of thy lawe, and louers of thee : bringe them to bliſſe in euerlaſtinge glorie.

Haue mercy alſo on the ſoules in Purgatory for thy bitter paſſion, I beſeche thee, and for thy glorious name, Ieſu.

The holy Trinitie, one very God

God, haue mercy on me.

Philippenf. 2.

Dominus nofter Iefus Chriftus humiliauit femetipfum pro nobis faëtus obediens vfque ad mortem, mortem autem Crucis.

Pater nofter. Aue Maria. Credo.

In nomine Iefu omne genu flettatur, celeftium, terreftrium & infernorum. Et omnis lingua confiteatur, quia Dominus Iefus Chriftus in gloria eft Dei patris.

The fixt petition.

i	Iefu. Iefu. Iefu.	lyght me.
ii	Iefu. Iefu. Iefu.	lyght me.
iii	Iefu. Iefu. Iefu.	lyght me.
iiii	Iefu. Iefu. Iefu.	lyght me.
v	Iefu. Iefu. Iefu.	lyght me.
vi	Iefu. Iefu. Iefu.	lyght me.
vii	Iefu. Iefu. Iefu.	lyght me.
viii	Iefu. Iefu. Iefu.	lyght me.
ix	Iefu. Iefu. Iefu.	lyght me.
x	Iefu. Iefu. Iefu.	lyght me.

Iefu

IEfu light me with ghoftly wifdome, to know thy goodnes,
and thofe thinges, which are moft
acceptable to thee.

Graunt me grace to geue good
enfample profitable to foules, that
none be hurt by me: and to helpe
thofe with good counfell, which
haue offended thee.

Make me to proceede from vertue to vertue, vnto fuch time, that
I fhal clearely fee thy Maieftie.

Lette me not turne to thofe
finnnes, which I haue forowed for
& by cõfeffiõ haue accufed me of.

The horrible fentence of endleffe death, the terrible iudgement
of damnation, thy wrath, ire, and
indignation, mercifull Lord, let
neuer fall vpon me.

Thy mercy and thy merites,
my Sauiour, euer be betweene
them and me.

Haue

Haue mercy on all finners, Iefu, I befeche thee: turne their vices into vertues, and make them
true obferuers of thy law, and louers of thee : bring them to bliffe
in euerlaftinge glory.

Haue mercy alfo on the foules
in purgatorye for thy bitter paffion, I befeche thee, and for thy
glorious name Iefu.

The holy Trinitie, one verye
God, haue mercy on me.

Pater nofter. Aue Maria.

The feuenth petition.

i   Iefu. Iefu. Iefu.   graunt me
     grace, to dreade thee.
ii   Iefu. Iefu. Iefu.   graunt me
     grace, to dreade thee.
iii Iefu. Iefu. Iefu.   graunt me
     grace, to dreade thee.
iiii Iefu. Iefu. fefu.   graunt me
     grace, to dreade thee.
v   Iefu. Iefu. Iefu.   graunt me
                 B   grace

grace, to dreade thee.

vi   Iesu. Iesu. Iesu.   graunt me
      grace, to dreade thee.

vii   Iesu. Iesu. Iesu.   graunt me
      grace, to dreade thee.

viii   Iesu. Iesu. Iesu.   graunt me
      grace, to dreade thee.

ix   Iesu. Iesu. Iesu.   graunt me
      grace, to dreade thee.

x   Iesu. Iesu. Iesu.   graunt me
      grace, to dreade thee.

IEsu graunte me grace inwardly to dreade thee, and to eschue those thinges, whereby I mighte offend thee.

Thy blessed Mother be mediatrice for me, and purchace me a contrite harte, for that I haue offended thee.

Remoue my sinfull dispositions, which dulle myne harte, and lyke leade doe suppresse me.

All thy Saintes praye for me,
that

that I be not feperated from thee,
and their bleffed felowfhippe in
the heauenly Citie.

Let me not forget, good Lord,
the rycheffe of thy goodnes, of thy
patience, of thy longe fufferaunce
and benignitie.

Let the threatning of paine and
torment, whiche fhall fall vppon
finners, the loffe of thy loue and
of thy heauenly enheritance, euer
feare me to offende thee.

Suffer me not to lye in finne,
but call me foone to penaunce,
when I haue difpleafed thee: haue
mercy on me.

Haue mercy on all finners Iefu, I befeche thee, turne their vices
into vertues, and make them true
obferuers of thy lawe, and louers
of thee: bringe them to bliffe in
euerlaftinge glorie.

Haue mercy alfo on the foules
in

in purgatorie for thy bitter passion, I beseche thee, and for thy
glorious name Iesu.

The holy Trinitie, one verye
God, haue mercie on me.

Pater noster. *Aue Maria.*

The eyght petition.
i Iesu. Iesu. Iesu. graunt me
grace, to loue thee.
ii Iesu. Iesu. Iesu. graunt me
grace, to loue thee.
iii Iesu. Iesu. Iesu. graunt me
grace, to loue thee.
iiii Iesu. Iesu. Iesu. graunt me
grace, to loue thee.
v Iesu. Iesu. Iesu. graunt me
grace, to loue thee.
vi Iesu. Iesu. Iesu. graunt me
grace, to loue thee.
vii Iesu. Iesu. Iesu. graunt me
grace, to loue thee.
viii Iesu. Iesu. Iesu. graunt me
grace, to loue thee.

Iesu

ix   Iefu. Iefu. Iefu.   graunt me
    grace, to loue thee.

x   Iefu. Iefu. Iefu.   graunt me
    grace, to loue thee.

IEfu graunte me grace, truely to loue thee for thy edleffe goodnes, and for thofe giftes, which I haue receaued, and trufte to receaue of thee.

Lorde, when I offende, fmite me not with foudeine death, I befeche thee.

Let the remembrance of thy kindenes & patience, conquere the malice and wretched defire in me.

Drawe me, Lord, to thee, by perfect loue and charitie.

By breaking of thy commaundements I haue difpifed thee.

Graunt me, good Lord, in keepinge of them, as greatly to honour thee.

From leffe finne that I fall not into
    to

to the greater, Lord, preserue me.

Do with me according to thy mercy, and not after my misery: withdraw thy sword of vengeance for thy greate mercye and pitye.

Graunte me, Lorde, to be the childe of saluation, in body and soule to haue glorification, cleare sighte and fruition of thy Diuinitie, aad euer presentlye to see the glorious Trinitie.

Haue mercy on all sinners, Iesu, I beseche thee: turne their vices into vertues, and make them true obseruers of thy lawe, and louers of thee: bringe them to blisse in euerlastinge glorie.

Haue mercy also on the soules in purgatorie for thy bitter passion, I beseche thee: and for thy glorious name, Iesu,

The holy Trinitie, one verye God, haue mercy on me.

Pater

Pater noster. Aue Maria.

The ninth petition.

i   Iesu.Iesu.Iesu.   graunt me
grace,to remember,my death.
ii   Iesu. Iesu.Iesu.   graunt,&c.
iii   Iesu. Iesu. Iesu.   graunt,&c.
iiii   Iesu. Iesu.Iesu.   graunt,&c.
v   Iesu. Iesu. Iesu.   graunt,&c.
vi   Iesu.Iesu. Iesu.   graunt,&c.
vii   Iesu.Iesu. Iesu.   graunt,&c.
viii   Iesu.Iesu.Iesu.   graunt,&c.
ix   Iesu. Iesu.Iesu.   graunt,&c.
x   Iesu. Iesu.Iesu.   graunt me
grace,to remember my death.

IEsu,graunt me grace,for to remember perfitly the danger of
death,& the great account,which
I muſt then giue to thee, and ſo
diſpoſe me,that my ſoule be acceptable to thee,and to thy glorious
Mother the bleſſed virgin Marie.

Then with the aſſiſtance of thy
glorious Angel S.Mighel,deliuer
me

me from the danger of my ghostly enemy. And thee, my good Angel, I beseche, than to helpe me.

Then, good Lorde, remēbre thy
mercy, & for myne offences turne
not thy louely face from me.

O my Lord, be mercyfull King,
and meke Iudge at that dreadfull
houre, of me. I may not heare the
rigour of thy righteousnes : therfore I appeale to thy mercie. Thy
mercy exalteth thy Iudgemente,
and to vs sinners it is saluation,
when we cry hartily to thee.

At that dreadfull houre helpe vs
most mercifull Lord , which for
the time now cal for mercie.

Haue mercy on all sinners, Iesu I beseche thee , turne their vices into vertues, and make them
true obseruers of thy lawe , and
louers of thee : bringe them to
blisse in euerlastinge glorie.

Haue

Haue mercy alſo on the ſoules in purgatorie for thy bitter paſſion, I beſeche thee, and for thy gloriousname,Ieſu.

The holy Trinitie, one verye God, haue mercy on me.

Pater noſter.   *Ane Maria.*

The tenth petition.

i   Ieſu. Ieſu. Ieſu.   Sende me here my purgatory.

ii   Ieſu. Ieſu. Ieſu.   Sende &c.

iii   Ieſu. Ieſu. Ieſu.   Sende &c.

iiii   Ieſu. Ieſu. Ieſu.   Sende &c.

v   Ieſu. Ieſu. Ieſu.   Sende &c.

vi   Ieſu.Ieſu. Ieſu.   Sende &c.

vii   Ieſu. Ieſu.Ieſu.   Sende &c.

viii   Ieſu.Ieſu.Ieſu.   Sende &c.

ix   Ieſu. Ieſu.Ieſu.   Sende &c.

x   Ieſu. Ieſu.Ieſu.   Sende me here my purgatory.

I Eſu ſende me heere my purgatory,& preſerue me from thoſe torments of fire, which euer ſhall puniſhe punifhe finne and iniquitie.

Let ful hope of thine helpe euer abide in me, that I neuer fall in defperation of thy endleffe mercie.

Mother of God, Patriarks, Prophets, Apoftles, Euangelifts, Martyrs, Confeffours, Virgins, wydowes, Matrones and Innocents, I offer me to your merites, and befeche you, to pray for me, and at my paffing helpe to protect me.

VVith thy Sacraments, Lord, then recomfort me, & bring me to the kingdome of endleffe felicity.

My Lord Iefu crucified for me, by the merits of thy glorious paffion, I befeche thee, graunte me thefe petitions, which I haue afked of thee.

Haue mercy on all finners, Iefu, I befeche thee: turne their vices into vertues, and make them true obferuers of thy law, and lo-

uers

uers of thee: bring them to blisse
in euerlastinge glorye.

Haue mercy also on the soules
in purgatorie for thy bitter passion, I beseche thee, and for thy
glorious name,Iesu.

The holy Trinitie, one very
God,haue mercy on me.

Philip. 2.

Dominus noster Iesus Christus hu-
miliauit semetipsum pro nobis, factus
obediens vsque ad mortem, mortem au-
tem Crucis.

Pater noster. *Aue Maria.* *Credo.*

In nomine Iesu omne genu flecta-
tur cœlestium, terrestrium & inferno-
rum. Et omnis lingua confiteatur, quia
Dominus Iesus Christus in gloria est
Dei Patris.

The eleuenth petition.

i   Iesu. Iesu. Iesu.   graunt me
      grace to flee euill compagnie
ii   Iesu. Iesu. Iesu.   graunt, &c.
                Iesu.

iii	Iefu. Iefu. Iefu.	graunt, &c.
iiii	Iefu. Iefu. Iefu.	graunt, &c.
v	Iefu. Iefu. Iefu.	graunt, &c.
vi	Iefu. Iefu. Iefu.	graunt, &c.
vii	Iefu. Iefu. Iefu.	graunt, &c.
viii	Iefu. Iefu. Iefu.	graunt, &c.
ix	Iefu. Iefu. Iefu.	graunt, &c.
x	Iefu. Iefu Iefu.	graunt, me

grace, to flee euill compagnie.

IEfu graunte me grace, to flee euill companye: And when I come amonge them, for thy glorious paffion, I befeche thee, preferue me, that none occafion of mortall finne ouercome me: And fend me ghoftly comfort, by fuch as be true louers of thee.

Keepe my mouth, good Lord, from flaunderous fpeaking, lying, falfe witneffe-bearing, curfinge, fwearing, vncharitable chidinge, diffolute laughing and wordes of vanitye.

Make

Make me, blessed Lorde, with dreade to remember, that thou presently hearest me, which of all my wordes shalt iudge me.

Suffer not my hart to be light of creditte in hearing detraction, and obloquie, rancour and ire.

Iesu, represse in me all inordinate affection of carnalitye, and where I haue by euill felowshippe offended, mekely I aske mercie of thee, and I besech thee for helpe to all that crie for mercie.

Thy power protecte me, thy wisdome directe me, thy fatherly pitie correcte me.

Sende me gratious lyfe, blessed endinge: and thy passion preserue me from euerlastinge damnation and terrour of mine enemie.

Haue mercye on all sinners, Iesu, I beseche thee: turne their vices into vertues, and make them
true

true obſeruers of thy lawe, and louers of thee, bring them to bliſſe in euerlaſtinge glorie.

Haue mercy alſo on the ſoules in purgatorye for thy bitter paſſion, I beſeche thee, and for thy glorious name Ieſu.

The holy Trinitie, one verye God, haue mercye on me.

Pater noſter.   Aue Maria.

The twelfth Petition.

i	Ieſu. Ieſu. Ieſu.	geue me

grace to call for helpe to thee.

ii	Ieſu. Ieſu. Ieſu.	geue, &c.
iii	Ieſu. Ieſu. Ieſu.	geue, &c.
iiii	Ieſu. Ieſu. Ieſu.	geue, &c.
v	Ieſu. Ieſu. Ieſu.	geue, &c.
vi	Ieſu. Ieſu Ieſu.	geue, &c.
vii	Ieſu. Ieſu. Ieſu.	geue, &c.
viii	Ieſu. Ieſu Ieſu.	geue, &c.
ix	Ieſu. Ieſu. Ieſu.	geue, &c.
x	Ieſu. Ieſu. Ieſu.	geue me

grace to call for helpe to thee.

Ieſu

IEſu graunt me grace, and ſpe-cially in the time of temptati-on, to call for helpe to thee, and then with faythfull minde to re-member thy paſſion, which thou ſufferedſt for me: then, moſte mer-ciful Lorde, keepe my ſoule from conſent of ſinne for very true loue of thee: then let ſinne appeare ſtin-kinge and abhominable to me.

Let the remembraunce of the paines of hell, and damnation hor-rible, and terrible, and full of thine enmitie, with the merites of thy meeke patience, through charitie and chaſtitie, mitigate the proni-tie to ſinne and frailtie in me.

In my temptations, Lorde, I beſeche thee, helpe me, for the tender loue, that thou dideſt ſhew to thy Mother, and ſhe to thee.

Repell the power of my aduer-ſaryes, which intende the damnation

tion of me.

Inhabite my foule, O Sauiour, which with all humble fubiection defireth the bleffed prefence of thee.

Make me pure in fpirite, meeke in fpeakinge, patient in fufferinge, hungrie of righteoufe workinge, and mercifull to all them that be in miferie.

Make me peafable in conuerfation, cleane in harte with holy meditation, and ioyfully to fuffer perfecution in the caufe of thee.

Let all my powers and defires be ruled according to the will of thee: and all my petitions order to thy wifdome, and to the euerlafting profite of me.

Haue mercy on all finners, Iefu, I befeche thee: turne their vices into vertues, and make them true obferuers of thy lawe, and
louers

louers of thee: bring them to blisse
in euerlastinge glorie.

Haue mercy also on the soules
in purgatorie for thy bitter passion, I beseche thee, & for thy glorious name, Iesu.

The holy Trinitie, one verye,
God, haue mercy on me.

Pater noster. Aue Maria.

The thirtenth Petition.

i Iesu. Iesu. Iesu. make me to perseuer in vertue acceptable to thee.

ii Iesu. Iesu. Iesu. make me. &c.

iii Iesu. Iesu. Iesu. make me. &c.

iiii Iesu. Iesu. Iesu. make me. &c.

v Iesu. Iesu. Iesu. make me. &c.

vi Iesu. Iesu. Iesu. make me. &c.

vii Iesu. Iesu. Iesu. make me. &c.

viii Iesu. Iesu. Iesu. make me. &c.

ix Iesu. Iesu. Iesu. make me. &c.

x Iesu. Iesu. Iesu. make me. &c.

IEsu, make me perseuerante in
the blessed seruice of thee.

C

In holy cuſtome and vertuous occupation, Lord, keepe my ſoule and my body.

Make me flee ſinfull delectation, and patiently to ſuffer iniuries and rebukes, in recompence of my diſobedient hart to thee.

Prouide, good Lord, that life to me, which thou knoweſt moſt to thine honour, and to my eternall felicitie.

Fyll myne heart with contrition, and myne eyes with teares, that I neuer be forſaken of thee.

Awake my dull ſoule frō ſlepe of ſinne: and ſend me helpe from heauen, my bleſſed Sauiour, to ouercome the olde ſerpēt with all his cautels, by exerciſe in vertue, & ſpeciall grace of thee.

The Angels of light deliuer me from the Angels of darkenes, and from their great crueltie.

Let

Let thy obedience, Lord, recompence for mine obstinacie, thy
abstinence, for my superfluitie, thy
meekenes and thy patience, for
my pride, irefull hart and enmitie.

Thy charitie for my malice, thy
deuotion for my dulnes, thy louing hart for mine vnkindnes, thy
holy death for my wretched lyfe,
and for all my miserie.

Haue mercy on all sinners, Ie
su, I beseche thee, turne their vices into vertues, and make them
true obseruers of thy lawe, and louers of thee: bring them to blisse
in euerlastinge glorie.

Haue mercy also on the soules
in purgatorie for thy bitter Passion, I beseche thee, and for thy glorious name, Iesu.

The holy Trinitie, one very Go d
haue mercy on me. *Pater*. *Aue*,

The fourtenth Petition.

Iesu

i   Iefu. Iefu. Iefu.   graunt me
grace, to fixe my mind on thee.

ii   Iefu. Iefu. Iefu.   graunt. &c.

iii   Iefu. Iefu. Iefu.   graunt. &c.

iiii   Iefu. Iefu. Iefu.   graunt. &c

v   Iefu. Iefu. Iefu.   graunt. &c

vi   Iefu. Iefu. Iefu.   graunt. &c.

vii   Iefu. Iefu. Iefu.   graunt. &c.

viii   Iefu. Iefu. Iefu.   graunt. &c.

ix   Iefu. Iefu. Iefu.   graunt. &c.

x   Iefu. Iefu. Iefu.   graunt me
grace, to fixe my mind on thee.

IEfu graunt me grace, specially
in the time of praier, to fixe my
minde on thee , and then remember my wretchednes, and faithfully to call for helpe to thee.

That time to remember the pe-
rills of body and foule, which I
haue efcaped, and the benifits that
I haue receaued through thy great
chari tye : and with all my harte
Lorde then to geue laude to thee.

In:

In this prayer I thanke thee, for all the creatures, which thou haste made to helpe man, and that thou hast made him to thine image finally in thy glory to honor thee.

The motions of my runninge minde, the desire of mine vnstable harte in the time of prayer, stoppe and staie, I beseche thee.

Represse the power of my ghostly enimies, which then drawe my minde from ghostly weale to many imaginations of vanitie.

VVith the hand of thy feruent loue then I beseche thee to take me: and strength me in thy power, and with thy goodnes glad me.

Keepe me so occupied in good workes, that my prayers may be acceptable to thee.

Heare nowe, sweete Sauiour Iesu, heare the voyce of a sinner, which would fayne loue thee, and

C 3   with

with the hart as greatly pleafe thee,
as euer it hath offended thee : and
if it pleafe thy grace, more largely
to recompenfe, it befecheth thee.

Iefu, faue mine enemies from
thine enmitie, and forgeue them
that they haue offended me, like
as I woulde be forgeuen in thofe
things wherby I haue offéded the.

Lord, helpe al thofe, which haue
holpen me, or prayed for me, or
fhewed to me any deede of pitie.

Thy grace, Lord, and the merites of thy pretious blood, defend me from the ftriking Angell
and the fpirite of peftelence, and
make him to ouerpaffe me.

Haue mercy on all finners, Iefu, I befeche thee : turne their vices into vertues, and make them
true obferuers of thy law, and louers of thee : bring them to bliffe
in euerlaftinge glory.

Haue

Haue mercy alſo on the ſoules in Purgatory for thy bitter paſſion, I beſeche thee, and for thy glorious name Ieſu.

The holy Trinitie, one very God, haue mercie on me. *Pater*. *Aue*.

The fiftenth Petition.

i Ieſu. Ieſu. Ieſu. geue me grace to order my life to thee.

ii Ieſu. Ie ſu. Ieſu. geue me. &c.

iii Ieſu. Ieſu. Ieſu. geue me. &c.

iiii Ieſu. Ieſu. Ieſu. geue me. &c.

v Ieſu. Ieſu. Ieſu. geue me. &c.

vi Ieſu. Ieſu. Ieſu. geue me. &c.

vii Ieſu. Ieſu. Ieſu. geue me. &c.

viii Ieſu. Ieſu. Ieſu. geue me. &c.

ix Ieſu. Ieſu. Ieſu. geue me. &c.

x Ieſu. Ieſu. Ieſu. geue me grace to order my life to thee.

IEſu geue me grace, to order my life and the workes of my body and ſoule with actual entēt finally to thee, & to the reward of thy infinite

finite ioy and eternall felicitie.

The water and blood, which ranne frō thy bleſſed heart, waſh my ſoule from ſinne and iniquitie, and purchace to me abundance of grace faithfully to ſerue thee.

O my Lord, my life, my might, my ſight, leade me, feede me, and ſpede me in the pilgrimage of this mortalitie.

Graunt me, Lord, by the merites of thy Paſſion, and vertue of thy moſte excellent and glorious Diuinitie, what ſo euer thy wiſedome knowethe moſte expedient to me, which my miſerable lyfe is not worthie to obtaine of thee.

At the houre of death (when I ſhall be accuſed before thee) for that death that thou ſufferedſt for ſinners, haue mercy on me.

Breake my froward harte, and make it obedient to thee. From
ſoudayne

foudayne and vnfore-feene death,
Lord,preferue me.

Graunt me grace, to departe
with contempte of this world,and
with ioyfull hart to come to thee.

Let the remembraunce of thy
Paffion, make me ioyfully to take
temptation and tribulation for the
loue of thee.

Make me mofte to loue that
ioyfull lyfe, that immortall glorie,moft excellent bliffe, and endleffe felicitie, which is ordeined
in the heauenly kingdome for the
feruauntes of thee.

By the vertue of thy Incarnation, Natiuitie, Paffion and Refurrection, graunt me thefe fupplica-
tions, which I haue made to thee.

This inuocation and Pfalter of
thee, by the meditation of thy
mofte intierly beloued Mother,
purchace to me gracious life and
bleffed

blessed ending, free from debt and deadly sinne, I beseche thee, & after my bodilie death, euerlastinge life, vvith endlesse blisse & felicity.

Haue mercy on all sinners Iesu, I beseche thee : turne their vices into vertues, and make them true obseruers of thy law, and louers of thee: bringe them to blisse in euerlastinge glorie.

Haue mercy also on the soules in Purgatorie for thy bitter passion, I beseche thee, and for thy glorious name Iesu.

The holy Trinitie, one verie God haue mercy on me.

Dominus noster Iesus Christus humiliauit semetipsum pro nobis , factus obediens vsque ad mortem, mortem autem Crucis.
Pater noster. Aue Maria. Credo.

Thus endeth this Psalter.

A 3

VNto such, as haue none opportunitie to say the whole
Psalter together, it is good that
they say the first v. petitions one
day, & the second v. another day,
and the last v. another day, and so
in three dayes they shall saye the
whole Psalter. But els if they may
haue conuenient time, it is better
to say the xv. principall petitions
euery day, & ech of them x. times,
with *In nomine Iesu,* in the begin-
ning, *Pater noster. Aue Maria.* and at
euerie fifth, like as it is writen in
the booke, with *Dominus noster. Pater noster. Aue Maria. Credo.*

*Here folovveth a hoolsome doctrine,
hovv to resiste and ouercome the ghostly temptations of the Fiende.*

DOctours do write, that in spirituall temptations we should
behaue our selfe otherwise, then
in

in carnall temptations. For carnall
temptations, we ought to refift and
wreftle withthem: but we may not
doe fo in fpirituall temptations:
VVifely & difcretely we muft re-
fiftethem, but in no wife wreftle
with them: as thus: when the enemie putteth a motion of infideli-
ty, reafon not with him: & likewife
when he caftethe a fuggeftion of
defperation, ftryue not with him,
but vfe this medicine.

Sufpend your reafon, reftraine all
your fenfes, and plucke vp all your
fpirits: and as the motion cometh,
fo let it paffe, without ftrife. If it be
onely of the difpofition of our
corrupt nature, this is fufficiét, if it
be vfed. If it come of the enemie,
he will not leaue fo, but he will
cleaue otherwyfe, & worke more
trouble. Than after the counfell of
Doctours, vfe] this remedie : Dif-
          femble

semble, & shew your selfe to set it
at nought,though it be great : and
lift vp your mind to God,remem-
bring his tender mercie in the redemption of man,and how it is his
ordinance,with such tentations &
paines to proue his seruantes, to
whom he entendeth to geue the
crowne of glorie. But if the enemie be fierce & will not cease for
this(as he is most subtill & crafty)
than meeke your selfe to God,&
offer your selfto suffer for his loue
(and for the fruit of penance for
your sinnes)gladly & with thanks
of heart,all paines,that it shal please his grace to sende you.And with
that, call and crie with heart and
worde on the holy name of Iesu x.
times, ether more or lesse,as your
deuotiõ serueth,with some holy &
swete meditation of reuerence to
the same,as God shall put in your
minde

minde. This vertue of mekenes, &
confeſſion of the name of Ieſu in
harte and worde, the enemie may
not abide. For although for a time
he will pretend and diſſemble, as
though he were not abaſhed for
that vertue & name: as the Serpēt,
of which Scripture ſaith, that for a
time ſhe will ſtoppe her eares, and
yet by the worde of the enchanter
in concluſion ſhe is ouercome and
taken: ſo certainly the enemie (that
holy name named) is ouercome,
although he will not be knowen,
but ſōtime will make inſurrection
more fiercely, after that holy name
ſpoken. Then ſtrongly purſewe
him with the ſame, & with mekenes: and ye ſhall ſee, how he will
flee: to the great comfort of al thē,
that abide as true ſeruantes perſe-
uerant in this their proofe, to their
great triumph, and vtter confuſion
of

of the enemie. This hath ben pro-
ued by experience.

A Narration.

A Certaine perſon there was,
which by the ſpace of two yeares and more was troubled with
ſuche motions oftētimes by water
and by lande. He had motions to
deſperation, & to the moſte abhominable that may be, to deſtroy
him ſelfe both by water, & other-
wiſe. And this ſaid perſon ceaſſed
not, but called to God daily, to
ſtrength him, euer confeſſing him
ſelfe his ſeruant, and the worſhip-
per of the holy name of Ieſu, cō·
mitting him ſelfe only and wholy
to the Paſſion of Chriſt and mercy
of God. And ſone after the ſaid
time, he had comfort, and was illu-
mined or lightened in his ſoule,
how to anſwere the enemie: to his
great comforte, & to the edifiyng
of

of others, and that was thus. It was geuen to him by a light, that whensoeuer such a motion came to his minde, he should take the motion for an occasion of remembrance to honour the Passion of Christ, & his blessed Mother the glorious Virgin Marie. And although that it came to his minde an hundred times in the daie, so oft to saye: *Adoramus te, Christe Iesu:* and to the Mother of mercy, *Aue Maria.* And thus the person was cleane deliuered from his great tentation and trouble, to the greate encrease of hope in his soule, to the vtter driuing away of the enemie, and to the glorie of God: to whome be all honour & praise world without end. Amē.

FINIS.

HEREAFTER FOLOVVETH

Certayne deuout and godly Petitions,
commonly called The Golden Litanie.

LOrde haue mercye vppon vs.
Chrifte haue mercy vppon vs.
Lorde haue mercy vppon vs: and
graunt vs vertue of foule & minde
in earth and aboue earth, that we
may ferue thee after the pleafure
of thy will.

God euerlafting Father, by thy
heauenly vertue, haue mercy vpon vs.

The Sonne of God Redeemer
of the world, haue mercy vpon vs.

The holie Ghoft, by thy goodnes, haue mercie vpon vs.

God the increate and vndeuided
Trinitie, haue mercie vpon vs.

By thy diuine nature, haue mercie vpon vs.

By thy infinite meekenes, haue
mercie vpon vs.

By thy selfe and all goodnes that in thee thou beholdest, haue mercie vpon vs.

By the creation of heauen and earth, and all thinges that in them are, haue mercy vpon vs.

By thy goodnes that didest create Angels, haue mercy vpon vs.

By the loue that thou haddest when thou created man to thine owne similitude, haue mercie vpon vs.

By the greate loue that thou haddest to redeeme man after his fall, haue mercy vpon vs.

By that ineffable loue that thou haddest, when thou didest chuse the worthy Virgin Mary to be thy Mother, haue mercy vpon vs.

By the holy name of Mary, haue mercy vpon vs.

By the Conception of the Virgin thy Mother, the which was sancfanctified in her Mothers wombe, haue thou mercy vpon vs.

By the holy natiuitie of her, haue mercy vpon vs.

By the perfecte puritie and meekenes of her, haue mercy vppon vs.

By the moste humble affection, which she toke of thee in the lap of the Father, in her Virgins wōbe, haue mercy vpon vs.

By the mekenes of thy high Maieftie, that thou difdained not to defcend into the wombe of the Virgin Marie, haue mercy vpō vs.

By the fraile nature of ours that it pleafed thee to take for our finne, not abhorring the fame, haue mercy vpon vs.

By thy holy Natiuitie, that thou wouldeft vouchefafe to be borne of a Maide, haue mercy vpon vs.

By the ineffable ioye, whiche thy Mother had in thy birth, haue mercy vpon vs.

By the colde Cribbe, in the which with vile clothes thou was wounde and put, and nourished with maidens milke, haue mercy vpon vs.

By the ioy of the shepherds, which honoured thee in the Cribbe, haue mercy vpon vs.

By thy painfull Circumcifion and shedding of thy precious Bloode, and by thy holy Name Iesus, and by all thy holy Saints, haue mercy vpon vs.

By the oblatiõ & praier of the three Kings, haue mercy vpon vs.

By the oblation, wherewith thou was offered vp in the Temple, haue mercy vpon vs.

By the fleeing into Egipt, and by all the necessitie that thou suffredst

fredſt there with the Virgin thy Mother, haue mercy vpon vs.

By thy going againe from Egipt into Nazereth, and obedience that thou was vnder thy parentes, haue mercy vpon vs.

By thy humble and meeke conuerſation, that thou hadſt on earth in the time of three and thirtye yeares that thou was conuerſant, haue mercie vpon vs.

By thy meeke obedience and paines, haue mercie vpon vs.

By thy holy meditations in worde and worke, haue mercie vpon vs.

By thy Baptiſme, and appearing of the holy Trinitie, haue mercie vpon vs.

By thy holy ſtedfaſt contemplations and kneelinges, and ouercomminge of the fiends temptation in deſerte, haue mercie vpon vs.

D 3

By thy thirst and hunger, colde and heate, which in this vale of miserie thou suffered, haue mercy vpon vs.

By the sorow of thy harte, labour and wearines, haue mercye vpon vs.

By thy greate pouertie and contemplation, haue mercie vpon vs.

By the obtrectation of thine enemies toward thee, haue mercy vpon vs.

By thy watchings and praiers, haue mercy vpon vs.

By thy holsome doctrine & benefites, and strength of resisting, in that thou yelded not to thine enemies, haue mercy vpon vs.

By the tokens, wounders, & miracles that thou diddest, haue mercy vpon vs.

By the meke, swete, and holy conuersatiõ, haue mercy vpon vs.

By

By thy holy teares, and thy meeke entring into Ierusalem on Palme-sonday, haue mercy vpon vs.

By the inflamed desire that thou had to redeeme vs, haue mercy vpon vs.

By thy meeke washing of thy Disciples and Iudas the traitours feete, haue mercy vpon vs.

By thy moste louing institution of the worthy Sacrament of thy blessed Blody & Blood, Lord haue mercy vpon vs.

By the profound loue, in that thou suffered thy disciple Sainte Iohn to rest on thy Breaste at thy laste Supper, haue mercy vpon vs.

By the peace that thou didst geue to thy Disciples, haue mercy vpon vs.

By thy holy wordes and sermons, haue mercy vpon vs.

D 4.   By

By thy Paſſing great heauines
that thou hadſt, when thou didſt
praie to thy Father in the garden
nigh to the Mount of Oliuete, haue mercy vpon vs.

By the vertue of thy praier
that thou offeredſt vp three times,
haue mercy vpon vs.

By thy painefull and fearefull
death, haue mercy vpon vs.

By thy agonie when thou of-
fredſt thy ſelfe willingly to the
death, in obeing thy Father, haue
mercie vpon vs.

By the ſhedding of thy Blood for
anguiſh, haue mercie vpon vs.

By the meekenes, in that thou
wouldeſte be comforted of the
Angell, comforte me in all times,
and haue mercie vpon vs.

By the triumphant will that thou
hadeſt, when thou wentſt to meete
them that ſought thee vnto death,

haue

haue mercie vpon vs.

By the fearefull taking and violent laying on hands of the Iewes,
haue mercie vpon vs.

By thy immutable goodnes that
thou refusedst not to take the kisse
of Iudas the traitour, and that thou
healedst the eare of the Bishopps
seruant, that was stricken of, haue
mercie vpon vs.

By the holie Bondes in the
which thou was taken, and led a-
waie, and by the braids in which
thou was made werie that night,
haue mercie vpon vs.

By the buffet which thou sufferedst at the Seate of Annas the
Bishop and others vnknowinge
thee, haue mercie vpon vs.

By the loue and charitie that
thou hadst, when thou was ledde
bounden before the Bishop Cai-
phas, haue mercie vpon vs.

By

By the false witnesse and lies by which thou vvas vniustlye condemned haue mercie vpon vs.

By the vile spittings and illusions, haue mercie vpon vs.

By thy buffetts and stripes, haue mercie vpon vs.

By the blind-foldinge of thy holie eies, & other reproches that thou sufferedst that nighte, haue mercie vpon vs.

By thy gracious beholding that thou beheldest Peter, and by all that labour & secrete vnknovven tormente, vvhich thou sufferedst that night, haue mercie vpon vs.

By thy presentation, and accusation vvhich they brought againt thee before Pilate the Iudge haue mercie vpon vs.

By the despisinge and illusion that thou suffredst before Herode, & the vvhite vesture in the vvhich

he

he sent thee to Pilate, haue mercie
vpon vs.

By all the labours that thou sufferedst in goinge from one Iudge
to an other, haue mercie vpon vs.

By thy great patience and stil-
nesse, haue mercie vpon vs.

By the shamefull pulling of thy
clothes and harde bindinge of thy
bodie to the piller, haue mercie
vpon vs.

By the harde beating of scour-
ges, haue mercie vpon vs.

By the innumerable vvounds
of thy precious body hugelie shed
out, haue mercie vpon vs.

By all thy paines, dollours, colde
aud shaking, and the glad shedding
out of thy bloode, haue mercie
vpon vs.

By the purple vestement, and
the crovvne of thorne thrust faste
vpon thy blessed Head vvith violence,

lence, haue mercie vpon vs.

By the innumerable paines wherwith thou was torméted whé they
fmote the croune of thorne with
the Kinges fcepter, and by the
greate effufion of thy precious
Blood, haue mercy vpon vs.

By the fcornefull honouring
and faluting of the Iewes, when
they faid: Haile King of the Iewes,
haue mercy vpon vs.

By their vile fpitting on thy
diuine face together with harde
ftrokes, haue mercy vpon vs.

By all the paines and heauy-
nes of heart that thou haddeft,
when Pilate ledde thee out vnto
the people bearing the Crovvne
of thorne, & the purple veftemét,
and faide : *Beholde the Man*: haue
mercy vpon vs.

By that dreadfull fentence of
death, and vile name, leading thee
vnto

vnto the mount of Caluarie, haue
mercy vpon vs.

By the loue wherewith thou
didſt beare the Croſſe to the place
of paine vpon thy backe, haue
mercy vpon vs.

By the labours, anguiſh, ſhame
and beatings which thou ſuffredſt
by the way, haue mercy vpon vs.

By al thy harde ſteppes that thou
hadſt, bearing the Croſſe when
thou wentſt to thy death, haue
mercy vpon vs.

By the great wearines of thy
ſhoulders, on whiche thou didſt
beare the Croſſe vnto the time
thou failed for weakenes, haue
mercy vpon vs.

By the compaſſion of harte
that thou hadſt in meting of thy
ſorowful Mother, and in bearing
of thy croſſe, haue mercy on vs.

By thy heauy loking & aſcen-
ding

ding vp the high Mount of Caluarie, on whiche thou was crucified, haue mercy vpon vs.

By the ftripping of and fpoi-
ling of thy clothes in moft confufion in the fight of the Virgin thy
Mother and all the people, haue
mercy vpon vs.

By thy being naked, full of
woundes, ladē with great forowes
enduring the colde of the vvind,
till the Croffe vvas made ready,
haue metcy vpon vs.

By thy painfull fteppes, vvhen
thou vventeft nere to the Croffe,
and thereon vvas faftened vvith
boyfteous nayles, haue mercy
vpon vs.

By thy tender teares & weeping, haue mercy vpon vs.

By the ache of thy veines and
finowes and all thy members on
thy Croffe, haue mercy on vs.

By

By the thyrling of thy right hande, and fhedding of thy precious bloode, Lorde make vs cleane from all finne, and haue mercy vpon vs.

By the thyrling of thy left hand, and by the holy wounde of the fame, and thy holy Bloode, faue vs, and haue mercy vpon vs.

By the fore driuing of the nailes into thy holy Feete, and by the woundes of the fame, and by the flovving out of thy precious Bloud, purge vs, and reconcile vs to thy father, and haue mercy vppon vs.

By the lifting vp of thy mofte holy Body on the Croffe, and by the violent paines where-withall thy holy membres vvere rufully pained, haue mercy vpon vs.

By the heauiues of thy harte and all the ftrengthes of thy foule,
faue

faue me, deféde me, and haue mercy vpon vs.

By the diuifion or parting of thy veftures, & the lot which they caft on thy cote vvithout feame in thine ovvne fight and beholding, haue mercy vpon vs.

By the loue that thou hadft hăging three houres on the Croffe aliue, haue mercy vpon vs.

By the reproches and wordes full of confufiŏ that thou heardft hanging on the Croffe, haue mercy vpon vs.

By the blafpheminges & curfes & fhamefull reuiling that thou fuffredft on the Croffe, haue mercy vpon vs.

By all the dolours that thou fuffredft in thy ribbes, loynes and fhoulders crucified, haue mercy vpon vs.

By all the paines that thou hadft

had beinge fprede on the Croffe in thy finowes, veines, feete and all thy members, haue mercy vpõ vs.

By thy great mekenes in praying to thy Father for thine enemies, haue mercy vpon vs.

By thy mercy, by which thou promifed to the theefe Paradife, haue mercy vpon vs.

By the care that thou had of thy Mother in thy tormente commending her to thy beloued Difciple, haue mercy vpon vs.

By the fword of forow that went vnto thy Mothers harte, and the compaffion & teares that fhe fhed out for forowe ftanding vnder the Croffe, haue mercy vpon vs.

By all thy holy Teares on the Croffe, and in all the time of thy life, fhedde out for the world, haue mercy vpon vs.

By thy thirft, gall and eyfell with
E   vine-

vineger, geue me to taste of thy sweete Spirite, and haue mercy vpon vs.

By all the holy words by thee pronoūced both vpon the Crosse, and in all thy whole life, haue mercie vpon vs.

By the weeping and crie, in the which thou diddest commend thy Spirit to thy Father, that our souls may be commended to thee, haue mercie vpon vs.

By the seperation of thy holie Soule from thy blessed and diuine bodie haue mercie vpon vs.

By the enclininge of thy holie Heade vpon thy breaste, encline sweete Iesus vnto vs, and haue mercie vpon vs.

By the huge dolefulnes of thy death, and intollerable brusinges in which thy harte was broken, haue mercie vpon vs.

By

By the opening of thy fide, and the redd wound of it, and the precious blood, good Lord, pearce our harte with the fpeare of thy loue, and haue mercy vpon vs.

By the precious blood & water that ranne out of thy holie Harte, wafh & make vs cleane in the fame holie water & bloode from all our finnes, and haue mercy vpon vs.

By the mercy that thou fhewed on the Croffe to the Centuriõ, and all the mercy that euer thou fhewed to man, haue mercy vpon vs.

By the defcending of thy holy Soule to Limbo Patrum, haue mercy vpou vs.

By the vertue of thy holy foule, wherewith thou brakeft vp the gates of hell, and deliuered ou the foules of thy friendes, hau mercy vpon vs.

By the taking downe of thy

E 2   holy

Holy Body from the Croſſe,& the
ſoléne Sepulture of it,& the lamē-
ting of the Virgin thy Mother and
Marie Magdalen,and other of thy
frindes,haue mercy vpon vs.

By all the labour, wearines,
ſorow,and heauines that thou ſuffered from the daie of thy Natiuitie vnto the houre of the depar-
ting of thy holy Soule from thy
bodie,haue mercy vpon vs.

By thy glorious and vertuous
reſurrection in Body and Soule,
haue mercy vpon vs.

By the ineffable ioye of thy
Mother,and other of thy frindes
and the glorie of thy Reſurrectiō
haue mercie vpon vs.

By the grace that thou appeared
to Marie Magdelen and other women,and to thy Diſciple in thy im-
paſſible body after thy Reſurrection,haue mercy vpon vs.

By

By thy marueilous and glorious Afcenſió cófort vs Lord in all our nedes, and haue mercy vpon vs.

By the diuine conſolation and ſending of the holy Ghoſt into thy Diſciples, glad vs, ſanctiſie vs, and ſtrength vs in faith, hope, and charitie, and haue mercy vpon vs.

By thy glorious and diuine maieſtie, & the vertue of thy holy name, kepe vs gouerne vs now & euer, and haue mercy vpon vs.

By the Sonne in thy holy Godhed together in thy Manhod hidden, haue mercy vpon vs.

By thy ſelfe, and all goodnes and merites that in thee and in thy Mother thou didſt beholde, haue mercy vpon vs.

By thy celeſtiall Miniſters Michaell and Gabriel, keepers deputed to me, & all other thy heauêly Spirits, haue mercy vpon vs.

By

By the interceſſion and merites of Saint Peter, Saint Paule, S. Iohn the Euangeliſt, and other of thine Apoſtles, haue mercy vpon vs.

By the merites & interceſſion of thy holy Martyrs S. Stephan, and Saint Laurence and all other, haue mercy vpon vs.

By the vertues and merites of the holy Fathers and Confeſſours Saint Auguſtine, Saint Hierome, S. Chriſoſtome, Saint Ambroſe, and all other, haue mercy vpon vs.

By the merites and praiers of holy Saint Anne, Saint Katherin, S. Barbara, and all other holy Virgins, and holy widowes and chaſte women, haue mercy vpon vs.

By the merits and praiers of all thy holy choſen Saintes, that are, were, & be for to come in heauen and in earth, haue mercy vpon vs.

Succour vs, ſweete Ieſu, in the
trem-

trembling and ſtrait daye of Iudgement,and graunt vs in this exile
and tranſitory life thoſe things that
be neceſſarie to the helth of our
body & foule, and after this life to
liue in ioy with thee euerlaſtingly
without end. Amen.

 Lorde heare gracioufly my
prayers and let my crie come vnto
thee, &c.

Praye vve.

LOrd geue to the quick grace,
to the dead reſt,in eſpeciall to
them,that I am bounden,N.and to
the Church holines,peace & con-
cord.And that thou wilt voucheſafe,to take this praier to the honour and glorie of thy holy name,
and that thou wilt vouchefafe to
haue mercy vpon vs,& to forgiue
vs all our fynnes: & graut euerlaſtingly, that we may perſeuer in all
goodnes,& that we may ſerue thee.
       And

And after this life, we may merite to raigne with thee, in euerlasting glory and life without end.

GODLYE AND DEVOVTE
Prayers made and collected by Syr
Thomas Moore vvhyle he vvas
Prisoner in the Tovver of
London.

GOod Lorde, geue me grace in all my feare and agonie to haue recourse to that greate feare and wounderfull agonie, that thou my sweete Sauiour haddest at the Mounte of Oliuete before thy moste bitter Passion, and in the meditation thereof to conceaue ghostlie comfort and consolation profitable for my soule.

Almightie God take from me all vaine-glorious mindes, all appetites of mine owne praise, all enuie, couetousnes, glotonie, slouth, and leacherie, all wrathfull affections,

ons, all appetite of reuenginge, all
defire or delite of other folkes
harme, all pleafure in prouokinge
anie perfon to wrathe and anger,
all delite of exprobration and in-
fultation againfte anye perfon in
their affliction or calamitie. And
geue me, good Lord, an humble,
lowlie, quiet, peaceable, patiente,
charitable, kinde, tender, and pitifull minde, with all my workes,
& all my words, & al my thoughts,
to haue a tafte of thy holy bleffed
Spirite.

Geue me, good Lorde, a full
faith, a firme hope, and a feruente
charitie, a loue to thee, good lord,
incomparable aboue the loue to
my felfe, and that I loue nothing
to thy difpleafure, but euery thing
in an order to thee.

· · Geue me, good Lord, a long-
ing to be vvith thee, not for the a-

uoy-

uoydinge of the calamities of this
vvretched vvorld, nor so much for
auoyding of the paynes of Purgatory, nor of the paynes of hell neither, nor so much for the atteining
of the ioyes of heauen in respecte
of mine ovvne commoditie, as e-
uen for a very loue to thee.

And beare me, good Lorde, thy
loue and fauour, vvhich thing my
loue to thee-vvard (vvere it neuer
so greate) coulde not, but of thy
great goodnes, deserue.

And pardonne me, good Lord,
that I am so bolde to aske so high
petitions, beinge so vile a sinfull
vvretch, and so vnvvorthy to obteyne the lovvest : but yet good
Lord, such they be as I am bounde
to vvish for, and should be nerer
the effectuall desire of them, if my
manifolde sinnes vvere not the let.
From vvhich, O glorious Trinity
vouch-

vouchfafe of thy goodnes to wafh me vvith that bleffed bloude that iffued out of thy tender body, O fvveete Sauiour Chrift, in the dyuers torments of thy mofte bitter paffion.

Take from me, good Lorde, this luke-vvarme fafhion, or rather key-colde maner of meditation, and this dulnes in prayinge vnto thee : and geue me warmnes, delight and quicknes in thinkinge vpon thee: and geue me thy grace to long for thy holy Sacraments, & fpecially to reioyce in the prefence of thy very bleffed bodye, fvveete Sauiour Chrift, in the holy Sacrament of the Aulter: And duely to thanke thee for thy gracious vifitation there-with : and at that high memoriall, with tender compaffion, to remember & confider thy mofte bitter Paffion.

Make

Make vs all, good Lorde, virtually participant of that holy Sacrament this day, and euery day make vs all lyuely members, sweete Sauiour Christ, of thy holy Misticall body, thy holy catholike Church.

Dignare Domine, die isto sine peccato nos custodire.

Miserere nostri domine, miserere nostri.

Fiat misericordia tua Domine super nos, quemadmodum sperauimus in te.

In te Domine speraui, non confundar in æternum.

Ora pro nobis, Sancta Dei Genitrix.

Vt digni efficiamur promissionibus Christi.

LOrde geue me patience in tribulation, and grace in euerye thing to cōforme my will to thine, that I may truely say: *Fiat voluntas tua sicut in cælo & in terra.*

The things, good Lord, that I pray for, geue me thy grace to labour

bour for.   Amen.

Pater noster.   Aue Maria.

Geue me thy grace, good lord,
to sette the world at nought.
To set my mind fast vpon thee.

And not to hange vpon the blast
of mens mouthes.
To be content to be solitarie.

Not to long for worldly companie.

Litle and litle vtterly to cast of
the world.

And rid my minde of all the busines thereof.

Not to longe to heare of any
worldly thinges.

But that the hearing of worldly
fantasies may be to me displeasant.
Gladly to be thinking of God.

Pitiously to call for his helpe.
To leane vnto the comfort of
God.
Busily to labour to loue him.

To

To humble and meeke my selfe vnder the mighty hande of God. ~~and wretchednes.~~

To knowe mine owne vilitie To bewayle my sinnes past.

For the purginge of them patiently to suffer aduersitie.

Gladly to beare my purgatorie here.

To be ioyfull of tribulation.

To walke the narowe way that leadeth to lyfe.

To beare the Crosse with Christ.

To haue the laste thinges in remembraunce.

To haue euer before mine eye my death that is euer at hand.

To make death no straunger to me.

To forsee and consider the euerlasting fyer of hell.

To praye for pardon, before the Iudge come.

To

To haue continually in minde the Paſſion that Chriſt ſuffered for mee.

For his benefites inceſſantly to geue him thankes.

To buy the time againe, that I before haue loſt.

To abſteine from vaine confabulations.

To eſchue light fooliſh mirth and gladnes.

Recreations not neceſſarie to cut of.

Of worldly ſubſtaunce, frends, libertie, life & all, to ſet the loſſe at righte nought, for the winning of Chriſt.

To thinke my moſt enemies my beſt friends.

For the bretherne of Ioſeph coulde neuer haue done him ſo muche good with their loue and fauour, as they did him with their

ma-

malice and hatred.

These mindes are more to be desired of euery man, then all the treasure of all the Princes & Kings Christian and Heathen, were it gathered and layde together all vpon one heape.

FINIS.

A SHORTE DIA-
LOGVE OF S. KATHE-
rine of Siene touching
perfection.

Vhen a certaine soule
(being illuminated by
the author of light)did
acknowledge her pro-
per frailtie and miserie,
that is to say her ignorance and nature
prone to sinne: & did beholde the great-
nesse of God,I meane wysdome, powre,
goodnesse,and other his parts of excel-
lencie : euen then she perceiued, how
meete and necessarie it were that the
same God should be worshipped in all
perfectiō and sanctetie:Meete : for sithe
he is the father and lord of all and hathe
ordeyned and created all things to praise his name and set forthe his glorie, it
is therfore verie good reason that the
seruant attéding vpō his maister should
serue and dewtyfully obey. Necessarie:
for that God him selfe, hathe made him
a reasonable creature consisting of soule
and bodye and hathe annexed ther vnto

E   this

this condition, that if withe a good will
and fideletie he ferue him faithfully vntill death, he may come to life euerlafting, other wife he can not obteine that
felycitie aboundantly flowing in all
goodneffe: but fewe they are which accomplifhe this fame, and therfore very
fewe are faued becaufe all for the moft
parte feeke that whiche is ther owne,
and not that whiche is of God.

This fame fowle did further fee, that
the dayes of man are fhort, his time vn-
certaine, the litle moment whiche we
haue to gain our faluatiõ quikly ended:
no redemption in hell, but that eche
mortall wight in the life to come, by the
immutable and ineuitable fentence, fhall
iuftly receiue reward, or punifhment,
according as in this life they haue de-
ferued. It did alfo perceiue how many
men fpeake many things, and diuerfly
talke of thofe vertues wherwith God
may be faithfully worfhypped. and how
the capacytie of the reafonable creature was but litle, his vnderftandinge dull,
his memorie weake, in fo muche, as he is
not able either to cõceiue muche, or yet
furely to reteine that which he haith
con-

conceiued Ald therfore though many-
studie to learne alwayes more, yet very
fewe reache to that full perfection of
pure integretie, in seruinge God as necessarie it were, and best should become
them: But all for the most part côtinually
liue in anxeytie and care, in trouble of
mynde, in extreame perill and danger.

This soule therefore well vew-
inge and notinge all this, began to raise
it selfe in spirite before God: and with
feruent desire, and vehement affection,
did beseche his maiestie that he wolde
vouchsafe (for the better direction of
our life and passing ouer the same,) to
deliuer her some compendiouse and
brieffe instructiôs which in pythy sen-
tences may so containe the truthe of all
preaching, and the effect of all the vni-
uersall scriptures, as by obseruing the
same his maiestie myght be worshipped
with all dewe seruice: and wee forthe of
this short, mortall , and miserable life,
might come to that felycitie and blisse,
which he hathe appointed for vs.

VVherupon, our lord God (who afwell inspireth into vs these good desires, as also maketh them profitable vnto

vs if we admitt them)furthwith appeared vnto the foule, as in an extafie or
traunce, and thus he faid.

GOD. My beloued, thefe thy defires do marualoufly pleafe me, yea
& they do fo greatly delite me, as
I defire more to fatilfie them then
they can defire to be fatiffied : for
great is my defire(vpon thy fuyte)
to beftow fuch benefits on the, as
may be profitable, fyt & neceffarie
for thy faluation: and therfore I am
mofte readie to fulfill thy requeft
and graunt thy defire. VVherfore
attend & diligently obferue thefe
things which I (the vnfpeakable &
infallible truthe) will fay: for con-
defcending to thy petition, I will
breifly fet down what that is which
conteineth the higheft perfection
and all other vertues, & therwithall the wholle volumes of fcriptu-
res and manifold exhortations: in
fo

so much, as if thou behold thy face in this mirror, frame thy selfe to it, and dispose thy selfe to keepe it: then thou shalt fulfill what soeuer lyeth open or hiddē within diuine scriptures: and thow shalt enioye euerlasting gladnesse & peace perpetuall.

Assure thy selfe therfore, that the saluation and perfection of my seruants cōsisteth in this one thing, that is to say to do my only will: & to endeuour with all care and diligence to fulfill the same: and to labour ech moment of their life to ebey me onely: to serue me only: to attend me onely : and the more diligently they goe about this, the nearer they come to perfection, becaufe they do adheere, are vnited, & ioyned more closely to me which am the highest perfection.

But to make the vnderstand

E 3   this

this short doctrine more plainly
(otherwise ineffable,)looke vpon
the face of my sonne Christ Iesus
*in vvhome I am vvell pleased,*for,*he*
abaising him selfe tooke vppon him the
forme of a seruant,and vvas made to a
*similitude of the flesh of sinne:*that you
oppressed in darknesse,& astrayed
from the way of truthe,might be
illuminated with the bewty of his
light, and conuerted to the right
waye both by word and example:
he became obedient vntill death, tea-
ching you by his continuall obedience that your saluation dothe
depend of the constant performing
of my only will,for if any man will
with diligent study & consideratiō,
looke vpon bothe his life and do-
ctrine:without doubte he shall see
the integretie & perfectiō of mortall creatures to cōsist in no other
thing,than in the cōtinuall,perpe-
tuall

tuall,& faithfull obferuance of my
will:the whiche thing he him felfe
(your guyde and Captaine)hathe
often found out and teftefied:for
thus he faith. *Not euerie one that faith
vnto me Lord, Lord,fhall enter in to the
kingdome of heauen : but he that dothe
the vvill of my father.*And here cofi-
der that he doth not in vain repeat
twife thefe wordes *Lord,Lord,*for
wher as the whole codition of tra-
fitorie and mortall ftate may be reduced to two generall points, to
wit,religious and fecular:his mea-
ning is therby to fignyfie, that no
man of what condition or degree
fo euer he be,can obtaine the glorie of euerlafting life,although he
geue to me all honor owtwardly,
except he doe my will. And in an
other place he faith,*I came not to doe
myne owne vvill,but the vvill of my
father vvhich fent me* and againe, *my*
E 4 *meate*

*meate is to do the vvill of him that sent,
me.* And once more: *not my vvill, but
thine be done.* And in an other place
*as the father hath geuen me commaun-
dement so do I.*

Therfore, if thou wilt imitate
the example of thy Sauiour to do
my will wherin thy goodnesse cõ-
sisteth, it is necessarie that in all
things thou abandone, remoue, &
vtterly extinguish thine owne will:
for the more thou dyest in thy selfe, so much more thou liuest in me:
and the more thou castest awaye
that which is thine, the more aboũ-
dantly I will requite thee with that
whiche is myne owne.

This soule, after she had heard these
moste comfortable and holesome docu-
ments and instructions of truthe, all ra-
uished with ioye saide.

SOVLE. My father and my God
these things do greatly delyte me,
more then I can expresse, whiche
thou

thou hafte vouchfafed to open to
me thy poore feruant, and with all
humiletie, I yeld vnto thy diuine
Maieftie all cōdigne thankes. For,
as far as my dull vnderftāding can
reache, it is euen fo as thou hafte
manifeftly and plainly declared by
the example of my Sauiour, for
feeynge thou art the chiefefte and
whole good: not willing iniquity,
but iuftice onely and vpright dea-
ling, I do all that is for me to do, if
I fulfil thy wil, & if I do fulfil it for
thee, I deny myne owne. But thou
wilt not haue it by violēce, & therfore thou haft geuē it me free, that
I frely fubmitting the fame to thee,
intending to do thine onely, may
be made more acceptable to thee,
and my merites of more valewe
with thee. My will therfore is, and
earneftly I defire, to fulfill that
which thou cōmaundeft : but yet
                              I doe

I do not plainly know wherin thy will confifteth, or how I may faithfully ferue thee. If I prefume not to farre, & my temeretie may not abufe thy lenetie : lett me intreat thee, (according to my requeft) breiffly alfo to informe me herin.

Then fayed our Lord.

GOD. If thy defire be, in fewe wordes to know my will, and that thou maift wholye fulfill the fame: this it is : That thou loue me alwayes and aboue all, as by my law I haue commaunded thee and all mankind, to loue me with all your hart, with all your foule, aand with all your ftrength , in the keepinge of this commaundemēt confifteth your whole perfection: *for the ende of the commaundement is charitie, and the fulneffe of the Lavv is loue.*

To thefe the foule anfwered.

SOVLE. I perceaue thy will and
my

my perfection to reste in a moste
feruente loue towardes thee: and I
for my parte would (as equitie requireth) in a feruente and vehe-
mente maner loue thee: but how I
may or ought to accomplish the
fame, as yet I am not fufficientlye
inftructed, wherefore I humblye
befeeche thee in this pointe alfo
breifly to informe me.

Then God anfwered.

GOD. Attend dilligently and geue
eare to that which I wil fay, if thou
wilt perfectly loue me, thou muft
of neceffity doe thefe three things.

1 Fyrfte thou muft vtterlye fe-
quefter, remoue and purifye thy
felfe from all earthlye and carnall
loue and affection : in fuch forte as
in this lyfe thou loue no frayle,
tranfitorie, nor temporall thinge,
but for me:nor yet (which in deed
is more, and a moft fpeciall point)
                    muft

must thou loue me for thine owne
sake, or thy selfe, for the loue of
thy selfe, but thou must loue me
for mine owne cause, thy selfe for
me,& thy neighbour for my sake:
for loue diuine can not suffer the
felowshippe of any earthly affection, or any other loue whatsoeuer.
VVhereupõ it foloweth: the more
contagiouslye thou arte infected
with corruption of earthly things,
so much more shalte thou sayle of
my loue and wante of thine owne
perfection. For to make thy soule
pure and holy, thou must needes
loath and abhorre euery thinge,
which the body sensibly affecteth.

Indeuour thou that none of
those thinges which are come to
your vse, may either hynder, or
with-drawe thee from louinge of
me, but rather further, stirre vp and
inflame thee to loue me, for to you

at

(at their firſt creatiõ) I gaue them:
to this end, that by them throughly deſcerning the largeneſſe of my
benignetie, you might more feruently loue me. Perſiſt therfore in
thy deſire, gird vp thy loynes, and
with a vigilante care and watch o-
uer thy ſelfe, cherefully and boldly withſtand theſe earthly concu-
piſcences, which the miſerie of this
life and corupt nature ſuggeſteth
vnto thee: that thou maiſt ſay with
my Prophete, *he hathe made my feete*
(that is my affections which are the
feete of my ſoule) *like the feete of*
harts to flee from doggs (that is from
the ſnares of concupiſcence of
earthly thinges) *and hath ſett me on*
high, in the toure of contẽplation.
2   VVhan thou haſt performed
this firſt rule, thow ſhalt come to
the ſecõd which is of more higher
perfection to. That thou direct all
                                   thy

thy cogitations, actions, and workes to my honour and glorie one-
ly:and (as one cõtinually defirous
to fett furth my praife)thow muft
by prayers and petitions, words
and God example, yea and by all
meanes poffible trauaile, and la-
boure,that not thow onely, but
all others afwell as thow, may be
thus mynded towards me : & that
all & euerie one may knowe loue
and,worfhippe me a lone : for this
doth pleafe me better thẽ the firft,
in that it doth more fulfill my wil.
3   To the third (whiche is the
laft,)if thow fhalt reache?be thow
affured,that thou wanteft nothing,
and hafte attained vnto the full &
perfect integretie:and that is,thow
muft with moft earneft defire feeke, endeuour, and ftudie to come
to fuche a difpofition of mynd, as
thow mayft be fo vnited to me,&
                                    thy

thy will fo like, and conformed to
mine (whiche is mofte perfect) as
nothing content thee whiche dif-
contēteth me, be it good or euell:
that happ what happ fhall, what fo
euer befall thee in the miferie of
this life, whether fpiritually or tē-
porally, thy peace muft in no cafe
be broken, nor the quiett of thy
minde difturbed: but with faith inuincible thow muft euer take faft
hold on this, that I thy God which
am omnipotent, do loue the more
than doeth thy felfe, and that I haue a verie diligent care ouer thee:
yea farr more greater then thou
haft thy felfe: thus the more thou
fhalt committ and yeld thy felfe to
me, fo muche the more I will helpe thee, and allwayes abide with
thee, and the more clearely fhalt
thow knowe, and more fenfibly
feele my loue about thee. But to
this

this perfection none can attaine,
without a stedfaste, constant , and
absolute renouncing of his owne
proper will,& who soeuer negle-
cteth to performe this,doth therwithall neglect that most excellēt
perfection:and he that doth performe it,doth soundly execute my
said will & cōmaūdemēts:he plea-
seth me marualously well, & hath
me alwayes in his cōpany.For nothinge is more gratefull to me,nor
more pleasaunt, than through my
grace to lyue among you, and to
dwell with you,*for it is my delyte to
be vvith the childrē of men*, and great
pleasure I haue that they with their
good wil(for the lawe of free will
I mind not to violate) may be all
one with me in participatiō,of my
perfection,and principall peace &
tranquillytie.

But to make thee vnderstande
more

more playnly, how feruently I defire to be among you, and for thy
further prouocation to fubmitte
and ioyne thy will vnto mine: now
marke & deepely côdfider, how it
was my mind & will, that my only
begotten fonne was incarnate, and
that my deitie fhould be adioyned
to your humanytie, to the end that
by fo great an example of loue &
charytie, and by fuch a demôftra-
tion of vnfpeakable affe
ction, I
might prouoke, allure, and drawe
you to come bynde your willes
and myne together, & to ftay your
felues continnally vpon me. And
further my minde and will was that
this my welbeloued fonne, fhold
endure that fo horrible, extreme
and cruell death vpon the croffe,
to take away by his tormêts your
fynne (your finne I fay, which had
made a diuifiô betwixt you & me,

P   and

and had fo turned my face frō you
as I could not looke vpō you, cō-
fider alfo, that I haue prouided for
you a table of that mofte great &
vnknown facramēt of his body &
blood, that yow receiuing it for
your foode might be tranfformed
and chaunged into me: and like as
bread and wyne (wherwith you
are feed) do paffe in to yowr cor-
porall fubftance, fo your eatinge
him, which is one with me, might
be conuerted into a fpirituall fubftance and in to my felfe and this is
it which I faide to my feruant Au-
guftine in thefe wordes, *I am the*
meate of the great and perfeʃt in faith:
increafe in faith and thovv fhalt eate,
yet thovv fhalt not chaung me in to thy
felfe but thovv fhalt be chāged into me.

VVhen the foule had harde what was
the will of God, and how (for the accom-
plifhment of the fame) perfeʃte charitie
                                                    was

was neceffarie : and how perfect charitie confifteth in the renouncing of her proper will:fhe fayed.

SOVLE. My Lord, my God, thou haft fignified vnto me thy will, and thou haft fignified (O Lord)that if I will loue thee perfectly I muft loue no earthly, nor mortall thing, nor yet myne owne felfe for mine owne fake: but whatfoeuer I loue, I mufte loue for thee, and for thy fake, thou haft fayed that with fpeciall care and ftudie I fholde allwayes feeke the praife, honour, and glorie of thee alone, and therwithall that I fhoulde endeuour & go about, that others might do the fame, and what aduerfytie fo euer befall vnto me in this miferable life I fhold trauaile to endure the fame with a calme, quiett and cherfull mynde. Nowe fith thefe things are to be obtayned by the

F 2   renown-

renowncing of oure owne proper
will, inſtruct me (I beſeche thee, o
Lorde) how and by what meane I
may do the ſame, and how I maye
attaine to this ſo great a vertue, for
as I perceiue by the light of thy
doctrine, ſo muche I liue in thee, as
I die in my ſelfe.

Then God (which neuer doth fruſt-
rate holy deſires) vpon theſe wordes did
thus inferre.

GOD. It is ſure and certaine, that
all good cōſiſteth in a full & abſo-
lute renowncing of thy ſelfe, for
ſo much I fill thee with my grace,
as thou arte emptie of thine owne
will: and thy perfectiō is eſſentially
wrought by participation of my
diuine benignytie through grace:
without the which mankinde (in as
much as appartaineth to his vertue
& worthineſſe) is nothing worth:
here vnto therfore then if thou art
                                    deſi-

defirous to attaine, this one thing
thou muft with perfecte humilitie
endeuour:and with true acknow-
ledging of thy miferie, want, and
pouertie,cõtinually,earneftly,and
vehemẽtly defire & affect:that is,
to obey me alone,to obferue, and
keepe my only wil.Nowe the better to bring this to paffe,thou muft
in the cõceit of thy mind,& imagi-
natiõ of thy foule builde vnto thy
felfe a clofe and well vaulted habitation, made of the matter of my
will,herein thou muft fhutt vp thy
felfe,and alwayes abide:fo as whether foeuer thou goeft,thou neuer
goe out of it : wherfoeuer thou
cafteft thine eye,thou neuer looke
out of it:but lett my will allwayes
enuirone thy fenfes,afwel ghoftly
as bodely:neuer fpeake any thing:
neuer do any thing:but that which
thou beleueft to ftãd with my will
F 3   and

and thus the holy ghoſt ſhall en-
forme the, what ſoeuer thou haſte
to do.

There is yet an other way, wherby thou maiſt come to this renouncing of thine owne propre
wil: that is, by ſubmitting it to thoſe
which are (and haue authoritie) to
inſtruct and gouerne thee according to my commaundements, and
by committinge thy ſelfe wholly,
and all thine, to them: by obeying
thē: & euer folowing their aduiſe
and connſayle, for he that heareth
my faithfull and wiſe ſeruants, heareth me. But yet I wolde haue thee
(with an aſſured faithe, attentiue
minde, and often cōſideration,) to
meditate & thinke, that I thy moſt
glorious god (which hath created
thee for the fruition of euerlaſting
bleſſedneſſe) am Eternall, moſte
highe, and omnipotent, and worke
all

al thinges in you according to my
will and pleasure:& that ther is no
creature able to resist my will,be it
neuer so litle:or that any thing can
happen vnto you,without my will
and suffrance.For euen as before
this I haue sayde by my Prophet,
*ther is no euill in the Cytie which I
haue not made:*that is to saye,which
I haue not permitted.

Thou must also meditate, that
I thy God am of moste highe wisdome of most perfecte knowledge
and vnderstanding,and that moste
certainly I beholde & sharply pe-
netrate the sight of all things:in so
muche as(in my iudgement,)ouer
the heauens,earthe,& the whole,
world and all creatures,I can in no
wise be deceiued,nor with any er-
ror disturbed.For if it were not so:
neither coulde I be God,nor yet
moste wise.

And yet (to make thee fom-
what to perceiue, the force of my
perfect wifdome,)affure thy felfe,
that out of the euill of finne and of
the punifhemēt for finne, I woork
muche more good than the euill
amounteth vnto. Thirdly I wold
haue thee confider, that I the felfe
fame God am alfo of no leffe perfection in goodneffe, nor no leffe
louing. It is therfore manifeft and
plaine, that I can not wifhe, nor
will any thing, but whiche is good
and profitable for thee & others:
that ther can no euill proceed frō
me: that I hate nothing: that as vpō
myne owne meere goodneffe I
haue created man : euen fo vpon
my meere motion alwayes I loue
him moft ineftimably. Now when
thow hafte made a collection of
thefe things in thy mynd by a fure
and faft faith : thou fhalt knowe
that

that tribulations, temptations, di-
ſtreſſes, wordly promotions, infir-
myties, & all aduerſities doe happē
for no other cauſe (by my direction) but for your profitt & ſal-
uatiō, that by theſe meanes which
ſeeme euill vnto you, you maye
be reclamed from your wicked-
neſſe, and led vnto vertue, which
is the very way and pathe to the
ſincere and principall goodneſſe,
as yet vnknowne vnto you. And
whan thow arte illuminated withe
this light of faith, thow ſhalt know
further that I thy God am more
able to worcke thy Good, & that
I know it better, and wiſhe it more
then thow doeſt thy ſelfe: and that
thow neither canſt procure it,
know it, nor deſire it without my
grace.

And ſithe it is ſo: thow muſt
endeuoure by all meanes poſſible,
vtterly

vtterly to submitt thyne owne wil
to my diuine will, for thus thy
minde shall allway be quiet, and
thou shalt alwayes haue me with
the : for my place is buylded in
peace : and thou shalte haue no
scandall of sinne, that is to saye,
no stumblinge blocke, to synne,
nether by impatience, nor by any
other meane. For muche peace remaineth to them that loue my name, and they take no scandale: for
they so muche tender my lawe (I
meane my will, and in deede it is
my lawe, wherby I work al things)
and by it they are so fast tyed vnto
me, and so delitedwith obseruatiō
therof, that what misfortune soeuer befall them, vpon what occasion so euer, and vpon what condition or estimation soeuer it be:
nothing can disquiett them , but
the iniurie onely whiche is done
                              vnto

vnto me through their fault: for
they see & beholde with the cleare
and bright eye of ther mynde, that
from me (the supreme gouernour
of all, ruling all things with maruailous wisdome, charitie, and order) nothinge can proceede but
that which is good: and that I doe
better & more profitably prouide
for them and others, than they thē
selues either know, could, or wold.

And thus in all thinges which
happen, and which they endure,
what-soeuer: these men conside-
ringe with a sure determination
that I am the author therof, (and
not their neighbour) are corro-
borated with a certaine inuincible
patience, as they beare all thinges
not onely with a quiet and peaceable, but also with a most chearfull
and glad minde what-soeuer happen: tastinge in all things inwardly

or

or outwardly a certaine sweetnesse
of my vnspeakable charity:which
is in a most perfect good maner to
thinke of me: I meane,in all tribulations, miseries, and distresses to
marke,obserue,beleeue,& thinke,
and with a glad and cherefull mind
to meditate that I dispose al things
sweetly: that all thinges proceede
from the deepe fountayne of my
loue. But no other thinge corrup-
teth, hindreth and distroyeth the
great good of this last consideration, and most holy settling of the
minde,but onely your meere proper will and selfe loue.And if these
were taken away from you: assure
your selfe, hell should be taken
from you:not only that hell which
is ordained for an eternall torment
of soule and body to the accursed:
but that hell also, which, duringe
mortall lyfe,by manifolde vexati-
ons

ons of mind, and varieties of cares,
in the bottomlesse pitte of ignorance and errour you susteine and
abide. Thus therefore, if you desire to liue, both in that slipperye
and transitorie world by grace: and
in this stable and euerlasting world
by glory, see thou dye to thy selfe
by renouncing thine owne selfe,
and layinge away thy proper will:
for *blessed are the dead which dye
in our lorde, and blessed are the poore
in spirite*, for such see me in their
pilgrimage by mutuall loue:
and afterward shall see me
in their country by glo-
rye and honour.
Amen.

THE VVORDES OF

BROTHER RICERIVS OF
Marchia, a companion to the blessed Father S. Francis, declaringe,
howe a man may come to the
knowledge of trueth in a
shorte time.

Vho so euer is desi-
rous to come to the
knowledge of trueth
in a short time by the
righte and streighte
way, and to haue a perfecte fruitiõ
of peace in his soule: it is necessary
for him to dispossesse him selfe of
the loue of all creatures, & of him
selfe also : in such sorte, as he may
caste him selfe wholly vpon God,
not reseruinge any thinge to him
selfe: no, not so much as time: to
the ende that he may procure him
selfe nothinge by his owne sense:
                                    but

bnt be alwaies readie to folow the directiõ and calling of God. VVho foeuer is defirous to be vnited vnto God : he muft referue nothing, that may be a ftop or 'et betweene him and God. And thefe ftoppes are fo many, as there be thinges, which a man loueth.

VVhere fore, that this coniunction with God maye not be hyndered, lett all loue of creatures be taken awaye. For this is the caufe why manie feeme to be great fpirituall perfones, keeping certaine good obferuations verie rigoroufly, côtinually, & carefully: yet are they alwayes not withftanding but onely luke warne, and neuer come to anye perfecte and firme ftate: becaufe they haue fome proprietie, which is a ftoppe betwene them and God. And by reafon of thefe ftoppes, which they referue in their fowles, they are euermore
fub-

subiecte to alterations. For if they
feele the goodnes of God at anye
tyme, if they continue in prayer &
other obseruations, and haue therby some feeling of God, yet afterwardes they returne vnto sables,
murmuring, talking of wordlie
matters, & other externall thinges
which they loue: as if they had had
no feeling of God at all. They do
as flies are wont to do: which pitch
at one tyme vpon honny, and at
an other time vpõ spetle or dung.
For what is the cause, whie the
Passion of Christ, (which is of such
efficacie and vertue, as it might &
ought with one meditation onely
to cleaue the hartes of men, and of
anie other thing were it neuer so
hard) doth not alter manie persõs,
whiche are exercised in meditating vpõ it fower or fiue or more
yeares: whoe although they are
moued with compunction, and do
take

take some delite & feeling in it: yet do they not chaunge their life, but when they departe from that exercise, they geue them selues to dissolute behauiour, as they dide before. Vndoubtedlye this cometh so to passe for none other cause, but onely because the stoppes which they reserue, will not suffer their soule to approch vnto Christ, nor Christ vnto it. And if these stoppes do cease sometimes, yet doe they returne againe afterwardes, as to a howse voyd of a tenant, & as to their owne. But whé the soule doth wholly dispossesse her selfe of all the loue of creatures: and hath the true pouertie of spirite at harte: then, because she delyteth not in anye creature, she is drawen and replenished with the loue of God, vpon whom she casteth her selfe wholly. And if it chaunce afterward, that these things, which she had once abandoned, doe returne againe vnto the soule, they can not enter in-

E   t?

to it,becaufe the howfe is full,and the
lodgings are alreadie taken vp by the
loue of God,and all the affections are
tyed vp. As (we fee) wayfaring men
do,who wil not turne into fuch Innes
as are taken vp by others before, but
into fuch as are voyde of gheftes, and
able to receaue the whole companie.

Nowe when a foule is taken vp
after this maner,and replenifhed with
the loue of God (which cometh to
paffe immediatly, when God feeth it
voyde of all other loue , euen of the
loue of it felfe alfo) then doeth that
foul beginne to be illuminated of the
trueth it felfe,whiche is God. And in
this trueth it feeth the bafenes of all
creatures, & it knoweth bafe thinges
for baffe thinges,and precious things
for precious things and in this light it
feeth the bafenes of all creatures, and
of all earthlie things:with the difpleafure and harme,whiche maye enfewe
by the defire of them:& therfore will
not

not suffer it selfe to be deceiued by them, although it see manie men foloweing after them. As if a mã knewe for certayn, that there were poison in a meate, which were set before him, although manie other did eate of it, and would say to him, eate, the meate is good enough: yet would he not eate, but would rather saye vnto thẽ: I knowe right well, that there is poisõ in this meate, and therfore I will not eate of it: & I account you for fooles, that doe eate of it: for ye shall take your bane by it. In like maner, if a man see a tower, that is readie to fall, howsoeuer mẽ should say vnto him, go thy way in, & dwell there without feare, for we will doe the like: yet woulde he not enter in, but woulde rather laugh at their folie.

A man therfore, beinge once directed by this light, will not onely not loue earthlie things, but also despise & hate them, as the occasions of
death

death, for they poison the soule: and
sithe it is moste certaine, that they
them selues shall decaie and come to
naught, they drawe the soule, that
cleaueth vnto thē, together with thē
selues into ruine and destructiō. And
if it seeme by some chaunce that any
temporall cōmoditie is offered vnto
a man, which is thus directed: yet is he
taught by this light to let it passe: because his hart is set vpō greater gay-
nes. As if a man should saye to an Emperour, that he would sell him a verie
pretie peece of ground, valewinge it
at three score powndes : the grownd
in deed being well worth three score
& ten powndes, so that he might well
gayne ten pownds by it: vndoubted-
ly the Emperour would make small
account of it: yea he wold disdaigne
to geue eare vnto him, because his
minde is set vpon the getting of Ci-
ties and townes, & vpon other great
affaires. Euen so a soule being once
bent

bent to heauenlie thinges, wolde dif-
daigne to fet her mynde vpon téporall and earthlie commodities.

In this light alfo is the perfection
of all vertues gyuen vnto the foule.
For what is humilitie, but only a certaine light of the truth? VVhat is charitie? VVhat is patiéce? VVhat is obedience? VVhat are the reft of vertues:
but only certaine lights of the trueth?
The foule therfore is directed by this
light, to come to knowe the force &
efficacie of vertues, to embrace the
exercife of them: and fo by that meanes to laye hand vpon them, and to
keepe them in poffeffion.

By this light alfo on the other fide,
the foule abhorreth and detefteth all
vices : in fo muche as, if a hundred
women of the faireft, that coulde be
fownde in the world, were fet before
a mã, which had receiued the brightnes of this light, he wold loathe thé,
and wold not be moued one iote vn-

to incōtinencie. And as for gloutonie he wold not only not feeke after it, but alfo, if fyne and deyntie meates were fet before him, he fhould eate them with paine & yrckefomnes.

By this light alfo, the foule abhorreth all vices in confideration of the naughtines that is in thē. And generally by this light the foule is directed in the doing of euerie particular acte: for it is illuminated by him, of whome it is replenifhed, to confider the honour & will of God in all that is to be done. For him only doth fhe honour, him only doth fhe loue: and therfore fhe tendreth his honour and will only in all thinges. And this fhe doth accordinge to the example of Chrift, who in his prayer, whiche he made at the tyme of his Paffion, obferued thefe two pointes: for inbowing him felfe downe in praier as euerie cōmon man doth, he honoured his father: & in faying thefe wordes

des

des (*Not my vvill, but thyne be done,*)
he fought his fathers will. In like maner the foule of man, by the meane of
this light, foloweth the example of
Chrift. For if the thing, whiche is to
be done, ftand wel with the honour
and will of God: this foule executeth
and fulfilleth it. But if fhe fee, that it is
contrarie to anie of the premiffes, fhe
refufeth & will not do it, for anie caufe or perfone. In fo much as fhe auoi-
deth idle woordes, euell thoughtes,
and all vices: becaufe fhe knoweth,
that they are côtrarie to the honour
& will of God, as fhe is fully infor-
med by this light.

Nowe when the foule hath bene
once accuftomed and throughly ac-
quainted in this waye: this light is not
hidden from it, by occafion of other
good exercifes(if they happē to come)as by bearing office in the Churche, by hauing charge to preache, or
to intēd anye other charitable worke

to the profit of our neighbour.For as
a man hauinge a wall before his eye
some-what diſtant from him,ſeeth at
once both the wall and all that is betwene him & the wall:euen ſo a ſoule
beinge illuminated with this light,
ſeeth God,& al things,that are requi-
ſite to be done. Thus none of theſe
things doe cauſe it to ſwarue frō the
waye wherin ſhe walketh, although
contemplation be intermitted for a
time.In this light alſo,the ſoule ſeeth
the trueth of her owne baſenes: and
the more ſhe is vnited vnto God,
the more baſe and vile ſhe eſteemeth
her ſelfe and the reaſon is for that ſhe
ſeeth her ſelfe the more cleerly. And
becauſe ſhe reſerueth nothing to her
ſelfe : nor accounteth anye of thoſe
thinges to be her owne, whiche ſhe
ether receiueth at gods hand, or doth
by his grace:but aſcribeth all to him:
and acknowledgeth all ſuch thinges,
as ſhe receiueth of his bowntifull
good-

goodnes, to be bestowed vpon her without any of her desertes: therfore she is not puffed vp with pride, nor vseth her selfe vnthākfully: and therfore she is not depriued of the graces receiued. Yea when God seeth, that she stealeth nothing from him, but yealdeth all thinges truely vnto him, he heapeth his treasures abundantly vpon her, and bestoweth more vpon her, than she can either demaunde or desire.

All these commodities doth the soule receiue by this dispossessiō of al proprieties. For when euell lustes and ambitious desires are chased awaye: when inordinate affectiōs and loues of creatures, with all sensuall stoppes & letts that doe obscure and darcken the soule are expelled, then entereth the loue of God by and by, whiche replenisheth her, making her bright and lightsome, and geueth her instructions, as is sayd before.

By

By this putting away of proprie ties the foule receiueth not onely the a-forefayd grace of the light of trueth, but alfo the grace of peace & cõftan-cie:and then doth God dwell in it in verie deede. For he neuer abideth in anye place, but onely in the houfe of peace & quietnes. And therfore fuch a foule in all troubles, loffes, iniuries, and oppreffions, keepeth a certaine tranquillitie and patience, and is firme and ftowte : partly, becaufe fhe hath cõmitted her felfe wholly to God, & hath cõformed her felfe to his will: & therfore cõfidering that thofe aduer-fities do happẽ vnto her by the mere will, & free gift of god, fhe accordeth with him, & beareth them, not onely patiẽtly, but alfo with a glad & chere-full hart: and partly, becaufe fhe hath caft her felfe wholly vpon God, and there fhe abideth. VVhere vpõ it fo-loweth, that neyther iniurious wor-des, temporall loffes, nor other thin-

ges

ges of like sort, no not the worlde it selfe can not towch her: for such thinges can not ascend vnto God, where this soule hathe chosen her inheritance: and much lesse are they able to approche nere vnto her, because she is not allyed with thē: neither do they find her in the place, where she was wount to be. As if a mā were desirous to find me, and should seeke me in all those places where I was wont to be, yea, if he should seeke me throughout the whole worlde besids the place, where I were, he could neuer find me: In like maner if a howse be burned, while the owner is absent: he careth not thē for it, nether doth he thē take any sorow for his house, because he is awaie, & seeth not that it is burned: euen so a man, which regardeth not temporall thinges, careth not for the losse of thē. An other cause why the soule is firme & stowte, is this: because it is strengthened and fortified by

by the example of Christ dwelling in
it, who hath susteined so manie & so
great thinges for the loue of it.

And therfore it hath an earnest
and feruent desire to folowe him in
tribulatió, and reioyseth in them, & is
troubled in effecte with nothing. And
by these thinges the soule atteineth
vnto a certaine firmnesse, and good
staye of the senses of her bodie. For
when she hath once reiected all creatures, for the loue of her creator, she
wandereth no more abroad in them,
by the vnlawfully course of her senses, but she ruleth and stayeth them,
cómending them boldly vnto God,
and saying, when she departeth from
prayer : O Lord, keepe me fast tied
vnto thee, and gouerne my senses, &
suffer me not to wander owt of thee.
And generally by this putting awaye
of proprieties, the sowle getteth the
soueraigntie & rule ouer her bodie:
and there is suche a peace & concord
among

among them, as they difagree in nothing, for the bodie fubmitteth it felfe willingly vnto the foule, and foloweth her in all thinges, that fhe lift
to exercife, as well in the roughnes of
abftinécie and watching, as alfo in all
other labour and trauailes. For when
the bodie remébreth the diftreffes &
greuous paines, which it was wont to
fuffer, through impatience, anger, enuie, ambition, and other tormoiles
about téporall things: and feeth now,
how great peace and quietnes it en-
ioyeth : then it beareth all the labours of penance willingly, to auoyd
thofe other labours, that are fruite-
leffe, hurtfull and full of payne. As if
a man were well affured, that for a
hundred pence he fhould receiue a
thowfande, he woulde not fticke to
geue a hundred: nay, he would rather
geue two húdred: eué fo the body (as
on that maketh a great gaine therby)
beareth all thefe labours cherefully:
yea,

yea, it endeuoureth to runne before them and to preuent them.

VVherfore it shalbe verie profitable & requisite for vs, to cast all stoppes & lettes awaie, to dispossesse our selues of all proprieties, to die vnto all creatures, to put away, whatsoeuer hope & comfort we haue in our selues, & in all creatures, & to cast our selues boldly vpon God, who will receiue vs louingly, gouerne vs amiably, and bring vs to a blessed end. For sythe we see, that marchāts for tēporall gaines do hazard thē selues and put their liues in a thowsand aduētures by land & sea: if souldiers for worldly honour do the like offering them selues to swoordes, battailes, and death: and yet manie tymes it falleth so out, that neither do the souldiers receiue such honour, nor the merchāts such gaines, as they desire: & if they do, they are well assured, that they shall leese it: howe muche more ought we to do it for
spiri-

piritua ll honour & gaine,& for good
and fownd wares which fhall endure
for euer: efpecially, confidering that
we do put our felues in no danger for
thē? yea moreouer,if a mā would thus
difpoffeffe him felfe of all proprietes
& do it well, faithfully, & fincerely:
with in a few daies he fhould beginne
in himfelfe to haue afeling of the thinges a fore mētioned,he fhould taft the
fwetenes of God, & by cōtinuing in
this abandoninge of proprieties, he
fhould find by a moft euident & certaine experiēce,that the things,which
we haue here declared,are verie true.
In fo much as rifing vp frō praier with
a certaine liuelineffe & amorous hart,
he fhould loue & embrace the thinges of god only,& loking vpon this
world with a certaine yrckefomenes,
as one that were aftonnied,& eftraun-
ged from it , and made an other man:
yea as if he were come out of an o-
ther world, he fhould vtterly difpife
this

this world , and fhould hardly abide
to fee it,but vvith paine & lothfome
nes, by reafon that he had befor
vvholly vvith-drawne his mind from
it, and had mofte fvveetely and plea-
fantlye tranfformed him felfe int o
God , vvhoe liueth and raigneth for
euer and euer.

Vnto the mofte holy and infepe
rable Trinitie: Vnto the humanitie o
our Lorde Iefus Chrift,vvhich vva
crucified:Vnto the vndefiled
puritie of the mofte bleffed Virgin Marie, be
euerlafting glorie
world without
end.Amen.

Prayfe be vnto God.

pirituall honour & gaine,& for good
and fownd wares which shall endure
for euer: especially, considering that
we do put our selues in no danger for
thē? yea moreouer, if a mā would thus
dispossesse him selfe of all proprietes
& do it well, faithfully, & sincerely:
with in a few daies he should beginne
in himselfe to haue afeling of the thinges afore mētioned, he should tast the
sweetenes of God, & by cōtinuing in
this abandoninge of proprieties, he
should find by a most euident & certaine experiēce, that the things, which
we haue here declared, are verie true.
In so much as rising vp frō praier with
a certaine liuelinesse & amorous hart,
he should loue & embrace the thinges of god only, & loking vpon this
vorld with a certaine yrckesomenes,
as one that were astonnied, & estraun-
ged from it , and made an other man:
yea as if he were come out of an o-
ther world, he should vtterly dispise
this

this world, and should hardly abide
to see it, but vvith paine & lothsome
nes, by reason that he had befor
vvholly vvith-drawne his mind from
it, and had moste svveetely and plea-
santlye transformed him selfe int o
God, vvhoe liueth and raigneth for
euer and euer.

Vnto the moste holy and insepe-
rable Trinitie: Vnto the humanitie of
our Lorde Iesus Christ, vvhich vva
crucified: Vnto the vndefiled
puritie of the moste blef-
sed Virgin Marie, be
euerlasting glorie
world without
end. Amen.

Prayse be vnto God.